Marvin A. Sweeney

Isaiah 1 – 4 and the Post-Exilic Understanding
of the Isaianic Tradition

Marvin A. Sweeney

Isaiah 1 – 4
and the Post-Exilic
Understanding
of the Isaianic Tradition

Walter de Gruyter · Berlin · New York
1988

Beiheft zur Zeitschrift für die alttestamentliche Wissenschaft

Herausgegeben von Otto Kaiser

171

Gedruckt auf säurefreiem Papier
(alterungsbeständig – pH 7, neutral)

Library of Congress Cataloging-in-Publication Data

Sweeney, Marvin A. (Marvin Alan), 1953 –
Isaiah 1 – 4 and the post-exilic understanding of the Isaianic tradition.

Beiheft zur Zeitschrift für die alttestamentliche Wissenschaft ; 171)
Bibliography: p.
Includes index.
1. Bible. O.T. Isaiah 1 – IV – – Criticism, interpretation, etc.
2. Bible. O.T. Isaiah – – Criticism, interpretation, etc. I. Title.
II. Series: Beihefte zur Zeitschrift für die alttestamentliche Wissenschaft ; 171. BS1515.2.S93 1987   224'.106   87-15561
ISBN 0-89925-403-9 (U.S.)

CIP-Titelaufnahme der Deutschen Bibliothek

Sweeney, Marvin A.:
Isaiah 1 [one] – 4 and the post-exilic understanding of the Isaianic tradition / Marvin A. Sweeney. – Berlin ; New York : de Gruyter, 1988
(Beiheft zur Zeitschrift für die alttestamentliche Wissenschaft ; 171)
Zugl.: Claremont, Graduate School, Diss., 1983
ISBN 3-11-011034-2
NE: Zeitschrift für die alttestamentliche Wissenschaft / Beiheft

Satz und Druck: Arthur Collignon GmbH, Berlin 30
Bindearbeiten: Lüderitz & Bauer, Berlin 61

Acknowledgments

This work is a revised version of a Ph.D. dissertation completed at Claremont Graduate School in the Spring of 1983. I am especially indebted to Dr. Rolf P. Knierim, my doctoral advisor, and committee members, Dr. James A. Sanders and the late Dr. William H. Brownlee. Without their scholarly insight and judicious guidance, this work could never have been completed. I would also like to thank Dr. David L. Petersen, Dr. Richard D. Weis, Dr. Stan Rummel, Dr. Gene M. Tucker, Dr. Roy F. Melugin, Dr. George W. Coats, Prof. Zev Garber, Dr. Daniel L. Pals, Dr. John T. Fitzgerald, Jr., Dr. Stephen Sapp, and Dr. Henry A. Green for their advice, assistance, and encouragement at various stages in the preparation of this study.

I wish to express my appreciation to Prof. Dr. Otto Kaiser for accepting this work for publication in the BZAW. I have learned much from his own work on Isaiah.

Thanks are due to the Research Council of the University of Miami for providing a Max Orovitz Summer Stipend in the Humanities which enabled me to complete this work and a Research Support Grant to assist in publication. Thanks are also due to Dr. Daniel L. Pals, Chairman of the Religion Department, and Dr. David L. Wilson, Dean of the College of Arts and Sciences, for securing additional funds for publication.

Finally, I would like to dedicate this work to my father, Jack H. Sweeney, and the memory of my mother, Leonore R. D. Sweeney.

Coral Gables, Florida, autumn 1987   Marvin A. Sweeney

Table of Contents

Abbreviations

1QIsa[a]	The Great Isaiah Scroll from Qumran Cave 1
1QS	The Order of the Community from Qumran Cave 1
AB	Anchor Bible
ALUOS	Annual of the Leeds University Oriental Society
AnBib	Analecta Biblica
ANET	Ancient Near Eastern Texts Relating to the Old Testament. 3rd ed. with Supplement. 1969
AO	Acta Orientalia
AOAT	Alter Orient und Altes Testament
AUM	Andrews University Monographs
AUSS	Andrews University Seminary Studies
BDB	A Hebrew and English Lexicon of the Old Testament. By F. Brown, S. R. Driver, C. A. Briggs.
BEvT	Beiträge zur evangelischen Theologie
BHS	Biblia Hebraica Stuttgartensia
Bibl	Biblica
BJS	Brown Judaic Studies
BKAT	Biblischer Kommentar, Altes Testament
BWANT	Beiträge zur Wissenschaft vom Alten und Neuen Testament
BZ	Biblische Zeitschrift
BZAW	Beihefte zur Zeitschrift für die alttestamentliche Wissenschaft
CB	Cambridge Bible
CBOTS	Coniectanea Biblica Old Testament Series
CBQMS	Catholic Biblical Quarterly Monograph Series
CTM	Calwer Theologische Monographien
ExpT	The Expository Times
FThL	Forum Theologiae Linguisticae
FZB	Forschung zur Bibel
HAT	Handbuch zum Alten Testament
HBT	Horizons in Biblical Theology
Herm	Hermeneia
HSM	Harvard Semitic Monographs
IB	The Interpreter's Bible
ICC	International Critical Commentary
IDB	The Interpreter's Dictionary of the Bible
IDB[S]	The Interpreter's Dictionary of the Bible Supplementary Volume
Int	Interpretation
JB	Jerusalem Bible
JBL	Journal of Biblical Literature
JBLMS	Journal of Biblical Literature Monograph Series

JPS	The Holy Scriptures. Jewish Publication Society. 1917
JQR	Jewish Quarterly Review
JSOT	Journal for the Study of the Old Testament
JSOTSS	Journal for the Study of the Old Testament Supplement Series
JSS	Journal of Semitic Studies
KAT	Kommentar zum Alten Testament
KHAT	Kurzer Hand-Commentar zum Alten Testament
KJV	King James Version
LXX	Septuagint
MT	Masoretic Text
NCeB	New Century Bible Commentary
NEB	New English Bible
NJV	New Jewish Version
OBO	Orbis Biblicus et Orientalia
OTL	Old Testament Library
PSB	Princeton Seminary Bulletin
RSV	Revised Standard Version
SBL	Society of Biblical Literature
SBLMS	Society of Biblical Literature Monograph Series
SBS	Stuttgarter Bibelstudien
SBT	Studies in Biblical Theology
SJT	Scottish Journal of Theology
SVT	Supplements to Vetus Testamentum
ThB	Theologische Bücherei
TB	Torch Bible Commentary
TDOT	Theological Dictionary of the Old Testament
TZ	Theologische Zeitschrift
TJ	Targum Jonathan on the Prophets
TThS	Trierer Theologische Studien
VT	Vetus Testamentum
WMANT	Wissenschaftliche Monographien zum Alten und Neuen Testament
ZAW	Zeitschrift für die alttestamentliche Wissenschaft
ZBK	Zürcher Bibelkommentare

Chapter I
Introduction

Ever since the publication of Duhm's famous commentary in 1892, modern Biblical scholarship has recognized that the book of Isaiah is a composite work.[1] The words of the eighth century prophet, Isaiah ben Amoz, are found exclusively in Isa 1 – 39. Isa 40 – 55 contains the words of an anonymous prophet from the period of the Babylonian exile, generally designated as Deutero-Isaiah, and Isa 56 – 66 contains post-exilic materials attributed to either an individual or various authors generally designated as Trito-Isaiah.[2] Consequently, chapters 40 – 66 are treated as if they constituted a separate book, or books, which were appended to the earlier Isaianic collection in chapters 1 – 39.

Scholars have also recognized that Isa 1 – 39 contains a great deal of later material in addition to the words of Isaiah ben Amoz.[3] Some passages, such as Isa 24 – 27, were identified as independent compositions which were secondarily inserted into the book. Other passages, such as Isa 4, 2 – 6, were seen as scribal expansions of an already existing Isaianic text. In the view of many scholars, these later scribal additions have somehow obscured or distorted the "authentic" messsage of the prophet himself which is of primary theological importance. Consequently, many studies have examined these chapters in an effort to identify and reconstruct the "authentic" sayings of Isaiah so that they might be recovered from the additions of later scribes which had grown up around them. Theological discussion of Isaiah therefore proceeded on the basis of passages that were viewed as accurately preserving the words or actions of Isaiah ben Amoz. Passages that were identified as independent compositions were treated in isolation from their contexts in the book of Isaiah. Passages that were identified as later editorial additions were generally viewed as having less, if any, theological significance and were

---

[1] B. Duhm, Das Buch Jesaia, 1968[5]. For a brief survey of critical problems in the book of Isaiah, see B. Childs, Introduction to the Old Testament as Scripture, 1979, 316 ff.

[2] For a survey of opinions on Trito-Isaiah, see O. Kaiser, Introduction to the Old Testament, 1975, 268 f.

[3] For surveys of research on Isa 1 – 39, see J. Vermeylen, Du prophète d'Isaïe à l'apocalyptique I, 1977, 1 ff.; H. Wildberger, Jesaja 28 – 39 (BKAT X/3), 1982, 1529 ff.

frequently disregarded or deemphasized in theological discussion of Isa
1–39.

This situation has begun to change in the last few decades as
scholars have reconsidered their evaluation of redactional materials. Past
scholarship viewed redactors in opposition to authors. Their basic task
was not creative, like that of authors, but mechanical, merely to collect
and transmit older literary works.[4] They were viewed as technicians,
"scissors and paste men," who may add irrelevant and dull comments
to their material, frequently distorting its message, but who had very
little of theological worth to say.[5] The studies of G. von Rad on the
Jahwist[6] and M. Noth on the Deuteronomist,[7] however, demonstrated
the role of theological intent and literary creativity in relation to the
work of redaction. While von Rad and Noth defined the Jahwist and
Deuteronomist as authors who employed redactional methods, later
scholars have recognized redactors as creative theologians who give a
"new interpretation" to the older materials which they transmit.[8] The
result has been a new interest in the study of the redactional materials
within the Biblical tradition.

This new interest in the theological intent of redaction has had a
special impact on the study of Isa 1–39. Thus, H. Barth has identified
a late seventh century "Assyrian redaction" in Isa 2–32. According to
Barth, this redaction interpreted and presented older Isaianic material
in order to claim that the rise and fall of the Assyrian empire was part
of a divine plan to rebuild the Davidic empire under Josiah.[9] Likewise,
Vermeylen's study of Isa 1–35 focused on the intent of each of seven
redactional stages in the formation of these chapters. For each stage,
Vermeylen claimed that the older material was "reread" in accordance

[4] G. Fohrer, Introduction to the Old Testament, 1968, 190; O. Eissfeldt, The Old
Testament: An Introduction, 1965, 239 f.

[5] Cf. K. Koch, The Growth of the Biblical Tradition, 1969, 57.

[6] Das formgeschichtliche Problem des Hexateuch, BWANT 4, 1938.

[7] Überlieferungsgeschichtliche Studien: Die sammelnden und bearbeitenden Geschichtswerke im alten Testament, 1957², 1 ff.

[8] Koch, The Growth of the Biblical Tradition, 57 ff.; H. Barth & O. H. Steck, Exegese
des alten Testaments: Leitfaden der Methodik, 1980⁹, 50 ff.; G. Tucker, Form Criticism
of the Old Testament, 1971, 19 f.; G. Fohrer et al., Exegese des alten Testaments:
Einführung in die Methodik, 1976³, 135 ff.; O. Kaiser, Old Testament Exegesis, Exegetical Method: A Student Handbook, 1981, 12 ff.; W. Richter, Exegese als Literaturwissenschaft: Entwurf einer alttestamentlichen Literaturtheorie und Methodologie, 1971,
165 ff.; J. A. Wharton, IDB[S], 729 ff.; R. Knierim, Criticism of Literary Features, Form
Tradition, and Redaction, The Hebrew Bible and Its Modern Interpreters, ed. D.
Knight & G. Tucker, 1985, 150 ff.

[9] H. Barth, Die Jesaja-Worte in der Josiazeit, WMANT 48, 1977; cf. R. E. Clements,
Isaiah 1–39, NCeB, 1980.

with the theological concerns pertaining to the contemporary situation of the redactors.[10] O. Kaiser's commentary on Isa 1 – 39 also emphasizes the redactional character of these chapters.[11] He argues that the editors have so reworked the materials of the book that it is impossible to trace any material back to the prophet. According to Kaiser, the Levitical circles of the Deuteronomistic movement began to assemble the book in the 5th century as a means of presenting their understanding of the catastrophe of 587 B.C.E. The book continued to grow until approximately the Maccabean era as later generations interpreted and expanded the Isaianic tradition in relation to contemporary concerns. Finally, H. Wildberger traces the redactional process which led to the final formation of Isa 1 – 39 as a book before 400 B.C.E.[12] He argues that the prophet himself fixed the basic form of the text, but various later groups expanded the tradition according to their view of the prophet's relevance to major events of their time. Thus, an exilic judgment recension appeared following the fall of Jerusalem and a salvation recension appeared in relation to the post-exilic restoration. Post-exilic expansions reflect tensions within the Jewish community until the final formation of the book in the time of Ezra and Nehemiah.

In their studies of the editorial history of Isa 1 – 39, the scholars mentioned above have treated these chapters as a self-contained whole, independent of Isa 40 – 66. Yet other scholars have raised the question whether the editorial history of Isa 1 – 39 should be considered in relation to Isa 40 – 66. Thus, S. Mowinckel argued that the entire book of Isaiah was the product of an Isaianic school that continued to develop the text and message of Isaiah ben Amoz through Deutero-Isaiah, Trito-Isaiah, and other anonymous figures.[13] He was followed by D. Jones who argued that the present arrangement of Isaiah 1 – 5 presupposed the fall of Jerusalem in 586 and that it was established by Isaiah's disciples who attempted to apply the prophet's message to the needs of their time.[14] He further maintained that the reference to the "former things" in Deutero-Isaiah indicated that the greatest of the prophet's disciples reflected on the collected oracles of Isaiah in formulating his own message. It was considerations such as these that prompted J. Becker to argue that the book of Isaiah must be interpreted as a redactional unity which was assembled by the Isaianic school during the Babylonian exile.[15] Becker sketched the redactional organization of the book arguing

---

[10] Du prophète d'Isaïe à l'apocalyptique, 1977 – 78.

[11] Isaiah 1 – 12: A Commentary, OTL, 1983²; Isaiah 13 – 39: A Commentary, OTL, 1974.

[12] H. Wildberger, Jesaja 28 – 39, 1529 ff.

[13] Jesaja-disiplene. Prophetien frå Jesaja til Jeremia, 1926, AO 11 (1933), 267 ff.

[14] ZAW 67 (1955) 226 ff.

[15] Isaias – der Prophet und sein Buch, SBS 30, 1968.

that its purpose was to apply the old Davidic covenant to all Israel so that the post-exilic Jewish community could be reconstituted as a theocracy under the kingship of God.

Other scholars are just beginning to consider the redaction of Isa 1 – 39 in relation to the book as a whole. In his study of Isa 1 – 12, P. Ackroyd questions the assumption that Isa 1 – 39 should be considered separate from the whole.[16] He argues that the structure of chapters 1 – 12 represents an attempt on the part of the book's redactors to present the prophet in relation to the needs of the post-exilic Jewish community. Thus, Isaiah's message of judgment was reinterpreted as one of salvation in relation to the expectations of post-exilic Judaism. Furthermore, his studies of Isa 36 – 39 establish the transitional character of these chapters in that they provide a redactional link between Isa 1 – 35 and Isa 40 – 66.[17] In this respect, the positive presentation of Hezekiah in these chapters, in contrast to that of Ahaz in Isa 6, 1 – 9, 6, provides the contextual basis for the salvation prophecies of chapters 40 ff.

Child's canon critical study of the entire book of Isaiah questions whether Deutero-Isaiah ever circulated independently from the first part of the book.[18] He argues that Isa 1 – 39 is structured in a clear theological pattern, integrally related with Deutero-Isaiah, which stresses the interrelationship between judgment and eschatological salvation as part of God's plan for His people in all ages. Thus, the major aim of the redaction of First Isaiah was to ensure that its message was interpreted in the light of Second Isaiah.

Clements points to the questionable nature of the assumption that the unity of the book of Isaiah is a unity based on authorship.[19] In arguing for a redactional unity of the book, he notes a number of thematic and textual connections between the first and second parts of the book which indicate an overall message of hope. Based on his view that the connection of chapters 40 ff. to the earlier materials was a deliberate step to clarify and fill out the divine message given to Israel, Clements argues that Deutero-Isaiah develops a number of themes from

[16] Isaiah I – XII: Presentation of a Prophet, SVT 29 (1978), 16 ff.
[17] Isaiah 36 – 39: Structure and Function, Von Kanaan bis Kerala, Festschrift für Prof. Mag. Dr. Dr. J. P. M. van der Ploeg, O. P. zur Vollendung des siebzigsten Lebensjahres am 4. Juli 1979, ed. J. R. Nelis, J. R. T. M. Peters et al. AOAT 211, 1982, 3 ff. Cf. SJT 27 (1974), 328 ff.; The Death of Hezekiah – A Pointer to the Future? De la Tôrah au Messie: Études d'exégèse et d'herméneutique bibliques offertes à Henri Cazelles pour ses 25 années d'enseignement à l'Institut Catholique de Paris (Octobre 1979), ed. M. Carrez, J. Doné, P. Grelot, 1982, 219 ff.
[18] Introduction to the Old Testament as Scripture, 325 ff.
[19] Int 36 (1982), 117 ff.

the first part of the book.[20] In this respect, he sees Second Isaiah as a supplement and sequel to the collection of First Isaiah's sayings which was intended to influence the way in which the older material was understood.

Finally, R. Rendtorff examines the appearance and usage of a number of key terms and themes of Second Isaiah, especially from chapter 40, in First and Third Isaiah.[21] On the basis of his observations, Rendtorff argues that Second Isaiah was the compositional core of the book of Isaiah and may have existed independently prior to its placement in the book. Neither First nor Third Isaiah can be understood apart from Second Isaiah. First Isaiah was redactionally shaped as a *précis* for Second Isaiah. Third Isaiah was composed to bind First and Second Isaiah together. Rendtorff argues that this compositional process represents the post-exilic community's attempt to interpret First Isaiah's message of judgment in relation to Second Isaiah's message of salvation. Like Ackroyd, Childs, and Clements, he presupposes that the redactional process is motivated by post-exilic Judaism's understanding of God's purposes in history.

These scholars have raised a number of considerations which support the view that the book of Isaiah is a redactional unity. Not only do their studies indicate that chapters 40 – 66 build upon themes, concepts, and language from chapters 1 – 39, but that the first part of the book is presented in such a way as to anticipate the concerns of the second. In other words, the two parts of the book cannot be properly understood in isolation from each other, they must be understood as two interrelated components of a redactionally unified whole.

The conclusions of these scholars also raise methodological issues in relation to the study of the redaction of Isa 1 – 39, the composition of the book of Isaiah as a whole, and redaction critical methodology in general. These issues pertain specifically to the structure of Isa 1 – 39 in relation to the structure of the book as a whole, the hermeneutical perspective of the redaction in relation to the earlier texts which it is editing, and the process of growth by which these texts reached their final redactional final form.

First, the view that Isa 1 – 39 must be understood in relation to Isa 40 – 66 has implications for the manner in which the structure of these chapters is considered. While none of these scholars has undertaken a detailed analysis of the structure of Isa 1 – 39,[22] their studies conclude that these chapters are structured in a manner that anticipates Isa 40 – 66.

---

[20] JSOT 31 (1985), 95 ff.

[21] VT 34 (1984), 295 ff.; The Old Testament: An Introduction, 1986, 198 ff.

[22] Cf. Child's brief overview of the structure of Isaiah 1 – 39 (Introduction to the Old Testament as Scripture, 330 ff.)

This indicates that, at the final redactional level, the structure of Isa 1 – 39 is determined not only in relation to the issues and concerns that are raised within these chapters themselves, but in relation to the issues and concerns of chapters 40 – 66 as well. Furthermore, because the structure of Isa 1 – 39 anticipates Isa 40 – 66, the concerns of the second part of the book are the dominant factor in determining the structure of the first part. Consequently, a complete understanding of the structure of Isa 1 – 39 at its final redactional level requires that these chapters be considered in relation to the structure of the entire book. In short, Isa 1 – 39 is a structural sub-unit of Isa 1 – 66.

Second, if the basic understanding and structure of Isa 1 – 39 is determined in relation to the interests and perspectives of Isa 40 – 66, this has implications for understanding the hermeneutical perspective of the redaction. For example, Clements has demonstrated that a number of Deutero-Isaiah's themes are developed from those of Isa 1 – 39.[23] Yet, Deutero-Isaiah's understanding of those themes is not determined exclusively by their context in Isa 1 – 39, but in relation to the historical events and theological impulses of his contemporary situation. Furthermore, one cannot always be certain that the specific examples of themes from Isa 1 – 39 predated Deutero-Isaiah. It is possible that the presentation of these themes was influenced or even introduced by a redaction which sought to relate First and Second Isaiah together. For example, do Deutero-Isaiah's references to the fall of Babylon presuppose the oracle against Babylon in Isa 13, 1 – 14, 23, or was this oracle introduced to the text or modified in relation to Deutero-Isaiah's message?[24] Certainly, in the final redactional form of the book of Isaiah, this oracle must be understood in anticipation of the message of Deutero-Isaiah regardless of the time of its composition or the intent of its author. This indicates that although the final redactional understanding of Isa 1 – 39 may be based on the redaction's interpretation of the text, this understanding is ultimately imposed from outside the text itself. This is because the redaction's interpretation of the text will not necessarily correspond to the intent of the original author. Instead, it will be determined in relation to later textual tradition and to the historical and theological circumstances of the time of the redaction. Consequently, the presentation of Isa 1 – 39 is determined not only by factors inherent in the text of these chapters, it is also determined by the hermeneutical

---

[23] JSOT 31 (1985), 95 ff.

[24] Cf. Wildberger, Jesaja 13 – 27, (BKAT X/2), 1978, 505 ff., 524 f., 536 ff., 539 ff., who sees the final composition of this material in relation to the death of Nebuchadrezzar. S. Erlandsson maintains that this material originally stemmed from Isaiah's condemnation of Assyria in the late 8th – early 7th centuries (The Burden of Babylon: A Study of Isaiah 13:2 – 14:23, CBOTS 4, 1970, 160 ff.).

viewpoint of the redaction which is actively shaping the final form of
that text. Again, the redaction's hermeneutical perspective is dominant
in determining the presentation of the text since it makes the final
decisions concerning inclusion, exclusion, editing, placement, expansion,
and excision.

Third, the conclusions of these studies have an influence on the
way in which scholars conceive the growth process of the book of Isaiah.
Rendtorff's work in particular has called into question the standard
model for the book's growth. Formerly, the composition of Isaiah was
seen to begin with one or more small collections of materials stemming
from the prophet or his disciples. From this base, the tradition would
expand as later writers would make additions to the text until the final
form of the book was achieved. In short, the Isaianic core determined
the basic pattern for the growth process in that additions and expansions
were built around this original deposit of material. Instead, Rendtorff
sees Isa 40 – 55 as the core around which the book is constructed.
Likewise, the studies of Ackroyd, Childs, and Clements implicitly support the contention that Isa 1 – 39 and 56 – 66 are constructed in relation
to chapters 40 – 55. While this does not deny the existence or influence
of earlier deposits of Isaianic tradition that were included in the book,
it does indicate the influence of the intentions of the redaction in
determining the pattern of growth for the book of Isaiah. For example,
the present form of Isa 5, 8 – 25 and 9, 7 – 10, 4 indicate that an early
collection of Woe oracles and an early collection of oracles including a
common refrain have been split apart and recombined in a form that
mixes the two types.[25] This is clearly a redactional decision that disrupted
the pattern of earlier tradition. In sum, both earlier deposits of Isaianic
tradition and the intentions of the redactors play a role in determining
the basic patterns of growth in the book of Isaiah. Nevertheless, the
redaction makes the final decisions and therefore determines the last
stages of the process of composition.

These considerations indicate that, in its present form, Isa 1 – 39 is
the product of the final redaction of the entire book of Isaiah. Although
Isa 1 – 39 undoubtedly contains a great deal of material stemming from
Isaiah ben Amoz and other writers, the final form of these chapters is
composed, structured, and understood in relation to Isa 40 – 66. In short,
Isa 1 – 39 is presented as the preface which looks forward to Isa 40 – 66,
and Isa 40 – 66 is presented as the completion which presupposes Isa
1 – 39. Consequently, any attempt to properly understand the redactional
formation of Isa 1 – 39 requires both synthetic and analytical proce-

---

[25] Cf. Kaiser, Isaiah 1 – 12, 96 f., 220 ff.

dures.[26] Analysis must begin with a synthetic procedure, a detailed examination of the final form of the entire book, including its structure, genre, setting, and intent.[27] This will facilitate a clear understanding of the purposes, perspective, and historical background of the final redaction of the book. Furthermore, it will also clarify how Isa 1 – 39 functions in relation to the purposes of the book as a whole, thus specifying the role which these chapters play as a component of the book of Isaiah. Once this synthetic step is completed, the study may then turn to its analytical stage, an inquiry into the process by which the text arrived at its final form. The analysis will employ the standard tools of critical Biblical scholarship to identify and date the earlier materials which stand behind the final redactional form of the text as well as the editorial additions and expansions which have organized these materials into their present form. This will allow for a reconstruction of any redactional stages that may be apparent in the text. Furthermore, it will serve as a basis for comparing the form, intent, and perspective of the final redaction with that of earlier stages in the composition of the text. By this means, the redaction's understanding of earlier text material can be established in that it can determine how the intent of the redaction grows out of the earlier texts as well as how it determines the presentation of those texts. This will clarify the hermeneutical perspective of the redaction in its interpretation and application of earlier textual tradition.

Limitations of space do not allow for a full study of the redactional formation of the entire book of Isaiah. Consequently, this study will be a preliminary attempt to understand the redactional formation of the book by focusing especially on Isa 1 – 4. These chapters were chosen because their position at the beginning of the book suggests a potentially programmatic character[28] and because most scholars maintain that they contain material from later writers as well as from Isaiah ben Amoz.[29] The plan of this study will therefore be as follows: Chapter II will

---

[26] For the distinction between analytical and synthetic procedures, see Barth & Steck, Exegese des alten Testaments, 10 ff.

[27] A number of scholars are beginning to recognize that a full understanding of the redactional character of Biblical materials requires that analysis begin with the final form of the book concerned. Cf. Knierim, Criticism of Literary Features, Form, Tradition, and Redaction, 156; K. Koch, Amos: Untersucht mit den Methode einer strukturalen Formgeschichte, AOAT 30, 1976, I 31 f., 78 ff.; L. Keck & G. Tucker, IDB[S], 299 ff.; J. Willis, Redaction Criticism and Historical Reconstruction, Encounter with the Text: Form and History in the Hebrew Bible, ed. M. Buss, 1979, 88; R. Clements, Prophecy and Tradition, 1975, 6.

[28] Cf. G. Fohrer, Jesaja 1 als Zusammenfassung der Verkündigung Jesajas, BZAW 99, 1967, 148 ff.

[29] E. g., Clements, VT 30 (1980), 421 ff.

examine the evidence for viewing the book of Isaiah as a redactional unity. Chapter III will analyze the book of Isaiah as a whole in order to determine its structure, genre, intent, and setting.[30] Chapter IV will analyze chapters 1–4 of the book of Isaiah in attempt to understand how the redaction of the book assembled this material in relation to its purposes in composing the book as a whole. Chapter V will present the results of this study for understanding the redactional formation of Isa 1–4, as well as its implications for further research into the redactional formation of the book as a whole.

---

[30] For the form critical methodology employed here, see R. P. Knierim, Int 27 (1973), 435 ff.

Chapter II
The redactional unity of the book of Isaiah

As noted in Chapter I, the studies of Ackroyd,[1] Becker,[2] Childs,[3] Clements,[4] and Rendtorff,[5] have indicated that there are grounds for considering the book of Isaiah as a redactional unity. There are a number of lines of evidence, including thematic, literary, and structural considerations, that support this contention. These lines of evidence require examination to establish the need for an analysis of the book as a whole.

The first line of evidence centers around the role which Babylon plays in chapters 1 – 39. While Babylon is a central concern in the works of Deutero-Isaiah, it comes as somewhat of a surprise that the oracle against Babylon (Isa 13, 1 – 14, 23) heads the collection of oracles against the nations in Isa 13 – 23. Here, Babylon is presented as the symbol of world power which is about to be overthrown as a major enemy of God.[6] Babylon would certainly have filled this role during the time of Deutero-Isaiah, but prior to the 6th century, such a portrayal would have been appropriate only for Assyria. Assyria is mentioned in a short appendix (Isa 14, 24 – 27) to the oracle against Babylon. Consequently, some scholars have claimed that this oracle, or at least the taunt against the king in Isa 14, 3 – 23, was originally directed against Assyria, but was changed to Babylon in the light of later historical circumstances.[7] While the view that Assyria was the original subject of this oracle is

---

[1] SJT 27 (1974), 328 ff.; Isaiah I – XII: Presentation of a Prophet; Isaiah 36 – 39: Structure and Function; The Death of Hezekiah – A Pointer to the Future?

[2] Isaias – Der Prophet und sein Buch.

[3] Introduction to the Old Testament as Scripture, 311 ff.

[4] Int 36 (1982), 117 ff.; JSOT 31 (1985), 95 ff.

[5] VT 29 (1984), 295 ff.; The Old Testament: An Introduction, 190 ff.

[6] A number of scholars likewise see the placement of Babylon at the head of Isaiah's oracles against the nations as a further indication of its status as the major world power and representative of the nations. Cf. Kaiser, Isaiah 13 – 39, 2; G. B. Gray, A Critical and Exegetical Commentary on the Book of Isaiah I – XXVII, I, ICC, 1912, 233; G. Fohrer, Das Buch Jesaja, ZBK, 1966², I 181 f.; R. B. Y. Scott, The Book of Isaiah, Chapters 1 – 39: Introduction and Exegesis, IB V, 254 f.

[7] Erlandsson, The Burden of Babylon, 160 ff.; E. J. Kissane, The Book of Isaiah, I 1960², 146 ff., 159 f.; Barth, Die Jesaja-Worte, 135 ff.; Clements, Isaiah 1 – 39, 139.

attractive, the evidence is tentative and most scholars recognize that the present form of the oracle against Babylon stems from the exilic period or later.[8] Nevertheless, this only underscores the fact that in the perspective of Isa 13, 1 – 14, 23, Babylon has replaced Assyria as the dominant world power and the major enemy of God. This portrayal and the expectation of Babylon's imminent fall to the Medes correspond to the perspective of the second part of the book of Isaiah. In this respect, the oracle against Babylon serves as a major thematic link between Isa 1 – 39 and Isa 40 – 66.

A second line of evidence may be traced through the transitional function of Isa 36 – 39 in which the theme of Babylon also plays an important role. These chapters include three narratives concerning God's deliverance of Jerusalem from the Assyrian siege of the city in 701 B.C.E., Hezekiah's sickness and recovery, and Hezekiah's reception of a Babylonian embassy from Merodach-baladan. These narratives are all interrelated in their present context by temporal formulas in 38, 1 (*bayyāmîm hāhēm*) and 39, 1 (*bā'et hahî'*) which indicate that the events described are contemporaneous. This is significant in that following the report of God's deliverance of Jerusalem from the Assyrians in Isa 36 – 37, Isa 39 reports Isaiah's announcement that the Babylonians will carry away all that their embassy has seen in their visit to Jerusalem. This is generally understood as a reference to the Babylonian exile.

These chapters correspond to 2 Reg 18, 13 – 20, 19 and were generally believed to have been added as a conclusion to First Isaiah, analogous to Jer 52. However, Ackroyd's studies in particular establish the transitional character of these chapters within the book of Isaiah in that the announcement of the Babylonian deportation in Isa 39 provides the context for the prophecies of Second Isaiah.[9]

Ackroyd's conclusions are not entirely based on this observation, however, but focus to a large extent on the role that Hezekiah plays in these narratives. He notes that the portrayal of Hezekiah in these chapters is presented as a deliberate contrast to that of Ahaz in Isa 6, 1 – 9, 6. When both kings were faced with similar circumstances, an invasion of the land by foreign armies, Hezekiah turned to God for deliverance whereas Ahaz rejected God's deliverance offered through Isaiah. There is certainly a strong basis for this view. Both Isa 36 – 39 and Isa 6, 1 – 9, 6 are historical narratives which include chronological introductions in 6, 1; 7, 1; and 36, 1. Both narratives report an encounter between the king and the prophet during a time of foreign invasion,

---

[8] E. g., Wildberger, Jesaja 13 – 27, 505 ff., 524 f., 536 ff., 539 ff.; Clements, Isaiah 1 – 39, 132 ff.

[9] SJT 27 (1974), 349; Isaiah 36 – 39, 3 ff.

although they differ in that Isaiah comes to Ahaz to offer deliverance whereas Hezekiah comes to Isaiah to request deliverance. Both narratives emphasize the location "by the conduit of the upper pool on the highway to the Fuller's Field" (7, 3; 36, 2). Both kings are offered signs of God's faithfulness in times of crisis. In Isa 7, 11, 14, Ahaz refuses a sign from God which demonstrates his own lack of faith. In Isa 37, 30, Hezekiah is given a sign concerning God's deliverance of Jerusalem and in Isa 38, 7, 22, he accepts a sign that he will be healed from his sickness. Both narratives employ the phrase, "the zeal of the Lord of Hosts will do this." In Isa 37, 32, it follows Isaiah's announcement of the sign promising deliverance of Jerusalem. In Isa 9, 6, it concludes the oracle promising the "Prince of Peace," which many scholars understand in reference to Hezekiah. This is particularly significant in relation to Isa 36 – 39 since in Isa 9, 1 – 6, the prophet looks forward to a bright future under a new king following his disillusionment (Isa 8, 16) with Ahaz. Finally, the reference to the "Dial of Ahaz" in Isa 38, 8 accentuates the contrast between the faithful Hezekiah who looks to God for his cure and the faithless Ahaz who refuses God's offer of deliverance to turn to the Assyrians instead.

Another aspect of this idealization of Hezekiah in Isa 36 – 39 involves the textual differences between these chapters and the corresponding account in 2 Reg 18, 13 – 20, 19.[10] These differences are generally attributed to scribal inconsistencies in the transmission of the text. A number of these differences, however, betray a deliberate attempt not only to idealize Hezekiah as a faithful servant of God but to emphasize God's immediate response to Hezekiah's demonstrations of faith.

This interest appears in several passages in Isa 36 – 37. For example, Isa 36, 1 ff. eliminates the reference to Hezekiah's capitulation to the Assyrian king which appears in 2 Reg 18, 14 – 16. This removes any suggestion that he did anything but turn to God (cf. Isa 37, 1 ff., 14 ff.). Likewise, Isa 36, 17 f. eliminates and modifies the text of 2 Reg 18, 32 which reads, "a land of olives, oil, and honey. So live and do not die and do not listen to Hezekiah because he will mislead you saying, 'YHWH will deliver us.'" The first part of this statement is completely absent in Isa 36, 17 and v. 18 reads simply, "unless Hezekiah misleads you saying, 'YHWH will deliver us.'" This modification eliminates a statement that encourages disparagement of Hezekiah and indicates that the Assyrian will accomplish his purpose despite Hezekiah's attempts to stop him. By stating "unless (*pæn*) Hezekiah misleads you," the text of

---

[10] Ackroyd notes the significance of the textual differences between Isa 36 – 39 and 2 Reg 18, 13 – 20, 19 but does not trace them fully (cf. Isaiah 36 – 39, 7, 19 f.; The Death of Hezekiah, 220).

Isaiah accentuates Hezekiah's opposition to the Assyrian monarch and anticipates that he will indeed thwart his plans to deport the Judean soldiers. Finally, Isa 37, 36 eliminates the statement, "and it came to pass that night," from the corresponding text of 2 Reg 19, 35. This removes any sense of delay in God's response to Hezekiah's petition for deliverance (Isa 37, 15 – 20) in that the angel of the Lord acts to save the city immediately after Isaiah's salvation oracle.

The text of Isa 38 has been extensively modified from that of 2 Reg 20, 1 – 11. Like the examples cited above, it also idealizes Hezekiah and emphasizes YHWH's immediate response to Hezekiah's demonstrations of faithfulness. 2 Reg 18, 4 f. reads, "And Isaiah had not gone out from the middle court when the word of YHWH came to him saying, 'Return and you shall say to Hezekiah, prince of my people. ...'" Isa 38, 4 f. reads simply, "And the word of YHWH came to Isaiah, saying, 'Go and you shall say to Hezekiah. ...'" By eliminating the reference to Isaiah's intended departure from the inner court and emending "return" to "go," the writer of Isa 38, 4 f. emphasizes that YHWH's response to Hezekiah's prayer in v. 2 f. occurred immediately, not while Isaiah was leaving.[11] Likewise in reporting God's response through Isaiah, 2 Reg 38, 5 f. reads, "Behold, I am healing you. On the third day, you shall go up to the House of the Lord and I shall add fifteen years to your days." Isa 38, 5 reads simply, "Behold, I am adding fifteen years to your days." By removing the reference to Hezekiah's going up to the House of the Lord on the third day after God heals him, the Isaiah text eliminates any indication of delay in God's action. Furthermore, the removal of the reference to God's healing Hezekiah deemphasizes a potential motivation for Hezekiah's piety.

Isa 38, 6 eliminates a major portion of 2 Reg 20, 6 – 9 which contains a number of important points. These include reference to God's motivation for deliverance (i. e., "for the sake of my Name and for the sake of David, my servant"), Isaiah's prescribed treatment for Hezekiah's boil and its application, and Hezekiah's asking for a sign that he will be healed and go to the House of the Lord on the third day. Thus, Isa 38, 6 eliminates God's concern for the continuation of the House of David and focuses on the individual figure of Hezekiah instead. This is in keeping with Isa 7, 9 which states that Ahaz, identified in 7, 2, 13, as the "House of David," will not be established if he is not faithful. The references to the treatment and the sign are moved to the end of the passage (Isa 38, 21 f.) but their absence from the present context

---

[11] Note that Isa 38, 2 adds "Hezekiah" as the subject of the verbs in the sentence. This emphasizes that Hezekiah prayed whereas 2 Reg 18, 2 f. does not specify the subject of the verbs.

aids in idealizing Hezekiah's character. Again, healing is deemphasized as a potential motivation for Hezekiah's faithfulness. The absence of Hezekiah's request for a sign eliminates any indication of doubt on his part. In Isa 38, 7, God simply announces the sign through Isaiah whereas in 2 Reg 20, 8 f., the announcement of the sign is God's response to Hezekiah's request.

Likewise, Isa 38, 7 eliminates 2 Reg 20, 9b – 11a. The missing verses include references to Isaiah's question to Hezekiah concerning the sign (i.e., should the shadow move ten steps forward or backward?), Hezekiah's response that it should follow the difficult course and move backwards, and the statement concerning Isaiah's compliance. The first two items indicate doubt on Hezekiah's part so that their removal aids in idealizing him. The removal of 2 Reg 20, 11a deemphasizes the prophet's role as intermediary between God and Hezekiah. Furthermore, whereas 2 Reg 20, 11b reads "and he (God) turned back the shadow. ...," Isa 38, 8a reads, "Behold, I (God) am turning back. ..." In the text of Isaiah, this verse is no longer part of a compliance report but part of a divine promise delivered to Hezekiah. Again, Hezekiah did not request this promise as he did in 2 Reg 18, God simply announced it. A newly formulated compliance report follows in Isa 38, 8b.

The Psalm of Hezekiah appears in Isa 38, 9 – 20. This is a major addition to the Isaiah text of this narrative which is entirely absent from 2 Reg 20. These verses constitute a psalm of thanksgiving by the king in which he thanks God for healing him from his sickness. This psalm is especially significant in the Isaiah version of this narrative in that it is the first speech by Hezekiah following God's promise of salvation. Here, Hezekiah does not question God, state terms of proof, or express doubt in any way as he does in 2 Reg 20. He simply expresses his thanks to God on the occasion of his being healed. Isaiah's statement concerning the fig cake and Hezekiah's question concerning the sign appear after the psalm. Their position here emphasizes Hezekiah's faithfulness in that the statement concerning the cure (v. 21) only appears after his psalm. Hezekiah's question (v. 22) is awkward in that it receives no answer. It contains no reference to healing (cf. 2 Reg 20, 8). Instead, it accentuates Hezekiah's piety in that his concern is only with going up to the House of the Lord, i.e, the Temple. In these respects, it prompts the reader to pause and reflect on Hezekiah as a model of faithfulness to God.

A final difference between the two versions also indicates that the writer of the Isaiah text intended to idealize the character of Hezekiah. Following Isaiah's announcement that Hezekiah's house will be exiled to Babylon, 2 Reg 20, 19 reports the king's response as, "'Good is the word of the Lord which you have spoken,' and he said, 'Is it not true that ($h^a l\hat{o}$' 'im) there will be peace and truth in my days?'" The wording of this statement implies conditionality and suggests doubt on the part of Hezekiah. In contrast, the wording of Isa 39, 8, "For (kî) there will be peace and truth in my days," implies no conditions and removes any indication that Hezekiah doubts God's promise of security in his own lifetime.

In sum, these differences between the text of 2 Reg 18, 13 – 20, 19 and Isa 36 – 39 are not the result of accidental scribal inconsistency in transmitting these texts. The modifications apparent in the text of the Isaiah version, especially the extensive restructuring of the account of Hezekiah's sickness, indicate a specific interest in presenting an idealized picture of the character of Hezekiah. Furthermore, the modifications indicate an interest in demonstrating God's immediate and favorable response to Hezekiah's demonstrations of faithfulness. The reason for this is to contrast the character of Hezekiah with that of Ahaz as Ackroyd's studies indicate. When placed in similar situations of national crisis, Ahaz refused YHWH's offer of deliverance whereas Hezekiah responded with faithfulness. The modifications of 2 Reg 18, 13 – 20, 19 apparent in Isa 36 – 39 emphasize this contrast. Hezekiah responds as Ahaz should have but did not.

The purpose of this contrast becomes apparent when one considers the transitional function of Isa 36 – 39 within the book of Isaiah. As Ackroyd notes, these chapters provide the context for the prophecies of chapters 40 ff. which immediately follow. He states that the basis for these prophecies of assurance rests on "the relationship between Hezekiah and Isaiah, idealised king and prophet of judgment and salvation."[12] Certainly, Hezekiah's contrast with Ahaz emphasizes this idealization but the contrast functions on more than just the personal level. As indicated by 7, 2, 13, 17 one of the major concerns of Isa 7, 1 – 9, 6 is with the House of David, not just the individual figure of Ahaz. When Isaiah declares to Ahaz in Isa 7, 9, "If you will not be faithful, surely you will not be secured," he speaks not only about Ahaz the individual, but about the House of David as a whole, and calls the whole Davidic covenant into question.[13] As Isa 55, 3 ff. indicates, Deutero-Isaiah reconceives the Davidic covenant in that he applies the eternal Davidic promise to the entire people, not just to the House of David.[14] Furthermore, Conrad's study of the "Fear not" oracles in Deutero-Isaiah (Isa 41, 8 ff.; 41, 14 ff.; 43, 1b ff.; 43, 5 ff.; and 43, 2b ff.) indicates that the prophet has

---

[12] Isaiah 36 – 39, 20.

[13] Clements, Isaiah 1 – 39, 85; Kaiser, Isaiah 1 – 12, 147 f.; O. H. Steck, TZ 29 (1973), 163.

[14] O. Eissfeldt, The Promises of Grace to David in Isaiah 55, 1 – 5, Israel's Prophetic Heritage: Essays in Honor of James Muilenburg, ed. B. W. Anderson & W. Harrelson, 1962, 196 ff.

employed a royal form of the "War Oracle" to the community of Israel.[15] This is particularly significant since Isaiah employed this genre to address both Ahaz and Hezekiah during their respective crises (cf. Isa 7, 4 ff.; 37, 6 f.). In this respect, the transitional function of Isa 36 – 39 becomes even clearer. Hezekiah establishes his faithfulness by responding positively to the oracle in 37, 6 f. whereas Ahaz responds negatively to the oracle in 7, 4 ff. When Hezekiah shows his stores to the Babylonian embassy in Isa 39, however, Isaiah condemns the king and announces that all that is in his "House" will be carried off to Babylon. This includes not only material goods but his sons as well. In short, Isaiah's announcement of exile is directed specifically against the House of David. In the context of the book as a whole, this condemnation of the Davidic House paves the way for the "democratized" Davidic covenant of Second Isaiah. Despite Hezekiah, the House of David has not proved to be sufficiently faithful for the eternal Davidic covenant. At the same time, Isa 9, 1 – 6 indicates that the promise will not be withdrawn. Consequently, the eternal Davidic covenant has been transferred to the people as a whole in Deutero-Isaiah.[16] Nevertheless, Hezekiah's faithfulness, as expressed in Isa 36 – 38, appears to serve as a model for faithfulness to the community in Second Isaiah.

A third line of evidence for the redactional unity of the book of Isaiah can be traced through Isa 35. Scholars have recognized that this chapter, with its themes of the transformation of the wilderness and the appearance of a highway for the return of God's ransomed people to Zion, corresponds closely to the major themes of Second Isaiah. Consequently, some scholars consider it to be the product of Second Isaiah,[17] but most reject this position and simply view it as a late

---

[15] Begrich, ZAW 52 (1934), 81 ff., identified these oracles generically as the priestly oracle of salvation. E. W. Conrad, Fear Not Warrior: A Study of the 'al tîrā' Pericopes in the Hebrew Scriptures, BJS 75, 1985, esp. 79 ff., argues that they are modified forms of a genre which he calls "War Oracle." According to Conrad, this prophetic genre is generally addressed to warriors before battle. The examples in Deutero-Isaiah represent a form of the Royal War Oracle, generally addressed to a king, which has been applied by the prophet to the community of Israel/Jacob (Cf. Conrad, The Community as King in Second Isaiah, Understanding the Word: Essays in Honor of Bernard W. Anderson, ed. J. T. Butler, E. W. Conrad, B. C. Ollenburger, JSOTSS 37, 1985, 99 ff.).

[16] This would explain the absence of the references to "prince of my people" (2 Reg 20, 5) in Isa 38, 5 and to God's motivation for delivering Jerusalem "for my sake and for the sake of my servant, David." (2 Reg 20, 6) in Isa 38, 6. The writer of the Isaiah text apparently wished to deemphasize the House of David in his portrayal of Hezekiah's faithfulness.

[17] H. Graetz, JQR 4 (1892), 1 ff.; C. C. Torrey, The Second Isaiah: A New Interpretation, 1928, 53 ff.; M. H. Pope, JBL 71 (1952), 235 ff.; J. D. Smart, History and Theology in Second Isaiah, 1965, 41, 292 ff.

composition.[18] Clements, Fohrer, and Kaiser have argued that this chapter is dependent on Isa 40 ff. and draws its themes from these chapters.[19]

Isa 35 also serves as a transitional chapter between the first and second parts of the book. In addition to anticipating the major themes of Second Isaiah, it draws on major themes from the preceding chapters which are then taken up in the second part of the book. These themes include the Exodus motif and that of the Blind and the Deaf.

Scholars have noted that the Exodus motif is a constitutive theme in the prophecy of Second Isaiah[20] but give little attention to its role in First Isaiah. The motif appears in Isa 35, 8 – 10 which describes a highway for the return of those redeemed by the Lord to Zion. The reference to the highway as the "Holy Way" and the exclusion of the unclean in v. 8 indicate an association with the Jerusalem Temple,[21] but as Clements, Kaiser, and Wildberger point out, parallel passages in Isa 11, 12, 16; 19, 23; 27, 12 f.; and 51, 11 associate the highway with the Exodus from Egypt.[22] The highway imagery appears frequently in Second Isaiah together with the transformation of nature and the return of the redeemed (i.e., Isa 40, 3 ff.; 42, 14 ff.; 43, 14 ff.; 48, 20 ff.; 49, 8 ff.; 51, 9 ff.; 52, 11 f.; 55, 12 f.). As indicated above, this imagery also appears in Isa 11, 10 ff. and 19, 10 ff. In addition, these passages, together with Isa 10, 20 ff. and 27, 1, 12 f., emphasize the analogy between the Egyptian oppression which led to the Exodus and the Assyrian oppression which is the concern of First Isaiah, an analogy which also appears in Second Isaiah (Isa 52, 3 ff.). In the context of First Isaiah, these passages look forward to the time when God will redeem Israel from Assyrian oppression just as Israel was redeemed from Egypt at the time of the Exodus.

The Exodus motif appears in other passages from First Isaiah as well. Isa 4, 2 – 6 speaks about the restoration of the remnant in Jerusalem after the city is cleansed from its iniquity. In describing the purified Mt. Zion, this passage states that God will create a cloud by day and the shining of flaming fire by night over the holy site. These images symbol-

---

[18] E. g., Wildberger, Jesaja 28 – 39, 1357 ff.

[19] Clements, Isaiah 1 – 39, 271 ff.; Fohrer, Das Buch Jesaja, II 1967², 144; Kaiser, Isaiah 13 – 39, 361 ff.

[20] B. W. Anderson, Exodus Typology in Second Isaiah, Israel's Prophetic Heritage: Essays in Honor of James Muilenburg, ed. B. W. Anderson & W. Harrelson, 1962, 177 ff.; Exodus and Covenant in Second Isaiah and Prophetic Tradition, in F. M. Cross, Jr., et al., (eds.) Magnalia Dei: The Mighty Acts of God, 1976, 339 ff.; K. Kiesow, Exodustexte im Jesajabuch, OBO 24, 1979.

[21] Kaiser, Isaiah 13 – 39, 365.

[22] Clements, Isaiah 1 – 39, 276 f.; Kaiser, Isaiah 13 – 39, 365 f.; Wildberger, Jesaja 28 – 39, 1363 f. Note also that in Ex 15, 13 ff. the procession of the redeemed Israelites leads to the sanctuary.

ized God's presence among the people, including protection at the Red Sea and guidance through the wilderness, during the Exodus (cf. Ex 13, 21 f.; 14, 19 f., 24; 33, 9 f.; 40, 34 ff.; Num 10, 11 f., 34; 14, 14). In their present context, they symbolize God's presence at Zion. The imagery also corresponds to Isa 52, 11 f. which indicates that God will go out before the returning exiles and act as their rearguard in a manner similar to that of the pillar of cloud and flame at the Exodus.

Scholars have long recognized the relationship between the Song of Thanksgiving in Isa 12 and the Song of the Sea in Ex 15.[23] Thus, Isa 12, 2b, "For the Lord God is my strength and song, and He has become my salvation," is nearly identical to Ex 15, 2a, "The Lord is my strength and song, and He has become my salvation." Likewise, Isa 12, 5a, "Sing praise to the Lord for He has done gloriously," is very similar to Ex 15, 1b, "I will sing to the Lord, for He is highly exalted." As Ackroyd notes, Isa 12, 3 may continue the Exodus theme by alluding to the motif of water from the rock.[24] Furthermore, the commands to make God's deeds known among the nations in v. 4a and 5b recall the witness of the nations at the Red Sea in Ex 15, 14 ff. The concluding function of this psalm indicates that it employs the Exodus motif in anticipation of the future redemption promised in the preceding chapters of Isaiah.

Other references to the Exodus motif appear in Isa 27, 8 and 37, 36. The mention of the East Wind in Isa 27, 8 calls to mind the strong East Wind that parted the Red Sea in Ex 14, 21; 15, 8 ff. (cf. Isa 11, 15; Hos 13, 15). Likewise, the angel of the Lord that kills 185,000 Assyrian troops in Isa 37, 36 corresponds to the "destroyer" (mašḥît), or angel of death (cf. 2 Sam 24, 16), who slays the first born of Egypt at the Passover (Ex 12, 23) or to the angel of the Lord who fights on behalf of Israel at the Red Sea (Ex 14, 19; cf. Ps 35, 5 f.).

Finally, Isa 6, the prophet's call narrative, includes a number of associations with the Exodus tradition. N. Habel has already called attention to the similarities between Isaiah's call narrative and that of Moses in Ex 3.[25] Furthermore, the appearance of the Seraphim in this chapter is noteworthy. Apart from two other references in the book of Isaiah (14, 29; 30, 6), Seraphim, or fiery serpents, appear elsewhere in the Bible only in texts that are associated with the Exodus tradition (Num 21, 6 ff.; Deut 8, 15). Their appearance here reinforces this chapter's message of judgment in that they were sent to punish the Israelites

---

[23] E. g., Duhm, Das Buch Jesaia, 111.

[24] Isaiah I – XII, 37.

[25] ZAW 77 (1965), 297 ff. Other scholars have seen the call narratives of Isaiah and Moses as representatives of two distinct types (cf. H. Wildberger, Jesaja 1 – 12, BKAT X/1, 1972, 234 ff.).

when they spoke against God during the wilderness period.[26] Likewise, Isaiah's lament that he is a man of unclean lips in v. 5 calls to mind Moses' objections that he is slow of speech (Ex 4, 10 ff.) and a man of uncircumcised lips (Ex 6, 12, 30) and therefore unfit to speak to the people of Israel or to Pharoah. Finally, Isaiah's commission is to make the heart of the people fat, their ears heavy, and their eyes closed so that they will be unable to understand and repent. This corresponds to God's hardening of Pharoah's heart in the Exodus accounts (Ex 4, 21; 7, 3 ff., 13 f., 22 f.; 14, 4, 8, 17). The reason for this in both the Exodus and Isaiah traditions was to allow God's plan to be carried out.

Most scholars would agree that, with the exception of Isa 6, these passages are late additions to the book of Isaiah.[27] Nevertheless, in their present context in First Isaiah, they point forward to a new Exodus in which Israel will again be redeemed following its punishment at the hands of Assyria. As indicated above, Second Isaiah announces this new Exodus. Consequently, these texts aid in establishing a redactional connection between the first and second parts of the book of Isaiah.

The theme of Israel's blindness and deafness appears in Isa 35, 5 ff. where it introduces the transformation of nature and the new Exodus. These verses stress that Israel's eyes and ears will be opened at the time of redemption. Clements has identified this theme as one of the factors which indicates the redactional unity of the book of Isaiah.[28] According to Clements, Israel's blindness and deafness is of central importance to Isa 40 – 55. It appears in four passages (Isa 42, 16; 42, 18 ff.; 43, 8; 44, 18) which indicate that the time for the redemption of the blind and deaf has come (cf. Isa 40, 21 ff.; 42, 6 f.; 48, 6 ff.). Clements maintains that the appearance of this theme in Deutero-Isaiah is intended as a conscious allusion to its occurrences in First Isaiah. Isa 29, 18; 32, 3; and 35, 5 anticipate that Israel's eyes and ears will be opened at the time of redemption. Clements traces the origin of the theme to Isa 6, 9 f. where it serves as a constituent element of Isaiah's prophetic commission. As noted above, the theme is associated with the hardening of the heart motif which ultimately derives from the Exodus tradition. Ex 4, 11 indicates that the blindness and deafness theme is likewise a part of the Exodus tradition although in Isaiah, it is specifically applied to Israel. Isa 6, 9 ff. argues that Israel must be blind and deaf in order that God's

---

[26] N. B. 2 Reg 18, 4 reports that Hezekiah destroyed the image of Nehushtan, the bronze serpent that Moses made to protect the people from the Seraphim (cf. Num 21, 9). If this image was in the Temple prior to Hezekiah's reign, it could aid in explaining the appearance of Seraphim in Isaiah's vision. Isa 14, 29 and 30, 6 simply refer to Seraphim as desert snakes.

[27] E. g., Wildberger, Jesaja 28 – 39, 1563 ff.

[28] JSOT 31 (1985), 101 ff.; Int 36 (1982), 125.

judgment may be carried out. Isa 29, 18; 32, 3; and 35, 5 ff. anticipate that Israel's blindness and deafness will end when God redeems Israel through a new Exodus and Second Isaiah announces that this time of redemption has come. Consequently, the theme of Israel's blindness and deafness functions as part of the Exodus motif which aids in establishing the redactional unity of the book of Isaiah. Insofar as Isa 35 summarizes this motif from First Isaiah and anticipates it in Second Isaiah, it is a key text in making the transition between the two parts of the book.

A fourth line of evidence centers around the relationship between Isa 1 and the rest of the book. Fohrer demonstrates that this chapter serves as a programmatic introduction to First Isaiah.[29] He maintains that a post-exilic compiler collected and edited five originally independent oracles from Isaiah (Isa 1, 2 – 3, 4 – 9, 10 – 17, 18 – 20, 21 – 26) and expanded them by adding v. 27 f.[30] He argues that the five oracles summarized the major themes of the message of First Isaiah: sin and its subsequent judgment as well as the possibility of salvation and the means for attaining it. According to Fohrer, this chapter was intended as a compendium or cross-section of the prophet's teaching and was placed at the beginning of the book in order to serve as an introduction to the Isaiah collection.

Becker builds upon Fohrer's observations by focusing on Isa 1, 27 f. and 1, 29 ff.[31] Fohrer views these units as editorial additions to the original Isaianic oracles in 1, 2 – 26 and therefore gives them little attention in his analysis. Becker, on the other hand, views them as essential for understanding the intent of the redactor who assembled this chapter. He argues that the reference to "her (i. e., Zion's) returnees" in 1, 27 indicates the exilic or post-exilic perspective of the redactor who understood this material in relation to the return of the exiles from Babylon, a major concern of Second Isaiah. Furthermore, he claims that 1, 29 – 31, which elaborates on the content of 1, 28, functions in a manner similar to the threats against the apostates in Isa 56 – 66. As a result of these redactional additions, the original Isaianic oracles of this chapter were reinterpreted in relation to the fall of Judah to Babylon and the end of the Babylonian exile. Consequently, Isa 1, with its themes of judgment and salvation, serves as an introduction to the entire book of Isaiah, not only to Isa 1 – 39.

Scholars have also noted that Isa 1 has a close relationship with Isa 65 – 66. Thus, L. Liebreich finds an exceptional degree of correspondence between the vocabulary of Isa 1 and that of Isa 65 – 66 which he

---

[29] BZAW 99, 1967, 148 ff.

[30] Fohrer claims that Isa 1, 29 ff. is a fragment of an oracle that was added at a later time.

[31] Isaias – Der Prophet und sein Buch, 45 ff.

interprets as a deliberate attempt to provide connecting links between the beginning and end of the book.[32] R. Lack follows by noting thematic links between these chapters as well.[33] Both Isa 1 and 65 – 66 focus on cultic abuse which disrupts the relationship between the people and God. Both sections maintain that a normalization of the relationship with God requires a separation between the righteous and impious among the people. In both sections, this separation is effected by judgment against the impious and leads to a resumption of relations between God and the people. Finally, Isa 65 – 66 goes beyond Isa 1 by adding eschatological themes of non-violence on the holy mountain, the fecundity of Zion and the rebirth of the people, and the revelation of God's glory. Lack's comments suggest that these additional themes are drawn from other parts of the book of Isaiah. He concludes from these observations that Isa 1 and 65 – 66 form an inclusion for the entire book.[34]

Lack is correct to point to the correspondence in the themes and vocabulary of Isa 1 and 65 – 66 as a basis for claiming that these chapters form an inclusion for the book of Isaiah. Certainly the materials in Isa 1, 2 – 28 support this claim. Thus, Isa 1, 2 – 3 and 1, 4 – 9 indicate that there is a separation between the people and God due to the people's rebellion. Isa 1, 10 – 17 and 1, 18 – 20 claims that their iniquity is based in cultic improprieties but that the people have a chance to correct their ways. Finally, Isa 1, 21 – 26 and 1, 27 – 28 speak about God's judgment against Jerusalem which will redeem the city by destroying the apostates within her.

Lack seems somewhat uncertain about the role of Isa 1, 29 – 31 which is concerned with the sacred gardens and terebinths of the Canaanite fertility religion. A number of scholars are perplexed by the appearance of this passage in Isa 1 in that it appears to have little relation to the preceding material.[35] An analysis of the structure of this chapter, however, indicates that 1, 29 – 31 is an integral part of Isa 1 in that it specifies the punishment which will come upon the apostates mentioned in 1, 28[36] It would, therefore, be surprising to see these verses overlooked

---

[32] JQR 46 (1955 – 56), 276 f.; JQR 47 (1956 – 57), 126 f.

[33] La Symbolique du Livre d'Isaïe, AnBib 59, 1973, 139 ff.

[34] Vermeylen carries this conclusion further by tracing the thematic and lexical relationship between chapters 56 – 66 and chapter 1, arguing that the editor of Trito-Isaiah constructed this material according to the concerns and pattern of Isa 1 (Du prophète Isaïe, II, 1978, 504 ff.).

[35] Fohrer also had problems in relating this pericope to the rest of Isa 1 and simply claimed that it was a fragment that was secondarily added to v. 2 – 28 on the basis of a thematic association between the "burning" of v. 31 and the "smelting" of v. 25 (BZAW 99, 150).

[36] For an analysis of the structure of Isa 1, see Chapter IV.

by a writer who was attempting to create an inclusion between Isa 1 and 65 – 66. Lack, however, simply notes the concern with syncretism in Trito-Isaiah and claims that the erratic v. 17 of chapter 66 appears there only to lock up the inclusion. This comment suggests that the reference to Isa 1, 29 – 31 was an afterthought and indicates a potential weakness in the hypothesis that Isa 1 and 65 – 66 form an inclusion for the entire book.

Lack has overlooked the extent to which the writers of Isa 65 – 66 employed Isa 1, 29 – 31 in their portrayal of judgment against the apostates and triumph for the righteous. Thus, Isa 65, 3 speaks of those who sacrifice in the gardens to describe the people guilty of rebellion against God. This is a clear reference to the gardens of Isa 1, 29 – 31 but it also includes the sacrificial abuses mentioned in Isa 1, 10 – 17. The association between these concerns is probably based on a word play involving the Hebrew terms, *'êlîm*/*'êlîm* in both passages. In 1, 29, *'êlîm* refers to "terebinths" whereas in 1, 11, *'êlîm* refers to "rams." This association appears again in Isa 65, 12 where God condemns the apostates because they "chose" (*b^{e}ḥartæm*; cf. 1, 29) that in which God "did not take delight" (*lô' ḥāpaṣtî*; cf. 1, 11). Likewise, Isa 65, 13 claims that the apostates will be "ashamed" (*tebošû*; cf. 1, 29, *yebošû*[37]). On the other hand, Isa 65, 22 f. claims that the days of God's elect will be like the days of a tree, that they will not labor in vain and bring forth terror, an image that contrasts sharply with the rotten tree used to characterize the apostates in Isa 1, 29 – 31. Isa 66, 3 repeats the concern that the apostates have "chosen" (*bāḥ^{a}rû*; cf. 1, 29) that in which they, not God, "delight" (*ḥāpeṣâ*; cf. 1, 11). Isa 66, 4 repeats the language of Isa 65, 12 which previously expressed this concern. This is followed by Isa 66,5 which again states that the apostates will be ashamed (*yebošû*; cf. 1, 29). Isa 66, 15 f. employs the imagery of fire to describe God's coming judgment against the apostates. Lack related this imagery to the smelting in Isa 1, 25,[38] but the imagery of the burning tree in Isa 1, 31 is much more appropriate in the context of Isa 66, 17 which explicitly refers to the gardens. Likewise, Isa 66, 17 claims that the apostates "will be consumed together" (*yaḥdāw yāsupû*), using language that echoes Isa 1, 31, "and the two of them shall burn together" (*ûbā^{a}rû š^{e}nêhæm yaḥdāw*). Finally, Isa 66, 24 states that the fire which destroys the apostates will never be quenched (*w^e'iššam lo' tikbæh*). This corresponds to the final statement of Isa 1, 31 which claims that the fire that destroys the tree will never be quenched (*w^e'ên m^{e}kabbæh*). These observations

---

[37] Note that the 2nd person perspective of Isa 1, 29 f. indicates that *yebošû* may have originally read *tebošû*.

[38] La Symbolique du Livre d'Isaïe, 140.

demonstrate that the imagery of Isa 1, 29 – 31 permeates all of Isa 65 – 66 and indicate that the writers of Isa 65 – 66 employed the imagery and language of this oracle in presenting their views on the coming punishment of the apostates and triumph of the elect.

The considerations presented above indicate that Isa 1 and 65 – 66 form an inclusion which is intended to unite the entire book of Isaiah. Furthermore, the work of Fohrer and Becker indicates that Isa 1 serves as a programmatic introduction to the book which summarizes its basic themes and message. Likewise, the work of Liebreich and Lack indicates that Isa 65 – 66 serves as a conclusion to the book as a whole in that these chapters take up language and themes from earlier passages as a means of summarizing the message of the book.

A final line of evidence involves the structure and presentation of the materials in First Isaiah. Because a major purpose of this monograph will be to establish the structure of the book of Isaiah in an effort to demonstrate its post-exilic concerns, discussion of this line of evidence will be brief. However, a number of scholars have begun to consider this issue. Studies of Isa 1 – 5 by Jones,[39] Isaiah 1 – 12 by Ackroyd,[40] and of the fall of Jerusalem in First Isaiah by Clements[41] have concluded that the presentation of material in First Isaiah reflects the concerns of post-exilic Judaism, particularly its concern to understand the destruction of Jerusalem, the Babylonian exile, and the post-exilic restoration. Furthermore, Childs[42] and Clements[43] argue that Isa 1 – 39 is presented in a manner that anticipates Isa 40 – 66 and that Isa 40 – 66 presupposes Isa 1 – 39. Thus, Isa 1 – 39 anticipates a judgment by Assyria and a subsequent restoration once the Assyrian judgment is complete. Isa 40 – 66 presupposes that a judgment by Babylon is complete and that the restoration is about to take place. In this context, the two parts of the book function as a whole so that the "former things" mentioned in Second Isaiah refer to the prophecies of First Isaiah and the "new things" refer to the future restoration which Second Isaiah anticipates.

In sum, there are a number of lines of evidence, including thematic, literary, and structural considerations, which indicate that the book of Isaiah is a redactional unity. Furthermore, the considerations presented above indicate that the material in First Isaiah has been presented in such a way as to anticipate the concerns of the second part of the book. Insofar as Isa 40 – 66 stem from the late-exilic and post-exilic periods, this means that the material in Isa 1 – 39 has been interpreted and

---

[39] ZAW 67 (1955), 226 ff.
[40] Isaiah I – XII, 16 ff.
[41] VT 30 (1980), 421 ff.
[42] Introduction to the Old Testament as Scripture, 325 ff.
[43] Int 36 (1982) 117 ff.

presented by its redactors in a manner which addresses the concerns of the late- or post-exilic Jewish community. In order to prove this hypothesis, this study will now turn to an analysis of the structure, genre, setting, and intent of the book of Isaiah. This analysis will be an attempt to elucidate the conceptual structure of the book of Isaiah, a conceptual structure which demonstrates the intentions of the book's redactors to address their own generation with the message of the prophet Isaiah. Afterwards, Isa 1 – 4 will be analyzed in an attempt to determine how the book's redactors interpreted the oracles of the prophet and presented them in order to achieve their purpose.

Chapter III
The structure of the book of Isaiah

A. STRUCTURAL OVERVIEW: ISAIAH 1 AND ISAIAH 36–39

Discussion of the structure of the book of Isaiah may begin by considering its most obvious structural markers, the superscriptions. G. Tucker defines a superscription as a "statement prefixed to a written work, such as a book, a song, a collection, or individual prophetic sayings."[1] Generally, superscriptions provide information about the works they precede such their type (e. g., oracle, psalm), author, date, or the use for which they were intended.[2] Their basic function is to identify the work in question so that it may be distinguished from surrounding material. There are fourteen superscriptions in the book of Isaiah (1, 1; 2, 1; 13, 1; 14, 28; 15, 1; 17, 1; 19, 1; 21, 1, 11, 13; 22, 1; 23, 1; 30, 6; and 38, 9). However, these do not necessarily constitute the basic structural divisions in the text since the relationship of these superscriptions to one another or to their contexts must also be considered. In this respect, nine of these superscriptions (14, 28; 15, 1; 17, 1; 19, 1; 21, 1, 11, 13; 22, 1; and 23, 1) relate to 13, 1 on formal grounds since they all identify their respective units as *maśśā'* and together comprise a collection of *maśśā'ôt* in chapters 13 – 23.[3] Likewise, 30, 6 relates to its immediate context in that it is part of a larger unit concerned with a diplomatic embassy sent to Egypt (30, 1 – 33).[4] The superscription in 38, 9 relates directly to the Psalm of Hezekiah in 38, 10 – 20.

This leaves three superscriptions to consider as basic structural markers in the book of Isaiah: 1, 1; 2, 1; and 13, 1. A problem emerges in that while superscriptions determine the beginning of a distinct unit, they provide no clue of its end. Therefore, the extent of the units covered by these superscriptions must be determined on other grounds.

---

[1] Prophetic Superscriptions and the Growth of a Canon, Canon and Authority, ed. G. W. Coats and B. O. Long, 1977, 57 f.

[2] Tucker, Superscriptions, 58. Tucker also defines title as "a word or concise phrase that constitutes the name of a particular literary work." Certainly, the superscriptions for the *maśśā'ôt* in Isaiah could qualify as titles but these are mixed cases where the superscription also serves as title (Superscriptions, 58 f.)

[3] Wildberger, Jesaja 13 – 27, 497; Fohrer, Das Buch Jesaja, I 177 f.

[4] Kissane, The Book of Isaiah, I 322 ff.

On the surface, the superscription in 1, 1 appears to be the title of
the book so that the primary structural division of the book of Isaiah
would be between the first verse and body of the book in 1, 2 – 66, 24.
Certainly, the first words of the superscription, $ḥ^azôn$ $y^eša'yāhû$, have
been understood from ancient times in this sense since they are cited as
the title of Isaiah in 2 Chr 32, 32 and serve as the basis for ben Sira's
designation of the book in Ecclus 48, 22.[5] This may be only a result of
the placement of this superscription at the beginning of the book. It
does not necessarily mean that 1, 1 was intended to serve as the title of
the book. The problem here is to determine the block of material to
which 1, 1 refers. Scholars have already suggested a number of possibili-
ties: that Isa 1, 1 introduces the entire book,[6] chapters 1 – 39,[7] chapters
1 – 12,[8] or only chapter 1.[9] The second and third options may be
automatically eliminated since the superscriptions in 1, 1 and 2, 1 could
easily include the materials in chapters 40 – 66 or 13 – 66. Both of these
verses claim concern with Judah and Jerusalem and certainly, the entire
book is ultimately concerned with Judah and Jerusalem even though the
immediate topic is Ephraim[10] or a foreign nation.[11] It would be arbitrary
to assign the superscription in 1, 1 to chapters 1 – 12 or 1 – 39 when the
rest of the book could easily come under its purview.[12] This leaves two
options. Either the superscription in 1, 1 introduces the entire book of
Isaiah, since the entire book is ultimately concerned with Judah and
Jerusalem, or the superscription in 1, 1 functions only in relation to
chapter 1, since the superscription in 2, 1 could cover the rest of the
book with its concern for Judah and Jerusalem.

There are a number of reasons for considering Isa 1, 1 as the
superscription to chapter 1 only. Isa 1, 1 appears to be a comprehensive
title which refers to the reigns of four kings. This would suggest that it

---

[5] Unfortunately, the Hebrew remnants of Ecclesiasticus do not include this verse. The
Greek reads *horasei autou* which would refer to *horasis* in the LXX for Isa 1, 1. On
the Hebrew text of Ecclesiasticus, see F. Vattioni, Ecclesiastico: Testo ebraico con
apparato critico e versioni greca, latina e siriaca, 1968.

[6] Wildberger, Jesaja 1 – 12, 2; G. Fohrer, ALUOS 3 (1961), 6; Kissane, The Book of
Isaiah, I 8; F. Delitzsch, Biblical Commentary on the Prophecies of Isaiah, 1954, I 72;
Clements, Isaiah 1 – 39, 29.

[7] Scott, IB, V 165.

[8] Duhm, Das Buch Jesaia, 23; K. Marti, Das Buch Jesaja, KHAT X 1; J. Skinner, The
Book of the Prophet Isaiah, Chapters I – XXXIX, CB, 1905, 1; Gray, Isaiah
I – XXVII, 1; O. Procksch, Jesaia I, KAT IX/1, 1930, 29 (n. b., Procksch adds chapters
28 – 33 as well).

[9] Wildberger, Jesaja 1 – 12, 6; Vermeylen, Du prophète Isaïe, I 41, n. 4.

[10] E. g., Isa 9, 7 – 10, 4; 28, 1 – 4.

[11] E. g., Isa 10, 5 – 19; 13, 1 – 23, 18; etc.

[12] Delitzsch, The Prophecies of Isaiah, I 71 f.

is intended to function in relation to the book as a whole since references to these kings appear throughout the book. However, as noted above, Isa 1 is a compendium of the prophet's sayings which summarize the message of the book. In this respect, the chapter can be viewed as a summary of the message which the prophet spoke during the reigns of all four kings. Furthermore, Isa 1, 1 characterizes the material which it introduces as a ḥāzôn, "vision." It is worthwhile to note that in addition to the collective or abstract meaning of ḥāzôn, it can also refer to an individual visionary event.[13] Although chapter 1 is a composite text, it appears in its present form as a unified prophetic utterance concerning Judah and Jerusalem just as Obadiah, which is labeled ḥᵃzôn ᶜobadyâ, is a unified prophetic utterance against Edom.[14] Finally, the appearance of the superscription in 2, 1 may limit the material to which 1, 1 applies.

The arguments which support the view that Isa 1, 1 functions as the title for the entire book of Isaiah appear to override these considerations, however. The placement of this verse at the beginning of the book and its concern with Judah and Jerusalem, one of the foremost concerns of the book, has already been mentioned. The noun ḥāzôn, which appears at the beginning of 1, 1, is derived from the root ḥzh, an Aramaic loanword which basically means "to see."[15] When the word is used in connection with a prophet, however, it takes on a specialized meaning in that it refers to a vision that is a "revelation of a divine word, usually at night during a (deep) sleep and sometimes associated with emotional agitation."[16] In this sense, ḥāzôn is particularly oriented toward the future,[17] an orientation which the book of Isaiah shares as demonstrated by its many references to "that day" as well as the many promises of the restoration of Judah and Jerusalem in the future. Furthermore, ḥāzôn has no plural, a feature which lends itself to the interpretation of the word in a collective sense as including many visions or in an abstract sense as the totality of a prophet's revelatory experience.[18] In this connection, it is important to note explicit visionary elements which occur elsewhere in the book, such as Isaiah's vision of YHWH and His court in chapter 6, the attack by the nations against Ariel and YHWH's deliverance of the city in chapter 29, the vision concerning Midbar Yam

---

[13] E.g., 1 Chr 17, 15.

[14] The unity of Obadiah is disputed but the dispute centers around the dates of composition, not the final form of the book (Kaiser, Introduction to the Old Testament, 259 f.).

[15] A. Jepsen, TDOT, IV 280 ff., esp. 281.

[16] Jepsen, TDOT, IV 284.

[17] See especially Jepsen's citation of the Aramaic ḥzyn, "interpreter of the future," TDOT, IV 285.

[18] Wildberger, Jesaja 1–12, 6. On the formation of abstract nouns with the ending -ôn, see M. H. Segal, A Grammar of Mishnaic Hebrew, 1927, 119 f.

in chapter 21, the vision of the king and Jerusalem in 33, 17–22, the appeal to see (*ḥzh*) the restoration in 48, 6, and the vision of the new Jerusalem in chapters 60–62 (cf. esp. 60, 4). It should also be noted that the "word" and "oracle" mentioned in the other two major superscriptions in the book (2, 1; 13, 1) are qualified in relative clauses by the verb *ḥzh* which indicates that these are subsumed under the vision mentioned in 1, 1. This is particularly important here in that the purpose of the *ḥāzôn* was to transmit the divine message which might take the form of a *dābār*[19] or a *maśśā'*.[20] Further evidence for considering the superscription in 1, 1 in relation to the entire book occurs in the second relative clause of the verse which specifies the date of the material in question. As noted above, this clause defines the date according to the reigns of four kings of Judah, all of whom are mentioned elsewhere in the book outside of chapter 1.[21] It therefore appears likely that such a chronological statement functions to define the date for the entire book, not just for chapter 1. One might object that at least chapters 40–66 were written during a much later period than that described in 1, 1. Whatever the original dating of the elements of the book may be, however, they are here presented as a prophecy of Isaiah which he made during his own historical period.

With respect to Isa 2, 1, the evidence indicates that this verse does not serve as the title to chapters 2–66, but to a much more limited text unit within the book. There are no explicit factors which tie this superscription to the rest of the book such as those which apply to 1, 1; the chronological relative clause with its mention of kings, the association of the visionary elements in the rest of the book with *ḥāzôn*, and subordination of *dābār* to *ḥāzôn*. Furthermore, while *dābār* may be understood in a comprehensive sense as the entire prophetic message of the prophet, the usual formula for this is *dᵉbar yhwh*, which occurs as part of the initial superscription for a number of prophetic books.[22] Frequently, the singular use of *dābār* without the divine name is used to indicate an individual prophetic utterance whereas the plural *dibrê PN* can be used as a comprehensive title to gather together all the individual "words."[23] Thus, Isa 2, 1, with its singular *haddābār* uncon-

---

19 Cf. 1 Sam 3, 1; 1 Chr 17, 15; Jepsen, TDOT, IV 283.
20 Thr 2, 14; Hab 1, 1; Nah 1, 1; Jepsen, TDOT, IV 283.
21 Uzziah, 6, 1; Ahaz, Jotham, Uzziah, 7, 1; Ahaz, chapter 7 and 14, 28; Hezekiah, chapters 36–39.
22 E. g., Jeremiah, Ezekiel, Hosea, Joel, Jonah, Micah, Zephaniah, Haggai, Malachi.
23 Cf. Am 1, 1 (*dibrê ʿāmos*) and the individual occurrences of *dābār* in 3, 1; 4, 1; and 5, 1 (cf. J. L. Mays, Amos, OTL, 1969, 19; H. W. Wolff, Joel and Amos, Herm, 1977, 119). Jer 1, 1 begins with *dibrê yirmᵉyāhû* followed by numerous occurrences of *dᵉbar yhwh* (1, 5, 11, 13; 2, 1, 4, etc.). There are grounds, however, for considering *dibrê*

nected to the divine name,[24] was meant to apply to a limited body of text and not to the rest of the book. Some have suggested that this limited text might be chapters 2 – 12, since 13, 1, with its superscription *maśśā' bābæl*, begins a section devoted to the foreign nations.[25] This seems unlikely, however, in view of the culmination of this section with the restoration of Judah and Israel, whereas the superscription states "Judah and Jerusalem."[26] Instead, Isa 2, 1 must be the superscription for chapters 2 – 4, a self-contained unit which explicitly states its concern with Judah and Jerusalem.[27]

With respect to Isa 13, 1, it is clear that this verse does not serve as the title for the balance of the book. Instead, its form and content indicate that it functions only in relation to the oracles against the nations in chapters 13 – 23.

The above considerations lead to the conclusion that 1, 1 functions in a comprehensive sense as the superscription for the entire book of Isaiah. The superscriptions in 2, 1 and 13, 1 must be considered in a more limited manner as heading chapters 2 – 4 and 13 – 23 respectively. Their form and the contents of the material which they introduce indicate that they are subordinate to Isa 1, 1. As noted above, however, Isa 1, 1 functions in relation to the prologue in chapter 1 as well, although this function is clearly secondary to its role as superscription for the entire book. Thus, 1, 1 serves a dual role, as superscription for the whole book of Isaiah and as superscription for chapter 1. For the sake of convenience, the Masoretic practice of including 1, 1 as a part of chapter 1, while noting its larger role in relation to the rest of the book, will be followed here.[28] This indicates that the basic structural division of the book of Isaiah is between chapter 1, which serves as the prologue in that it summarizes the message of Isaiah,[29] and chapters 2 – 66, which form the body of the book. In this respect, while 2, 1

---

yirmᵉyāhû as "The History of Jeremiah" in analogy to Neh 1, 1 (W. Rudolph, Jeremia, HAT XII, 1968³, 3).

[24] Note that a number of LXX manuscripts specify, "the word which was from the Lord to Isaiah … (cf. Rahlfs, Septuaginta, 1935, on Isa 2, 1).

[25] Gray, Isaiah I – XXVII, 40; Clements, Isaiah 1 – 39, 3, 38 f.

[26] Cf. Isa 11, 12 – 16.

[27] Cf. Isa 3, 1, 8. For detailed arguments on the unity of this section, see Chapter IV below, and Delitzsch, The Prophecies of Isaiah, I 110; Skinner, Isaiah I – XXXIX, 12 f.; Duhm, Das Buch Jesaia, 36. The unity of this section and its concern with Jerusalem and Judah throughout make Ackroyd's hypothesis that 2, 1 applies only to 2, 2 – 4 unlikely [cf. ZAW 75 (1963), 320 f.].

[28] The Masoretes included neither setuma nor petucha after 1, 1.

[29] See above, Chapter II. Cf. Fohrer, BZAW 99, 72; Clements, Isaiah 1 – 39, 28 f.; Skinner, Isaiah I – XXXIX, 2 f.; Delitzsch, The Prophecies of Isaiah, I 72; Procksch, Jesaia I, 20.

serves as the superscription for 2, 2 – 4, 6, its placement in relation to the prologue and the body of the book serves as a convenient indication to the reader of the basic division of Isaiah.[30] The relationship between these elements may be indicated with the following structural outline:

I. Prologue	1, 1 – 31
A. Superscription (dual function)	1, 1
B. Prologue Proper	1, 2 – 31
II. Body of the Book	2, 1 – 66, 24

Thus, chapter 1 contains a succinct summary of the book's basic themes which are dealt with in more detail in chapters 2 – 66:[31] condemnation of Judah and Israel for disobedience, YHWH's punishment which will cleanse the people, a promise of restoration for Zion, and the distinction between the righteous and the wicked which reappears at the end of the book. The body of the book, chapters 2 – 66, still requires detailed investigation, but it may be noted that this portion begins and ends with a description of the nations coming to YHWH at Zion to offer their obeisance to Him (2, 2 – 4; 66, 18 – 24).

Turning to the structure of chapters 2 – 66, there are immediate problems in determining patterns in the material due to the great formal diversity among the elements which comprise these chapters. Yet, as Chapter II above indicated, chapters 36 – 39 form a bridge or transition between the two major parts of the book of Isaiah, the "Assyrian" section in chapters 1 – 35 which anticipates a judgment by Assyria followed by a restoration, and the "Babylonian" section in chapters 40 – 66 which presupposes a judgment by Babylon and announces that the restoration is about to take place.[32]

Chapters 36 – 39 are set off formally from their surrounding material in that they form a narrative block concerned with the reporting of events whereas the surrounding material is poetic and concerned with proclaiming comfort and restoration for Zion. Furthermore, there is no syntactical connection between chapters 35 and 36, on the one hand, and chapters 39 and 40 on the other. Internally, chapters 36 – 39 include three self-contained narratives (36 – 37; 38; 39) which are linked by connecting temporal expressions in 38, 1 (*bayyāmîm hāhem*) and 39, 1

---

[30] Delitzsch, The Prophecies of Isaiah, I 72.

[31] An analogous situation is that of Ps 1 or Ps 1 – 2 (cf. the variant reading of Acts 13, 33 which cites Ps 2 as the first Psalm; bBer 9b) which many scholars see as the introduction to the book of Psalms in that Ps 1 or Ps 1 – 2 draw out many basic themes of the Psalter (Childs, Introduction to the Old Testament as Scripture, 513 f., 516).

[32] Ackroyd, Isaiah 36 – 39, 3 ff.; Clements, Isaiah 1 – 39, 277 ff.; Delitzsch, The Prophecies of Isaiah, II 157.

(*bā͡ʿet hahî*). These connecting temporal expressions aid in presenting the three narratives as three episodes related to the same circumstances.[33]

By connecting these narratives in this manner, Isa 36 – 39 presents the figure of Hezekiah as a paradigm for the nation of Judah. As noted above in Chapter II, Hezekiah is the key figure in each of these narratives. Because of his piety, God miraculously delivers Jerusalem from the Assyrians in Isa 36 – 37. Likewise, Hezekiah's piety prompts God to deliver him from sickness in Isa 38. Finally, Hezekiah's reception of the Babylonian embassy in Isa 39 results in Isaiah's announcement that Hezekiah's house would be carried off to Babylon. In this respect, Hezekiah's personal fate is tied up with that of the nation.[34] Jerusalem is saved and Hezekiah is cured. These respites are temporary, however. Hezekiah is granted fifteen more years of life, but at the end of fifteen years, he will die. Likewise, Jerusalem is spared from the Assyrians, but the Babylonians will ultimately carry out the judgment.

Thus, chapters 36 – 39 form a bridge or transition between chapters 2 – 35 and 40 – 66. Chapters 2 – 35 look forward to a judgment of Judah by means of Assyria and her subsequent restoration. Chapters 40 – 66 presuppose that the judgment has already taken place and restoration is imminent. Chapters 36 – 39 explain the delay in the judgment and the change of agent from Assyria to Babylon as due to the piety of King Hezekiah. In this respect, these chapters revamp the expectations of Isaiah's prophecies in the light of history. Jerusalem was not destroyed by Sennacherib.[35] The deliverance of Jerusalem would have called Isaiah's prophecies of punishment into question as time and legend changed Hezekiah's submission to Sennacherib into a victory by YHWH. However, when Jerusalem was later conquered by Nebuchadrezzar, the "deliverance" of Jerusalem by Hezekiah would have to be understood as a temporary respite and the validity of Isaiah's word of judgment would then be confirmed. Hezekiah's piety only delayed the punishment of Jerusalem. The passage of time and the new historical situation required the change of YHWH's agent from Assyria to Babylon, but the judgment and the promise of restoration stood.

---

[33] Ackroyd, SJT 27 (1974), 330 f.; Wildberger, Jesaja 28 – 39, 1374.

[34] Cf. Ackroyd, SJT 27 (1974), 344 ff.

[35] The report of Hezekiah's paying tribute to Sennacherib in 2 Reg 18, 14 ff. and Sennacherib's account of the siege (ANET, 287 f.) indicate that Hezekiah submitted to Sennacherib, thus saving the city from destruction. Later legend idealized this reprieve as a victory by God (and Hezekiah) over the Assyrians (Clements, Isaiah 1 – 39, 278 ff.). For full discussion of this issue, see B. Childs, Isaiah and the Assyrian Crisis, SBT 3, 1967; R. E. Clements, Isaiah and the Deliverance of Jerusalem, JSOTSS 13, 1980; as well as the standard histories and commentaries.

The structure of chapters 36 – 39 and their relationship to the rest of the book may be illustrated with the following structural outline:

I. Prologue	1, 1 – 31
A. Superscription (dual function)	1, 1
B. Prologue Proper	1, 2 – 31
II. Body of Book	2 – 66
A. (Prophecies predicting judgment by Assyria and promising subsequent restoration)	2 – 35
B. Transition: Narrative concerning the temporary deliverance of Jerusalem	36 – 39
1. Narrative report of deliverance of Jerusalem from Sennacherib	36 – 37
2. Narrative report of deliverance of Hezekiah from sickness	38
3. Narrative report of the visit of Babylon's embassy and Isaiah's prediction of Babylonian exile	39
C. (Prophecies presupposing the punishment by Babylon and the imminent restoration)	40 – 66

This leaves two very large units which require close investigation, chapters 2 – 35 and chapters 40 – 66. General observations about their concerns have already been made. However, a full understanding of their relation to the book as a whole requires an investigation of their respective structures and functions.

Two blocks of material have already been identified in chapters 2 – 35, chapters 2 – 4 and chapters 13 – 23. Detailed reasons for identifying these blocks have not been given yet nor has there been a discussion of their relationship to the rest of chapters 2 – 35. Discussion of the relationship of these two blocks to the whole of chapters 2 – 35 requires some understanding of what that whole is. Unfortunately, chapters 2 – 35 do not lend themselves to easy analysis in determining the whole since these chapters contain much diverse material which at first glance does not fit well together. In addition to chapters 2 – 4 and 13 – 23, scholars have identified a number of other blocks, including 5 + 9 – 11; 12; 6, 1 – 9, 6; 24 – 27; 28 – 32; and 33 – 35 as well as variations of these.[36] Since there is evidence that a number of relatively homogeneous units do exist within chapters 2 – 35, it seems best to begin the investigation at the level of these lesser units rather than try to characterize the whole and then study its components. Unfortunately, there is no consensus on the delimitation of all blocks of material in chapters 2 – 35. Therefore, these blocks will be defined in the course of the discussion. The inquiry may then turn to how these blocks relate to each other in forming the larger unit, chapters 2 – 35.

1. Isaiah 2 – 4

The first of the blocks is Isa 2 – 4. Earlier discussion noted that this unit is set off at the beginning by the superscription in 2, 1. The unit is concerned mainly with Judah and Jerusalem (cf. 3, 1, 8) and extends as far as 4, 6 where there is a major formal change. There is no syntactic connection between 4, 6 and 5, 1 and the first person address in 5, 1 – 7 contrasts sharply with the third person perspective of chapters 2 – 4. Finally, 5, 3 addresses the "inhabitant of Jerusalem" and the "man of Judah," but this does not establish that chapter 5 should be considered a part of the unit in chapters 2 – 4. Chapters 2 – 4 are concerned with the fate of Judah and Jerusalem. In 5, 3, however, the reference merely indicates that the parable is spoken to the "inhabitant of Jerusalem" and the "man of Judah." Ultimately, the parable is concerned with the fate of Israel *and* Judah, as indicated by the explanation of the parable in 5, 7, not with the fate of Judah and Jerusalem. Therefore, chapter 5 can not be included as part of the block of material in chapters 2 – 4.

---

[36] Cf. Kaiser, Introduction to the Old Testament, 224 ff.

The structure of chapters 2 – 4 will be discussed in detail in Chapter IV below. Here, a simple outline of the blocks of material in these chapters and a brief discussion of their interrelationships will suffice. After the superscription in 2, 1, there is a block of material in 2, 2 – 4 which portrays the ideal future when Zion will be established as YHWH's royal residence where the nations come to acknowledge His rule. This is followed in 2, 5 by an invitation to Jacob to walk in the light of YHWH, a metaphorical way of inviting Jacob to join the nations. There follows in 2, 6 – 22 a block of material which discusses Jacob's inability to accept this invitation on account of his self-pride and an announcement that YHWH will come on His "day" to overturn this state of affairs, thus acknowledging the need to cleanse the people. Afterwards, in 3, 1 – 4, 6, there are two blocks of material which deal with the process of cleansing Zion. Isa 3, 1 – 15 and 3, 16 – 4, 1 form a sub-unit which discusses the punishment of Jerusalem's and Judah's leaders and women respectively. Isa 4, 2 – 6 speaks of YHWH's protection of Jerusalem after He has cleansed the city. The blocks in 3, 1 – 4, 6 and 2, 6 – 22 are linked by *kî* in 3, 1 and their common theme of punishment for the purpose of correction. Isa 2, 6 – 22 is in turn linked by another *kî* in 2, 6 to the invitation to Jacob in 2, 5. Since 2, 5 has no syntactic connection to 2, 2 – 4 and portrays a picture of corruption rather than the piety of 2, 2 – 4, 2, 5 – 4, 6 must form a block which contrasts with 2, 2 – 4. The two blocks are formally separate but linked by their common concern with the role of Zion as YHWH's capital for His rule over the world. Therefore, Isa 2, 1 – 4, 6 is a "Prophetic Announcement concerning the Cleansing of Zion for its Role as the Locus for YHWH's Rule over the World." The structure of this unit is as follows:

Prophetic Announcement Concerning the Cleansing of Zion for its Role as the Locus for YHWH's Rule over the World	2, 1 – 4, 6
I. Superscription	2, 1
II. Announcement Proper	2, 2 – 4, 6
A. Concerning the future establishment of Zion as the Locus for YHWH's rule over the world	2, 2 – 4
B. Concerning the cleansing of Zion for this role	2, 5 – 4, 6
1. Announcement concerning the need for cleansing	2, 5 – 22
a. invitation to Jacob to join YHWH	2, 5
b. prophetic acknowledgement of the need for cleansing	2, 6 – 22
2. Announcement concerning the process of cleansing	3, 1 – 4, 6
a. prophetic judgment speech against the people of Zion	3, 1 – 4, 1
1) against the leaders (male)	3, 1 – 15
2) against the women	3, 16 – 4, 1
b. prophetic announcement of salvation for the cleansed remnant in Jerusalem	4, 2 – 6

2. *Isaiah 5 – 12*

The next section, chapters 5 – 12, presents a problem due to the diversity of form and content in the materials which it contains. As a result, scholars have tended to treat this section not as a unified whole, but as a combination of elements which have only broad thematic relations to one another in their concern for Israel, Judah, and Jerusalem. They define the sub-units of chapters 5 – 12 on the basis of earlier text forms which were later rearranged and combined to create the present form of the text. Thus, on the basis of their formal similarity in the use of the exclamation *hôy*, 5, 8 – 24 and 10, 1 – 4 are believed to have originally stood together as a self-contained unit, although the original order is disputed.[37] Likewise, 9, 7 – 20 and 5, 25 – 30 are formally associated on the basis of the recurring "outstretched hand" formula and are believed to have formed an independent unit.[38] These reconstructed units are then considered to have formed the basis of a larger unit, chapters 5 + 9 – 11, which was later split apart by the insertion of Isaiah's "*Denkschrift*" or "memoir" in 6, 1 – 9, 6.[39]

Although it is likely that these theories are correct, it is unfortunate that so little attention is given to the interpretation of the text in its final form. If one accepts the opinion that 6, 1 – 9, 6 at one time was inserted into 5 + 9 – 11 so that this section was rearranged, then one must inquire into the purpose of this insertion and dislocation. Some have claimed that such machinations were accidental,[40] but such an explanation appears unlikely. There is reason to suspect that the present organization of chapters 5 – 12 has purpose. The entire section seems to be concerned with the fate of Israel and Judah in relation to the threat by Assyria. Furthermore, the present arrangements of the "woe" speeches in 5, 8 – 24; 10, 1 – 4a and the "outstretched hand" passages in 5, 25 – 30; 9, 7 – 10, 4 suggest a chiastic framework for the "memoir" in 6, 1 – 9, 6 which would very likely be an intentional arrangement. Finally, there are a number of observations of details in the units of this section which suggest a deliberate association of originally unconnected units.[41] These details will appear in the course of the discussion. Due to the great

---

[37] Kaiser, Isaiah 1 – 12, 96 f.; Wildberger, Jesaja 1 – 12, 180 ff. Clements sees the order as 10, 1 – 4a; 5, 8 – 24 (Isaiah 1 – 39, 60 f.).

[38] Kaiser, Isaiah 1 – 12, 220 ff.; Wildberger, Jesaja 1 – 12, 207 ff.; Clements, Isaiah 1 – 39, 66 f.

[39] Kaiser, Introduction to the Old Testament, 224. For discussion of Isa 6, 1 – 9, 6 as Isaiah's "memoir," see K. Budde, Jesajas Erleben. Eine gemeinverständliche Auslegung der Denkschrift des Propheten (Kap. 6, 1 – 9, 6), 1928.

[40] Duhm, Das Buch Jesaia, 61. Cf. Fohrer, ALUOS 3 (1961), 24 f.

[41] Cf. Barth, Die Jesaja-Worte, 17 ff., 57 ff., 109 ff. etc.

diversity in the materials of chapters 5 – 12, it is best to examine the constituent units of this section and then explain their interrelationships rather than attempt to characterize the whole unit at the outset. These constituent units are 5, 1 – 30; 6, 1 – 8, 15; and 8, 16 – 12, 6.

The first unit, 5, 1 – 30, has no syntactical connection with the preceding material in chapter 4 which is concerned with the future restoration of Jerusalem. Here, the book returns to a concern with judgment, but instead of judgment for Jerusalem only, the subject is judgment against Israel and Judah (5, 7). Furthermore, chapter 5 begins with a first-person poetic style as opposed to chapter 4 which is a third-person description of events. This first-person poetic style is maintained in 5, 9 and 5, 13. Because the woe speeches are a direct address to the parties concerned,[42] all of chapter 5 must fall under a first-person addressing perspective.[43] This changes at 6, 1 where the first-person perspective still appears but the language is narrative reporting language rather than the direct address proclaiming language of chapter 5. There are also some thematic considerations throughout the chapter. These include concern with the perversion of justice (v. 7, 23), drunkenness (v. 11 – 12, 22), the clouds as an indication of judgment (v. 6, 30), and the mention of trampling (v. 5) along with the suggestion of trampling in the mention of sandals, hooves, and wheels (v. 27 f.).

Scholars have identified three basic units in chapter 5. Isa 5, 1 – 7 is the vineyard parable which metaphorically describes YHWH's disappointment with the corruption of His people and the judgment which He proposes to carry out as a result. Isa 5, 8 – 24 contains a series of woe speeches which spell out the shortcomings of the leaders whose corrupt modes of behavior led to the downfall of the people. Isa 5, 25 – 30 announces YHWH's anger against the people and the punishment which He proposes to bring upon them, the Assyrian army. It is evident from 'al-ken at the beginning of v. 25 that 5, 25 – 30 is meant to describe the punishment or sentence that YHWH will bring upon His people for the crimes announced in the indictment in 5, 8 – 24. On this basis, 5, 8 – 24 and 5, 25 – 30 comprise the two elements of a larger unit concerned with accusing the people and announcing their punishment.[44] Since the

---

[42] J. J. M. Roberts, PSB 3 (1982), 296 ff., 305, n. 42.

[43] This does not mean, however, that the material in this section was all written by the same author at the same time.

[44] It should be noted here that while v. 25 – 30 may not have been composed for their present position, they certainly function in relation to v. 8 – 24 now. Scholars have noted that v. 24, with its introductory *lāken*, adequately describes the consequences of the crimes referred to in the preceding verses (cf. Barth, Die Jesaja-Worte, 109 f. and n. 38). However, v. 24 seems to relate specifically to v. 18 – 23 which discuss crimes of wisdom and justice, thus rejecting YHWH's instruction and word, the source of true

parable in 5, 1 – 7 also describes corruption and its punishment,[45] 5, 8 ff. spells out in detail what is parabolically stated in 5, 1 – 7.[46] Thus, 5, 1 – 30 is a proclamation of judgment against Judah and Israel. Its structure is as follows:

Proclamation of Judgment against Judah and Israel	5, 1 – 30
I. Stated Parabolically	5, 1 – 7
II. Stated Specifically	5, 8 – 30
A. Indictment (expressed in woe speeches)	5, 8 – 24
B. Sentence (punishment)	5, 25 – 30

The second unit, 6, 1 – 8, 15, has no syntactical connection with the preceding chapter. Furthermore, as mentioned above, the sixth chapter begins with reporting language which continues through 8, 15. For the most part, the perspective is first person.[47] Isaiah 8, 16 ff. is also expressed in first-person style and is generally considered part of the "memoir" of the prophet. However, the language here no longer reports what YHWH said to the prophet.[48] Instead, the language in 8, 16 ff. proclaims what Isaiah plans to do in the future and what his expectations for the future are. As is evident from the narrative language, the purpose of this section is to report events, specifically, events from Isaiah's prophetic career. However, it functions in a much broader sense in relation to the surrounding material and the book as a whole.

Isa 6, 1 – 8, 15 falls into two main sections: 6, 1 – 13 and 7, 1 – 8, 15. Isa 6, 1 – 13 is a self-contained narrative which reports Isaiah's encounter with YHWH in the divine council at the time of his prophetic commission.[49] It begins with a statement of time and employs the first-person perspective throughout. Here, Isaiah enters into the council of YHWH and volunteers for an assignment to proclaim a message of evil to his people. YHWH has already proclaimed judgment for the people and all that remains is to find a prophet who will proclaim that judgment before He carries it out. Furthermore, he is told to make sure that the people do not understand that judgment is taking place, lest they repent and

---

wisdom. Likewise, v. 13 – 17, also containing *lāken*, relate specifically to v. 8 – 12, which discuss crimes of greed and gluttony and subsequent swallowing by Sheol. V. 25 – 30, with the introductory *'al-ken*, are more comprehensive in scope in that they announce the consequences of all of v. 8 – 24.

[45] Wildberger, Jesaja 1 – 12, 166, labels 5, 1 – 7 as *"Gerichtsrede"* or, more precisely, *"Anklagerede."*

[46] Cf. Fohrer, Introduction to the Old Testament, 366; Wildberger, Jesaja 1 – 12, 180.

[47] The narrative in Isa 7, 1 – 25 is third person. See below for discussion of this unit.

[48] This is not to deny that 8, 16 – 9, 6 was originally a part of the "memoir." The dissociation of these verses is due to their function in the present form of the book in that they are now related structurally to the material which follows. See below.

[49] See R. Knierim, VT 18 (1968), 47 ff., on Isa 6.

avoid that judgment. This explains how YHWH could use Isaiah to proclaim salvation to Ahaz and how his response serves as the basis for Isaiah's message of judgment.

Isa 7, 1 – 8, 15 is much more complicated, especially since its narrative language appears as third person in 7, 1 – 25 and as first person in 8, 1 – 15. This would indicate that these sections did not originally belong together. Yet, it is clear that these sections belong together in the present context since they contain reports concerning Isaiah's encounters with the king and people of Judah. The first section, 7, 1 – 25, relates Isaiah's meeting with Ahaz. Following a narrative introduction in v. 1 – 2 are two sections which relate to different stages in the encounter. The first of these stages, 7, 3 – 9, reports YHWH's instructions to Isaiah to meet Ahaz and use his son, Shear Yashub, to announce that Judah would be delivered from the Syro-Ephraimitic coalition. There is no explicit report that these instructions were carried out, but this is presupposed by the following section which is linked to v. 3 – 9 by the connecting formula *wayyôsæp yhwh dabber 'æl 'āhāz le'mor*. The second section, 7, 10 – 25, reports a dialogue spoken between YHWH and Ahaz, presumably through Isaiah,[50] in which Ahaz refuses to place his trust in YHWH for deliverance from the Syro-Ephraimitic threat. As a result, YHWH proclaims that He will indeed save Judah from the immediate danger but at the price of Assyrian suzerainty which will be much worse for Judah than the Syrians and the Israelites. Thus, the message of deliverance in 7, 3 – 9 is changed into a threat in 7, 10 – 25.[51] This point is reiterated in the second main section, 8, 1 – 15, but in relation to the people. V. 1 – 4 report YHWH's instructions to Isaiah concerning a sign to announce the defeat of Syria and Israel together with Isaiah's compliance. V. 5 – 15 make it clear that the defeat of the Syro-Ephraimitic coalition will not bring deliverance to Judah as expected, but even greater danger. This point is simply stated in the speech by YHWH in v. 5 – 8 which interprets *'immānû 'el* in the sense that "God is with us" (v. 10). This is qualified by the report of a speech by YHWH in v. 11 – 15, connected by *kî*, which explains that the threat is not from the nations as claimed in v. 9 – 10, but from YHWH Himself. Thus, this section returns to the point made in chapter 6 that the punishment of YHWH's people is authorized by YHWH.[52]

Since Isa 6, 1 – 8, 15 is largely autobiographical in character and since it is a narrative concerning Isaiah's experiences in relation to the

---

[50] Cf. TJ on Isa 7, 10.

[51] Cf. O. H. Steck, BZ 16 (1972), 199 f., n. 29.

[52] Cf. Vermeylen, Du prophète Isaïe, I 225 ff., who claims that 8, 11 – 15 forms an inclusion of 7, 1 – 8, 10 together with Isa 6. His claim that *kᵉhæzqat hayyād* in 8, 11 refers back to the vision in Isa 6 cannot be accepted, however.

Syro-Ephraimitic War, i. e., his commission and his confrontation with the king and people, this section may be labeled, "Autobiographical Report of Isaiah's Experiences relating to the Syro-Ephraimitic War." It also reports Judah's rejection of YHWH and projects the resulting judgment of Judah by means of Assyria. The section may therefore be subtitled "The Basis for the Assyrian Punishment." The structure is as follows:

Autobiographical Report of Isaiah's Experiences Relating to the
Syro-Ephraimitic War: The Basis for the Assyrian Punishment   6, 1 — 8, 15

   I. Encounter with YHWH: Prophetic Commission to Bring
      about Judgment against Judah   6, 1 — 13

  II. Encounter with Judah: Judah's Rejection of YHWH   7, 1 — 8, 15
    A. Encounter with the King   7, 1 — 25
      1. Introduction to the situation   7, 1 — 2
      2. Report of encounter   7, 3 — 25
        a. first stage: offer of deliverance to Ahaz   7, 3 — 9
        b. second stage: Ahaz's rejection of deliverance and
          subsequent announcement of disaster   7, 10 — 25
    B. Encounter with People (through signs)   8, 1 — 15
      1. Concerning Israel and Syria: Punishment   8, 1 — 4
      2. Concerning Judah: Punishment by Assyria   8, 5 — 15
        a. YHWH speech: announcement of Judah's pun-
          ishment by Assyria   8, 5 — 8
        b. reinterpretation of popular Zion protection slo-
          gan   8, 9 — 15
          1) slogan: summons to battle for protection of
             Zion   8, 9 — 10
          2) reinterpretation: God is not with us   8, 11 — 15

The third major section of chapters 5 — 12, 8, 16 — 12, 6, begins with imperatives, presumably addressed to the audience of disciples mentioned in the opening verse and also to the reader. In spite of the thematic connections and first-person perspective, which have caused many scholars to view 8, 16 — 9, 6 as the closing section of the "memoir," this imperative address separates this unit structurally from the narrative sections in 6, 1 — 8, 15. The language here is proclamatory and as such, is oriented toward the future whereas the narrative language is oriented toward the past. Isa 6, 1 — 8, 15 reports what happened during the Syro-Ephraimitic crisis, i. e., the circumstances leading to the decision to implement the Assyrian punishment. Isa 8, 16 — 12, 6 announces what will result from that decision.

Isa 8, 16 — 12, 6 is composed of two major sections as indicated by the syntactical and thematic break at 9, 7. The first of these sections, 8, 16 — 9, 6, concisely announces Isaiah's withdrawal from prophetic activity to await YHWH's announced actions in relation to His people. These actions are portroyed in the following verses as a period of distress and hunger followed by a period of restoration ushered in by the birth of a new king.[53]

The second section, 9, 7 – 12, 6, deals with Isaiah's expectations of a period of distress and a period of restoration in greater detail. The period of distress is described in 9, 7 – 10, 4 which contains a series of oracles directed against Jacob (9, 7) and united by the "outstretched hand" formula.[54] Isa 10, 5 – 11, 16, which begins with a syntactically independent *hôy* exclamation, describes the process and period of restoration. YHWH's agent for punishing Jacob will first be judged as too arrogant in that she attributed her success to her own strength and prowess rather than acknowledging that the success was granted by YHWH. This will result in YHWH's punishing Assyria in her own turn. A noted consequence of this will be the end of the reliance by the remnant of Israel on Assyria and its return to YHWH. This first stage of the restoration process is described in 10, 5 – 23. The second part of the restoration process, the reestablishment of Israel and Judah under a Davidic king, is described in 10, 24 – 11, 16. In its present form, this section is closely related to 10, 5 – 23 by the introductory *lāken* in v. 24.[55] This *lāken* section, v. 24 – 26, assures the people of Zion that the Assyrian suzerainty is soon to end. These verses are then expanded by a number of sections introduced by the formula *wᵉhāyâ bayyôm hahû'* which describe the fall of Assyria and the reestablishment of the Davidic empire. Each of these sections, 10, 7 – 11, 9; 11, 10; and 11, 11 – 16, elaborates on the previous section, developing the picture of the restored kingdom into a world empire. These sections are followed by a composite hymn of thanksgiving in 12, 1 – 6[56] which forms a section following 10, 5 – 11, 16.

Isa 8, 16 – 12, 6 announces Isaiah's expectations of what will result from the Assyrian punishment, distress followed by restoration. The structure of this section is as follows:

Announcement of Expectations Concerning Assyrian Punishment: Distress followed by Restoration   8, 16 – 12, 6

    I. Announcement of Isaiah's Withdrawal to Await YHWH's Actions: Distress for Judah Followed by Restoration   8, 16 – 9, 6

    II. Elaboration on YHWH's Awaited Actions: Distress Followed by Restoration   9, 7 – 12, 6

---

[53] Cf. Clements, Isaiah 1 – 39, 103 ff.

[54] Note that scholars consider the woe oracle in 10, 1 – 4a to be a secondary addition affixed to 9, 7 – 21 by the addition of the "outstretched hand" formiia in 10, 4b (cf. Wildberger, Jesaja 1 – 12, 200 f.).

[55] Cf. Barth, Die Jesaja-Worte, 45. On the relation of chapter 11 to chapter 10, see Barth, pp. 57 ff.

[56] Wildberger, Jesaja 1 – 12, 478 f.

A. Period of distress for Jacob	9, 7 – 10, 4
B. Period of restoration for Davidic empire	10, 5 – 12, 6
1. Fall of Assyria and rise of David	10, 5 – 11, 16
a. punishment of Assyria by YHWH	10, 5 – 23
b. restoration of Davidic empire	10, 24 – 11, 16
2. Hymn of thanksgiving	12, 1 – 6

Having delineated the three major blocks of chapters 5 – 12, it still remains to determine how they relate to one another. It seems quite clear that 8, 16 – 12, 6 should be closely associated with 6, 1 – 8, 15. Both take the form of first-person speeches.[57] Also, the mention of children which YHWH gave to Isaiah as signs and portents provides a direct reference to the use of the children, Shear Yashub and Maher-shalal-hash-baz, in chapters 7 and 8. This relationship seems clear when one considers that 6, 1 – 8, 15, an autobiographical section, reports past events, whereas 8, 16 – 12, 6 projects future expectations which will result from the past events outlined in 6, 1 – 8, 15. Thus, the two sections work together to outline past events and project the future. While chapter 5 is also cast in a first-person perspective,[58] its relation to the following materials is not as clear. Chapter 5 is a proclamation of judgment against Judah and Israel. As such, it seems to duplicate to a large extent the function of 6, 1 – 8, 15, which also deals with punishment. Chapter 5 announces punishment and the accusations for which punishment is deserved. The material in 6, 1 – 8, 15 is more explanatory in nature. It explains how it was that YHWH's decision to judge Judah and Ahaz's decision to reject YHWH led to the Assyrian punishment. By describing the events which led to the reversal of YHWH's relationship with His people, 6, 1 – 8, 15 explains how the people became corrupt and deserving of punishment. YHWH made them blind and deaf so that they would act corruptly and Ahaz demonstrated incorrect actions by refusing to accept YHWH's protection, preferring to rely on Assyria instead. Thus, 6, 1 – 12, 6 explains how the situation of judgment in chapter 5 came about and where it was meant to lead.[59] Isa 6 – 12 is therefore an "Explanation of Judgment against Israel and Judah." The

---

[57] Note the first-person character of 6, 1 – 13 and 8, 1 – 15 as well as that of 8, 16 – 18. Even though this perspective never explicitly appears throughout the rest of the unit, it still dominates the whole.

[58] See Isa 5, 1 – 7, 9, 13.

[59] Cf. Barth, Die Jesaja-Worte, 115 f. Barth points to 5, 24b, which states that the people have rejected the Torah of YHWH, etc., as the redactional connection which joins chapter 5 to the following "memoir" material. In his view, this connection allows the "memoir" to serve as the reason (Begründung) for the proclamation of disaster in 5, 24a. To support his claim, he points to the use of m's, "reject," in 8, 6, which demonstrates the people's deficiency, and tôrâ in 8, 16, to which Isaiah wishes to return.

entire unit would then be an "Announcement of YHWH's Judgment against Israel and Judah." The structure of Isa 5 — 12 is as follows:

Announcement of YHWH's Judgment Against Israel and Judah	5 – 12
I. Proclamation of Judgment against Israel and Judah	5, 1 – 30
II. Explanation of Judgment against Israel and Judah	6, 1 – 12, 6
A. Autobiographical Report explaining the Basis for the Assyrian Punishment	6, 1 – 8, 15
B. Announcement of Expectations concerning the Outcome of the Assyrian Punishment	8, 16 – 12, 6

3. Isaiah 13 – 23

The next major section in the book of Isaiah, chapters 13 – 23, is a collection of oracles which concern various nations. This concern and the extensive use of the title, *maśśāʾ PN*, "oracle concerning PN,"[60] demarcate chapters 13 – 23 as a well-defined sub-unit within the book of Isaiah.[61] Despite this formal consistency, there are problems in determining the structure of this section. A number of oracles do not have the characteristic *maśśāʾ PN* title.[62] Others do not even concern the nations.[63] These inconsistencies have fueled an unresolved debate over what constitutes the basic structure of these chapters. Some have held that the *maśśāʾ PN* titles mark the basic divisions.[64] Others have concluded that the differentiation according to nations serves as the basic structural principle.[65] Still others have opted for the traditio-historical explanation of the phenomenon in that a collection of oracles with the title *maśśāʾ PN* was combined with oracles which lacked such titles.[66] The position taken here is that the *maśśāʾ PN* titles mark the basic

---

[60] For a detailed discussion of the genre *maśśāʾ* and the *maśśāʾ* texts in Isa 13 – 23, see the recent Claremont Ph. D. dissertation by R. D. Weis, A Definition of the Genre *Maśśāʾ* in the Hebrew Bible, 1986, esp. 105 ff., 264 ff., 343 ff. Weis argues that the *maśśāʾ* is a prophetic genre which expounds, on the basis of a particular revelation, how YHWH's action/intention is manifested in human affairs. Its purpose is to give instruction for the present or insight into the future (p. 271).

[61] Almost all scholars agree in seeing chapters 13 – 23 as a well-defined section within the book of Isaiah. Refer to the standard commentaries and introductions.

[62] E. g., Isa 14, 24 – 27; 14, 28 – 32; 17, 12 – 14; 18, 1 – 7; 20, 1 – 6.

[63] E. g., Isa 14, 3 – 23; 22, 15 – 25.

[64] Note Wildberger's remark that *maśśāʾ PN* titles serve as the redactional devices for organizing this section (Jesaja 13 – 27, 497).

[65] Kaiser, Isaiah 13 – 39, 1 ff.; Kissane, The Book of Isaiah, I xxiv ff.; Clements, Isaiah 1 – 39, 129 f.

[66] Fohrer, Jesaja, I 177 f.; *idem.*, ALUOS 3 (1961), 16 ff.; Wildberger, Jesaja 13 – 27, 498; Gray, Isaiah I – XXVII, li. Cf. Vermeylen, Du prophète Isaïe, I 286.

structural divisions with this section although these titles do not necessarily serve as the title for all of the material contained within their respective units. This will be demonstrated in the course of the discussion of each of the constitutive units of chapters 13–23.

The first sub-unit, Isa 13, 1–14, 27, presents all of the problems mentioned above. The unit begins with the superscription, "The oracle of Babylon which Isaiah ben Amoz saw," but the unit contains not only the material concerned with Babylon, but material concerned with Israel (14, 1–2), the king of Babylon (14, 3–23), and Assyria (14, 24–27). This would suggest that the superscription does not apply to these materials, but only to 13, 2–22. In the cases of 14, 1–2 and 14, 3–23, their relation to the Babylonian oracle in 13, 2–22 is clear. Thus, 14, 1–2, which is connected directly to 13, 2–22 by *ki*,[67] spells out the implications of Babylon's fall for Israel. The section containing the taunt (*māšāl*) against the king of Babylon (14, 3–23) is addressed directly to Israel as indicated by its second-person introduction in 14, 3–4a. YHWH's threat against Babylon in v. 22–23 makes it clear that although this taunt is addressed to the king of Babylon, he serves as the representative of his entire empire. Therefore, 14, 3–23 may be placed as a unit alongside 13, 2–14, 2. The superscription in 13, 1 introduces the whole.

The Assyrian oracle in 14, 24–27 presents problems. It contains no syntactical connection to the preceding Babylonian material[68] and there can be no mistake that Babylon is addressed here since Assyria is explicitly named in v. 25.[69] In order to understand the relation of this oracle to the preceding material, the perspective of the entire book must be considered. Chapters 40–66 were composed during the exilic and post-exilic times and presuppose the period of Babylonian domination. This presupposition explains the placement of an oracle against Babylon at the head of the collection of oracles against the nations in the book of Isaiah.[70] From the perspective of the book, Babylon is, or was, the dominant world power. Assyria had ceased to exist as a force to be reckoned with. Furthermore, as demonstrated in the discussion of Isa

---

[67] Wildberger, Jesaja 13–27, 524.

[68] Wildberger, Jesaja 13–27, 566, takes the introductory statement in v. 24a as evidence that the oracle is not connected to the preceding material.

[69] A number of scholars have claimed that the mention of Assyria in these verses supports a claim that the oracle against Babylon was originally directed against Assyria, but was later changed in light of historical circumstances (Erlandsson, The Burden of Babylon, 160 ff.; Kissane, The Book of Isaiah, I 146 ff., 159 f. Erlandsson's contention, that 14, 22–27 forms the epilogue of 13, 1–14, 27, indicating that both Babylon and Assyria are addressed in the oracle, can not be accepted here.

[70] Cf. Kaiser, Isaiah 13–39, 2; Clements, Isaiah 1–39, 132; Gray, Isaiah I–XXVII, 233; Fohrer, Das Buch Jesaja, I 181 f., Scott, IB, V 254 f.

36 – 39, Babylon will replace Assyria as the agent which carries out YHWH's punishment of His people. Despite Hezekiah's piety, the punishment will still come, thus upholding YHWH's word as announced by Isaiah. It is evident from the contents of 14, 24 – 27 that the same concern with upholding YHWH's word appears here, even under changed circumstances. V. 24b and the summary-appraisal in v. 26 – 27[71] make it clear that YHWH's purpose is unchanged. Just as YHWH had previously determined to destroy Assyria, His agent for Israel's and Judah's punishment (cf. 10, 5 – 19), so He now determines to destroy Babylon. V. 26 states that the destruction of Assyria is part of YHWH's plan for the entire earth. Likewise, the oracle against Babylon in 13, 2 – 22 makes it clear that the overthrow of Babylon has world-wide significance (cf. 13, 4 – 5, 11, 13). Furthermore, Babylon is YHWH's agent for punishing His people. Thus, the placement of 14, 24 – 27 after the oracle against Babylon points out that the old promises to destroy Assyria will be applied to Babylon. Even though the oppressor changes, the word of YHWH remains constant. Therefore, the entire section is ultimately concerned with Babylon and the superscription in 13, 1 applies to the entire unit. Since this is the case, Isa 13, 1 – 14, 27 may be labeled "Announcement of Babylon's Fate." The structure is as follows:

Announcement of Babylon's Fate	13, 1 – 14, 27
I. Superscription	13, 1
II. Announcement Proper	13, 2 – 14, 27
A. Concerning Babylon's fate	13, 2 – 14, 23
1. oracle against Babylon	13, 2 – 14, 2
a. oracle proper	13, 2 – 22
b. implications for Israel	14, 1 – 2
2. taunt against Babylonian king	14, 3 – 23
B. Summary-appraisal: Assyria's example applied to Babylon	14, 24 – 27

The oracle concerning Philistia in 14, 28 – 32 is much less difficult. It contains a superscription in v. 28 which introduces the oracle[72] and the oracle follows in v. 29 – 32. The structure of this passage is as follows:

Oracle concerning Philistia	14, 28 – 32
I. Superscription	14, 28
II. Oracle Proper	14, 29 – 32

---

[71] For discussion of the summary-appraisal form, see Childs, Isaiah and the Assyrian Crisis, 128 ff., esp. p. 39.

[72] The superscription does not follow the standard *maśśā' PN* pattern so common elsewhere in chapters 13 – 23. For the significance of this difference, see below.

The oracle concerning Moab is likewise simply structured. A supplement in 16, 13 – 14 contains a new announcement of judgment against Moab.[73] The structure is as follows:

Oracle concerning Moab with Supplement	15, 1 – 16, 14
I. Oracle concerning Moab	15, 1 – 16, 12
A. Superscription/Title	15, 1a
B. Oracle proper	15, 1b – 16, 12
II. Supplement: New Word concerning Moab	16, 13 – 14

Isa 17, 1 – 18, 7 is much more complicated. Following the superscription in v. 1a, the unit begins with an oracle against Damascus in 17, 1b – 3. This is expanded by three supplements in v. 4 – 6, 7 – 8, and 9 – 11. These supplements all concern Israel and were suggested by the mention of Ephraim/Israel in v. 3. This indicates that the oracle concerns not Damascus alone, but the Syro-Ephraimitic alliance.[74] The problems begin with 17, 12 – 14, a *hôy* speech which addresses the nations, and 18, 1 – 7, another *hôy* speech which addresses Ethiopia. Scholars have a great deal of difficulty relating these units to 17, 1 – 11.[75] Most maintain that the Ethiopian oracle lends itself much more readily to the Egyptian and Ethiopian oracles which follow in chapters 19 – 20.[76] Nevertheless, these oracles should be associated with 17, 1 – 11.

Isa 17, 12 – 14 is a "woe" speech which threatens unspecified nations with destruction. The language is mythological and seems to derive from the traditions concerning the defeat of nations which threaten Zion. This represents the overthrow of chaos which threatens to overturn world order.[77] It is on the basis of this motif of protection of Jerusalem that Wildberger separates this section from 17, 1 – 11 which contains a threat against Israel.[78] Yet, such a position overlooks the fact that the Syro-Ephraimitic alliance was a direct threat to Jerusalem. Furthermore, similar material which referred to the "peoples" and "nations" that threatened Zion was applied to the situation of the Syro-Ephraimitic War in 8, 9 – 10. Finally, Israel (and Syria) is accused of forgetting YHWH in v. 10. Thus, in the present context, 17, 12 – 14 refers to Israel and Syria. They are warned against attacking Zion.

---

[73] Wildberger, Jesaja 13 – 27, 598 f., 630 f.
[74] Clements, Isaiah 1 – 39, 156 f.
[75] Wildberger, Jesaja 13 – 27, 665 f.
[76] Kaiser, Isaiah 13 – 39, 3 f.; Gray, Isaiah I – XXVII, 306; Clements, Isaiah 1 – 39, 163; Scott, IB, V 275; Vermeylen, Du prophète Isaïe, I 317.
[77] Wildberger, Jesaja 13 – 27, 665; Childs, Isaiah and the Assyrian Crisis, 50 ff.; Kaiser, Isaiah 13 – 39, 85 ff.; Fohrer, Das Buch Jesaja, I 218.
[78] Wildberger, Jesaja 13 – 27, 665.

Isa 18, 1 – 7 is sometimes interpreted as an oracle *against* Ethiopia since it begins with an introductory *hôy*, "Woe!"[79] The particle, *hôy*, however, does not always introduce a threat. It is sometimes used simply as a device for getting the audience's attention.[80] A close reading of chapter 18 shows that no threat is made against Ethiopia. The oracle simply reports the sending of messengers to Ethiopia to direct their attention to YHWH's trimming of shoots and branches. The language is metaphorical, of course, and elsewhere in Isaiah such imagery is used to describe YHWH's defeat of Assyria.[81] Thus, chapter 18 simply directs Ethiopia's (and the world's, cf. v. 3) attention to YHWH's responsibility for defeating Assyria so that they should pay homage to Him (v. 7). The relation of this oracle to the preceding material may be explained by another reference to 8, 9 – 10. Those verses applied in a context in which the Syro-Ephraimitic threat was about to give way to an even greater threat by Assyria. Likewise, the Zion passage in 17, 12 – 14 provides a bridge for material concerned with the Syro-Ephraimitic alliance and with Assyria. Isa 17, 12 – 14 warns the Syrians and Israelites of their inevitable defeat and precedes the announcement (to Ethiopia) of YHWH's defeat of Assyria.[82] As Delitzsch noted, "... Syria was the forerunner of Asshur."[83] Since the whole unit is concerned with announcing YHWH's protection of Zion, it should be labeled "Announcement of YHWH's Protection of Zion." The structure is as follows:

Announcement of YHWH's Protection of Zion	17, 1 – 18, 7
I. Oracle concerning the Syro-Ephraimitic Alliance	17, 1 – 11
A. Superscription	17, 1a
B. Oracle proper with expansions	17, 1b – 11
II. Warning of YHWH's Protection of Zion	17, 12 – 14
III. Announcement of YHWH's Victory over the Threat to Zion	18, 1 – 7

Isa 19, 1 – 15 contains the oracle against Egypt and its superscription. The oracle is elaborated upon by five expansions in v. 16 – 25, each beginning with the formula *bayyôm hahû'* which describe a sequence of events leading to Egypt's joining Israel and Assyria under YHWH's

---

[79] Vermeylen, Du prophète Isaïe, I 318.

[80] Cf. Isa 55, 1. Gray, Isaiah I – XXVII, 309; Roberts, PSB 3 (1982), 296 ff.

[81] Isa 10, 16 – 19, 33 – 34.

[82] Erlandsson, The Burden of Babylon, 74 ff.; Delitzsch, The Prophecies of Isaiah, I 346; Kaiser, Isaiah 13 – 39, 85; Kissane, The Book of Isaiah, I 194. Erlandsson's argument, that *ye'āz*ᵉ*bû* in 18, 6 must refer to Assyria since it has no subject, must be rejected (cf. Burden of Babylon, 75). The words, *hazzalzallîm* and *hann*ᵉ*ṭîšôt*, in v. 5 serve as implied subjects for this verb.

[83] The Prophecies of Isaiah, I 346.

blessing. These two units form a larger unit which stands over against the report of a symbolic action in 20, 1 – 6. The report, which describes Isaiah's walking naked and barefoot for three years as a sign of Egypt's coming defeat, underscores the oracle in 19, 1 – 15. Since 19, 1 – 20, 6 announces Egypt's fate, with regard to both a future disaster and a following time of blessing, the entire unit may be labeled, "Announcement of Egypt's Fate." The structure is as follows:

Announcement of Egypt's Fate	19, 1 – 20, 6
I. Oracle concerning Egypt	19, 1 – 25
A. Superscription	19, 1a
B. Oracle proper with expansions	19, 1b – 25
II. Report of Symbolic Action by Isaiah	20, 1 – 6
A. Superscription	20, 1
B. Report Proper	20, 2 – 6

The next three oracles, concerning Midbar Yam (21, 1 – 10),[84] Dumah (21, 11 – 12),[85] and Arabia (21, 13 – 17), each have relatively simple structures which may be outlined as follows:

Oracle concerning Midbar Yam	21, 1 – 10
I. Superscription	21, 1a
II. Oracle Proper	21, 1b – 10
Oracle concerning Dumah	21, 11 – 12
I. Superscription	21, 11a
II. Oracle Proper	21, 11b – 12
Oracle concerning Arabia	21, 13 – 17
I. Superscription	21, 13a
II. Oracle Proper	21, 13b – 17

The ninth unit of the oracles concerning the nations, 22, 1 – 25, begins with an oracle condemning the Valley of Vision in v. 1 – 14. While the superscription in v. 1a labels the addressee as the Valley of Vision, it is clear from the oracle itself that this refers to Jerusalem. This oracle is followed by a report of a speech by YHWH in which YHWH instructs Isaiah to tell Shebna, the steward over the royal household, that he is unfit for office and that he is to be replaced by Eliakim ben Hilkiah. Apparently, Shebna's ostentatiousness in constructing a monumental tomb for himself is considered paradigmatic of the people of Jerusalem

---

[84] Probably Babylon, cf. v. 9. The meaning of Midbar Yam has been widely discussed but scholars have reached no consensus. For a discussion of the options, see Kaiser, Isaiah 13 – 39, 119, n. a.

[85] Dumah is a city in the area of Edom (cf. LXX which translates this as "The Oracle of Edom,") Kaiser, Isaiah 13 – 39, 129 ff.

who continue in their revelry even when they are doomed.[86] The structure of this oracle is as follows:

Oracle against Jerusalem with Instructions concerning an Individual	22, 1 – 25
I. Oracle against Jerusalem	22, 1 – 14
A. Superscription	22, 1a
B. Oracle Proper	22, 1b – 14
II. Report of a Speech by YHWH concerning Instructions to Speak Judgment against Shebna	22, 15 – 25
A. Speech formula	22, 15a
B. Speech by YHWH to Isaiah	22, 15b – 25

The final unit of the series in 23, 1 – 18 concerns Tyre and Sidon. Following the superscription in v. 1a is a lament for the downfall of Sidon and Tyre in v. 1b – 14.[87] Two expansions project an end to the cities' despair (v. 15 – 16) and future prosperity in YHWH's service (v. 17 – 18). The structure is as follows:

Oracle concerning Tyre	23, 1 – 18
I. Superscription	23, 1a
II. Oracle Proper	23, 1b – 18
A. Lament for Sidon and Tyre	23, 1b – 14
B. Prediction of End of Despair	23, 15 – 16
C. Prediction of Prosperity in Service to YHWH	23, 17 – 18

There are ten basic units in chapters 13 – 23, each concerned with a country or city. The first unit of the series, 13, 1 – 14, 27, concerns Babylon as the greatest military power of the world. The tenth unit, 23, 1 – 18, deals with Tyre and Sidon, the world's foremost commercial powers of the time. Thus, chapters 13 – 23 begin and end with the greatest representatives of earthly power.[88] No reason for the order of the units is evident within the collection. However, the middle of the collection, the Syro-Ephraimitic (17 – 18) and the Egyptian sections (19 – 20), is concerned with YHWH's power to protect (17 – 18) and convincing a world power to turn to Him (19, 16 – 25). Thus, it is possible to see the power of YHWH at the center of the world powers in chapters 13 – 23. In any case, the structure of chapters 13 – 23 is composed of the sequential arrangement of the ten units contained

---

[86] This suggests a reason for the inclusion of Jerusalem with the nations in chapters 13 – 23. Since the people do not acknowledge YHWH's role in bringing about the Assyrian siege of Jerusalem, they are no better than the nations.

[87] Wildberger, Jesaja 13 – 27, 861 f.

[88] Kaiser, Isaiah 13 – 39, 4.

within them, each introduced by *maśśā'* formulation.[89] Since the whole unit is designed to announce YHWH's judgment against nations, it may be labeled as such. The structure is as follows:

Announcement of YHWH's Judgment against Nations	13 — 23
I. Announcement of Babylon's Fate	13, 1 — 14, 27
II. Oracle concerning Philistia	14, 28 — 32
III. Oracle concerning Moab with Supplement	15, 1 — 16, 14
IV. Announcement of YHWH's Protection of Zion	17, 1 — 18, 7
V. Announcement of Egypt's Fate	19, 1 — 20, 6
VI. Oracle concerning Midbar Yam	21, 1 — 10
VII. Oracle concerning Dumah	21, 11 — 12
VIII. Oracle concerning Arabia	21, 13 — 17
IX. Oracle against Jerusalem with Instructions concerning an Individual	22, 1 — 25
X. Oracle concerning Tyre	23, 1 — 18

4. Isaiah 24 — 27

The next major section in the first part of Isaiah is Isa 24 — 27, also known as the "Apocalypse of Isaiah." This unit has been widely discussed, yet scholars have reached no consensus on its interpretation.[90] Space does not permit reviewing the literature here.[91] Instead, an analysis of the structure of these chapters will be offered in an attempt to determine their function in relation to the rest of the book.

Isa 24 — 27 begins with the exclamation, *hinneh*, which is syntactically unconnected to the preceding oracle against Tyre in chapter 23. Likewise, 28, 1 begins with the exclamation *hôy* which is syntactically unconnected to chapter 27 and introduces a section concerned with Ephraim or Judah. Whereas the surrounding material is concerned with individual nations, chapters 24 — 27 are concerned with the fate of the entire earth.

---

[89] The superscription for the Philistine unit is a variant. This is probably because it was associated with the oracle long before the oracle became a part of the present collection (Wildberger, Jesaja 13 — 27, 498). In its present position, the superscription marks the oracle that immediately follows the Babylon section, which announces YHWH's plan for all the nations.

[90] Wildberger, Jesaja 13 — 27, 896.

[91] For brief reviews of scholarship on these chapters, see Wildberger, Jesaja 13 — 27, 893 ff. and W. R. Millar, Isaiah 24 — 27 and the Origin of Apocalyptic, HSM 11, 1976, 1 ff.

Within Isa 24 – 27, the first basic section is 24, 1 – 23, which is concerned primarily with YHWH's punishment of the earth. The unit begins with v. 1 – 13 in which judgment for the earth is determined because of its inhabitants' transgression of the "eternal covenant" (v. 5).[92] While it is evident that the whole earth is intended here (v. 1 – 3), the focus of the punishment in v. 4 – 13 seems to be on one unnamed city which serves as the representative for the earth.[93] From the first three verses of the second section of chapter 24, it is apparent that the inhabitants of the earth[94] do not understand that YHWH's appearance is for the purpose of punishment.[95] This requires the prophet to correct their misunderstanding by pointing out that the problems which brought about the punishment exist within themselves (v. 14 – 16). In v. 17 – 20, the prophet makes it clear that the punishment applies to the whole earth with a description of the punishment addressed to a collectively understood "inhabitant of the earth." He continues v. 17 – 20 with v. 21 – 23, which are linked with the formula, *wᵉhāyâ bayyôm hahû'*. These verses explain that YHWH's punishment of the earth, represented by its gods and kings, will lead to the establishment of His rule on Zion.

The second basic section of Isa 24 – 27 comprises the balance of the unit, 25, 1 – 27, 13. Chapters 25 – 27 continue and develop the situation portrayed in chapter 24 in that they discuss the aftermath of the earth's punishment and the establishment of YHWH's rule on Zion. According to chapters 25 – 27, the nations will turn to YHWH on Zion

---

[92] V. 13, "for thus it shall be in the midst of the earth," indicates that v. 4 – 13 are a projection. This and the projecting language in v. 1 – 3 demonstrate that judgment has been determined, but it has not yet been carried out.

[93] The identity of the city has been widely discussed (cf. Millar, Isaiah 24 – 27, 15 ff.), although without resolution. While the author of this poem would have had a specific city in mind when writing this section, he purposely did not identify his model. Instead, he labeled it *qiryat tohû*, a mythological designation which deliberately disconnects the image from any specific, historical city. Thus, the city of chaos seems to be intended as representative. Since the punishment affects all the nations of the earth (v. 13), the "city of chaos" must be representative of all the earth (cf. Clements, Isaiah 1 – 39, 202 f.).

[94] The understanding of "they" (*hemmâ*) in v. 14 is also disputed (cf. Clements, Isaiah 1 – 39, 203 f.). From the context, "they" appears to refer to the inhabitants of the earth (v. 5, 6, 16, 17). The inhabitants of the earth would rejoice thinking that YHWH's appearance would release them from the curse which devours the earth (v. 6). Yet, they do not realize that the guilt is their own and that YHWH's appearance will result in their own judgment.

[95] Cf. Isa 2, 6 – 22. Note the common misunderstanding that the appearance of YHWH at the "Day of YHWH" was meant as a day of deliverance (Am 5, 18 – 20). Yet, it is clear that the prophetic understanding of the "Day of YHWH" is as a day of judgment against His own people.

and this will result in the restoration of Jacob. The first sub-unit of chapters 25 – 27, 25, 1 – 12, opens with a thanksgiving song that praises YHWH for His victory over the alien foe (v. 1 – 5).[96] Two more sub-units follow this thanksgiving song, each of which is joined to the preceding material by a *waw*-consecutive perfect verb formation. Isa 25, 6 – 8 describes YHWH's blessing for the peoples on His mountain (Zion) and Isa 25, 9 – 12 describes the peoples' response to the blessing, claiming YHWH as their God (v. 9), together with the basis for their acceptance, YHWH's power (v. 10 – 12).[97] The mention of "this mountain" in v. 6, 7, and 10, together with the relation of blessing and response, indicates that v. 6 – 8 and 9 – 12 together form a sub-unit. In this context, the thanksgiving song in v. 1 – 5 would introduce the blessing of the peoples by YHWH and their response in v. 6 – 12. The results of this new situation are then described in three units, each introduced by the formula *bayyôm hahû'*. The first of these passages, 26, 1 – 21, describes Judah's praise of YHWH. The unit begins with a song of praise (with superscription in v. 1a) for YHWH's defeat of oppressors. This is followed in v. 7 – 21 by a description of the circumstances which will lead to this victory. V. 7 – 19 present a petition for deliverance by the people to YHWH and v. 20 – 21 give YHWH's answer that deliverance is coming.[98] The second *bayyôm hahû'* passage, 27, 1, briefly describes YHWH's defeat of the chaos monster, Leviathan, which is presumably representative of the chaotic state of all creation before YHWH's intervention. The third *bayyôm hahû'* passage, 27, 2 – 13, exhorts Israel to accept God's offer of reconciliation by describing the restoration of Jacob.[99] The vineyard allegory describing the restoration in v. 2 – 6 is applied to Israel in v. 7 – 13. V. 7 rhetorically questions Israel's attitude of defeat. V. 8 – 13 refute that attitude by explaining that the purpose of Jacob's punishment is to remove guilt and lead to Jacob's restoration at Zion. This restoration is the climax of YHWH's action.

---

[96] Cf. Wildberger, Jesaja 13 – 27, 899.

[97] Note that some scholars consider v. 10b – 12, which are concerned with the overthrow of Moab, to be a late interpretative addition (Clements, Isaiah 1 – 39, 209 f.; Wildberger, Jesaja 13 – 27, 900; cf. Kaiser, Isaiah 13 – 39, 202).

[98] Isa 26, 19, which announces the resurrection of the dead, is directed to YHWH as indicated by the second person address, "your dead." It is therefore a part of the people's petition. In this context, it is a petition for the restoration of the community, expressed metaphorically (cf. Clements, Isaiah 1 – 39, 216 f.).

[99] For a detailed study of the redactional unity of Isa 27, 2 – 13, see M. Sweeney, New Gleanings from an Old Vineyard: Isaiah 27 Reconsidered, Early Jewish and Christian Exegesis: Studies in Memory of William Hugh Brownlee, ed. C. Evans & W. F. Stinespring, 1987, 51 – 66.

Chapters 24–27 are concerned with YHWH's punishment of the earth and the resulting change in which the entire earth accepts YHWH as its God. They are also concerned with Israel's (Jacob's) return to YHWH at Zion. Such a change requires a fundamental shift in the world order. Because of this shift, and because of the projecting orientation of the whole passage, Isa 24–27 may be labeled as "Proclamation of the New World Order." The structure is as follows:

Proclamation of the New World Order	24, 1 – 27, 13
I. YHWH's Punishment of the Earth	24, 1 – 23
A. Judgment determined and announced	24, 1 – 13
B. Explanation of judgment	24, 14 – 23
1. the people's misunderstanding	24, 14 – 16
2. the punishment described and explained	24, 17 – 23
a. description: to the inhabitants	24, 17 – 20
b. explanation: leads to YHWH's rule on Zion	24, 21 – 23
II. Return of the Earth to YHWH at Zion	25, 1 – 27, 13
A. Nations turn to YHWH at Zion	25, 1 – 27, 13
1. hymn of thanks to YHWH for victory	25, 1 – 5
2. YHWH's blessing of the peoples and their response	25, 6 – 12
a. blessing	25, 6 – 8
b. response	25, 9 – 12
B. Results	26, 1 – 27, 13
1. Judah's praise of YHWH	26, 1 – 21
a. song of praise for YHWH's victory	26, 1 – 6
b. circumstances of victory	26, 7 – 21
1) people's petition for help	26, 7 – 19
2) YHWH's answer	26, 20 – 21
2. YHWH's defeat of Leviathan	27, 1
3. Exhortation to Israel to accept God's offer of reconciliation	27, 2 – 13
a. new vineyard allegory	27, 2 – 6
b. exhortation proper: application of oracle to Israel	27, 7 – 13
1) rhetorical question challenging defeatist attitude	27, 7
2) refutation of defeatist attitude	27, 8 – 13

5. Isaiah 28 – 35

The last major section of Isa 2–35 is chapters 28–35. Following Isa 24–27, which describe YHWH's establishment of sovereignty over the whole earth at Mt. Zion, chapters 28–35 focus on Jerusalem and, to some extent, Israel and Judah. These chapters are formally characterized by the repetition of the interjections *hôy* and *hen* which serve as the basic structural markers of the unit.[100] There is some question about the extent of the unit since many scholars claim that chapters 34–35 and possibly chapter 33 should not be joined with 28–32.[101] The following discussion will address these questions. For the present, it will suffice to note that chapter 36 begins a narrative section which discusses Sennacherib's siege of Jerusalem. As noted above, this section does not form a part of the preceding material in chapters 28–35.

The first sub-unit of chapters 28–35 is 28, 1–29, which is introduced by *hôy*. This section begins in v. 1–6 with a woe oracle directed against the Ephraimite crown (v. 1–4) and an elaboration, introduced by *bayyôm hahû'* (v. 5–6), which claims that YHWH will replace the ruler who is condemned in v. 1–4. There follows in v. 7–13, which are connected to v. 1–6 by *wᵉgam 'ellæh*, a section which also accuses the priests and prophets of corruption on account of their erroneous instruction to the people. In v. 14–22, which are joined to v. 7–13 by *lāken*, the prophet announces judgment against the leaders who were mentioned in v. 7–13. In addition to the close connection of v. 1–6 and 7–13 through the connective *wᵉgam 'ellæh*, is the common theme of drunkenness of the leaders which these two sections share. Structurally speaking, however, v. 7–22 form a unit over against v. 1–6.[102] V. 7–13

---

[100] Duhm, Das Buch Jesaia, 13; cf. Skinner, Isaiah I–XXXIX, 206.

[101] Whether scholars claim to see a larger unit, such as chapters 24–35 or 28–35, or a series of smaller units, such as 28–32, 33, 34–35, or any combination of these, the problem seems to hinge on the placement and function of chapter 33. The following is a brief overview of positions. The first listing of chapters is the scholar's determination of a larger unit. Chapter groupings which follow in parentheses are sub-units of the larger section: Ackroyd, Isaiah, The Interpreter's One-Volume Commentary on the Bible, 1971, 330, chapters 28–35; Barth, Die Jesaja-Worte, 297 f., chapters 24/28–35; Clements, Isaiah 1–39, 24 f., chapters 28–33, 34–35; Delitzsch, The Prophecies of Isaiah, I 54 f., chapters 28–33, 34–35; Duhm, Das Buch Jesaia, 13 f., chapters 24–35 (24–27, 28–33, 34–35); Fohrer, Das Buch Jesaja, I 2, 4 f., chapters 24–35 (24–27, 28–32, 33–35); Kaiser, Isaiah 13–39, 234 ff., 339 ff., 353 ff., chapters 28–32, (33), 34–35; Kissane, The Book of Isaiah, I xxv f., chapters 28–35; Marti, Jesaja, xvi f., chapters 28–35 (28–33, 34–35); Procksch, Jesaia I, 19, 22, chapters 28–35 (28–32 + 33, 34–35); Scott, IB, V 152, chapters 28–32, 33–35; Skinner, Isaiah I–XXXIX, lxix f., chapters 28–35; Vermeylen, Du prophète Isaïe, I 383 f., 439, chapters 28–33, 34–35. Some scholars see chapters 34–35 as the introduction to chapters 36–66 (Torrey, The Second Isaiah, 92 ff., 98 ff.; Pope, JBL 71 (1952) 235 ff.; W. H. Brownlee, The Meaning of the Qumran Scrolls for the Bible, 1964, 247 ff.). Others see only chapter 35 in relation to the rest of the book (Graetz, JQR 4 (1892), 1 ff.; Smart, History and Theology in Second Isaiah, 30 f., 292 ff.).

[102] Wildberger, Jesaja 28–39, 1068, is uncertain whether v. 14–22 should be joined to 7–13 or 1–13. J. C. Exum, Isaiah 28–32: A Literary Approach, SBL 1979 Seminar Papers, II 124, claims that they apply to 1–13. However, the mention of Jerusalem

do not mention that the prophets and priests are Ephraimite in contrast
to v. 1 – 6 which explicitly label the crown as such. This allows for some
ambiguity which is resolved by the mention of Jerusalem in v. 14. The
reader is purposely led to believe that v. 7 – 13 refer to Ephraimite leaders
whereas all along, the prophet was referring to Jerusalemite leaders.[103] This
transition from Ephraimite to Jerusalemite leaders would suggest that the
fate of the Ephraimite leadership, presumably the deportation of Ephraim's
leaders by Assyria, was meant to serve as an example for the leaders in
Jerusalem. Such a comparison would serve as a warning to the Jerusalem
leadership not to follow the example of their Ephraimite counterparts. To
underscore this warning in v. 1 – 22, v. 23 – 29 demonstrate the proper role
of the leaders. Just as YHWH properly instructs the farmer in his planting,
so the prophets and priests in Jerusalem must properly instruct the people.[104]
Since the purpose of this unit is to warn the leaders in Jerusalem to fill
their proper roles as leaders of the people, this unit may be labeled "Warning
to the Leaders in Jerusalem." The structure is as follows:

Warning to the Leaders in Jerusalem	28, 1 – 29
I. Warning Proper	28, 1 – 22
A. Judgment against the Ephraimite crown	28, 1 – 6
1. Woe oracle	28, 1 – 4
2. Elaboration: YHWH will be crown	28, 5 – 6
B. Threat against Jerusalemite leaders	28, 7 – 22
1. Accusation	28, 7 – 13
2. Threat proper	28, 14 – 22
II. Parable Illustrating Proper Role of Leaders	28, 23 – 29

The next unit, 29, 1 – 14, again begins with the exclamation *hôy*.
The first sub-section within this unit is the enigmatic Ariel oracle in v. 1 – 8.
It is clear that Ariel refers to Jerusalem, but scholars are not in agreement
over the significance of this name.[105] In any case, the oracle portrays
YHWH's afflicting Ariel with attackers who will lay siege to the city.
Miraculously, however, YHWH will deliver Ariel from the attackers so that
the whole experience will seem like a dream. This oracle seems to present an
encapsulated view of YHWH's plans for Jerusalem, affliction through foreign
invaders and eventual deliverance after His purposes are served (cf. the Assyrian attack and deliverance in chapters 36 – 37). A new sub-unit begins in
v. 9 with the appearance of the imperative verbs directed to the people of
Jerusalem. This unit, which continues through v. 12, stresses the people's

---

in v. 14 makes it clear that the prophet could not have intended his warning to include
the Ephraimite crown.

[103] Exum, Isaiah 28 – 32, 124.
[104] Cf. J. W. Whedbee, Isaiah and Wisdom, 1971, 51 ff., who claims that the parable is
disputational in that it argues for the purposefulness of YHWH's actions.
[105] Cf. Wildberger, Jesaja 28 – 39, 1104 f.

inability to see and understand. YHWH's speech in v. 13 – 14, which is connected to v. 9 – 12 by the *waw*-consecutive *wayyo'mær*, also focuses on the people's inability to comprehend YHWH's actions. Because of this inability, YHWH announces that He will perform even more wonders which will further demonstrate the leaders' inability to explain what He is doing. Their inability to understand is announced in v. 1 – 8. It is clear in both v. 9 – 12 and 13 – 14 that YHWH blames their leaders for the people's inability to understand. But it is also clear that YHWH has rendered the leaders incompetent (cf. Isa 6, 9 – 10). Clearly, this section relates to chapter 28. There, YHWH warned the leaders. Here, YHWH takes steps to render them incompetent so that they can be removed (cf. 29, 15 – 24). Therefore, this section may be labeled, "Announcement of YHWH's Rendering the Leaders Incompetent so that the People can not Understand." The structure of this unit is as follows:

Announcement of YHWH's Rendering the Leaders Incompetent so that the People can not Understand	29, 1 – 14
I. Illustration of YHWH's Plan for Jerusalem	29, 1 – 8
II. Command to Blindness	29, 9 – 14
A. Command proper	29, 9 – 12
B. YHWH's intentions stated	29, 13 – 14

In the next unit, 29, 15 – 20, the people's inability to comprehend will be reversed. The unit begins with a woe oracle in v. 15 – 16 which accuses the leaders of the people who have reversed their conception of their role vis-à-vis YHWH. Whereas YHWH is the true source of knowledge, these leaders believe that their knowledge comes from themselves and that their thoughts are therefore secret. V. 15 – 16 make it clear that this is not the case. In v. 17 – 21, YHWH announces His intention to grant knowledge to those who would not normally have it, the deaf, the blind, and the poor (v. 18 – 19) and deny it to the judges and the leading citizens who have used knowledge for their own unjust gain in the courts (v. 20 – 21). Since those who are wise have reversed their roles in their own minds, thus reversing justice, YHWH will reverse His gift of knowledge and grant it to those who did not have it before. V. 22 – 24, which are connected to the preceding section by *lāken*, describe the result of YHWH's reversal of knowledge in v. 17 – 21, Jacob's pride in his children for their piety and the acceptance of instruction by those who err. This section builds on the theme of the previous two sections. Here, the leaders are deposed on account of their corruption. The structure is as follows:

Announcement of YHWH's Reversal of Knowledge	29, 15 – 24
I. Accusation against the Leaders	29, 15 – 16
II. Announcement of Punishment: Reversal of Knowledge	29, 17 – 24
A. Announcement of Reversal	29, 17 – 21
B. Results	29, 22 – 24

The next section, 30, 1–33, discusses the punishment which the people will receive on account of their corruption. The unit begins with a woe speech directed against those who favor an alliance with Egypt. This woe speech accuses the people of not relying on YHWH as they should. There follows in v. 6–7 an independent oracle concerning the caravan which carries the embassy to Egypt, which concludes that the venture will be of no use. V. 8–14 are syntactically unconnected to the preceding material and serve as a proclamation of judgment.[106] The first part of this section, v. 8–11, relates a command, presumably by YHWH, to the prophet to record the iniquities of the people. This command functions as an accusation against the people. The judgment is announced in v. 12–14 which are connected to v. 8–11 by *lāken*. V. 15–17 are connected to v. 8–14 by the formula *kî koh ʾāmar ʾadonāy yhwh qᵉdôš yiśrāʾel*. They explain that the people could have avoided the preceding judgment by relying on YHWH. Instead, the people insisted on depending on military might and therefore, they must be judged. V. 18–33, a long composite unit which is connected to v. 15–17 by *wᵉlāken*,[107] explain that YHWH still intends to deliver His people after affliction and show them favor. These verses make it clear that the judgment is just a punishment and not a full break. After the people have received their punishment, they will be restored to the favor which they formerly enjoyed. The woe oracle concerning the Egyptian embassy in v. 1–5 and the *maśśāʾ* concerning the embassy's caravan together with the usefulness of the alliance in v. 6–7 provide background for the proclamation of judgment in v. 8–14. Furthermore, the judgment is only temporary. Therefore, this unit may be labeled, "Announcement of Punishment for Jerusalem." Its structure is as follows:

Announcement of Punishment for Jerusalem	30, 1–33
I. Woe Oracle: Accusation against the Egyptian Embassy	30, 1–5
II. Oracle concerning the Uselessness of the Embassy	30, 6–7
III. Proclamation of Judgment against Jerusalem	30, 8–33
A. Judgment against people proclaimed	30, 8–14
1. accusation	30, 8–11
2. proclamation proper	30, 12–14
B. Judgment explained	30, 15–33
1. reason for judgment	30, 15–17
2. limitation on judgment	30, 18–33

The next unit, 31, 1–9, continues the shift which preceded in chapter 30 from focus on judgment of Jerusalem to focus on protection. The unit begins in v. 1–3 with another woe speech directed against the

---

[106] Note the use of *ʿattâ* and imperative verbs.
[107] Cf. Kaiser, Isaiah 13–39, 297 f., 300 f., 305 f., for the divisions of this section.

afore-mentioned embassy to Egypt. In v. 4–5, however, there is an announcement that YHWH will defend Jerusalem, albeit in a qualified sense.[108] At first glance, v. 1–3 and 4–5 seem to have little to do with each other even though they are joined by the formula, *kî koh 'āmar yhwh 'elay*, in v. 4. Although v. 1–3 are concerned with the embassy to Egypt and v. 4–5 with Jerusalem, both share a common concern with defensive power. The embassy to Egypt emphasizes the people's trust in military alliance for defense against the Assyrian threat. V. 4–5 emphasize YHWH's power to defend. But since the people are willing to trust in Him, He will defend the city like a lion or a vulture would defend its prey. The city will be defended since that is what the people want from Egypt, but at what cost? V. 6–9, which begin with imperatives, follow and are an appeal to the people to return to YHWH, at which time Assyria will fall. The theme of this passage is similar to that of chapter 30, the futility of the embassy to Egypt and the contention that only YHWH can deliver the people from their distress. The difference between these units is one of emphasis. Chapter 30 stresses judgment on the people for their reliance on Egypt. Chapter 31 stresses the need for reliance on YHWH to protect the city and calls for the people to return to Him. Thus, chapters 30 and 31 deal with the two aspects of YHWH's plan announced in chapter 29, punishment and deliverance. Since the purpose of this passage is to convince the people to return to YHWH, it may be labeled, "Appeal to Jerusalem to Return to YHWH." The structure is as follows:

Appeal to Jerusalem to Return to YHWH	31, 1–9
I. Announcement that YHWH will "defend" the city	31, 1–5
A. Woe oracle: futility of reliance on Egypt	31, 1–3
B. Announcement proper	31, 4–5
II. Call to Repentance	31, 6–9

The next section, 32, 1–20, differs from the preceding sections in that the introductory exclamation is not the usual *hôy* but *hen*. The reason for this is because chapter 32 brings to resolution a number of problems which appeared in the preceding chapters. Thus, the first section of the unit, v. 1–8, proclaims the rule of a king who presumably

---

[108] There has been much discussion on the actual meaning of v. 4. The problem centers on the meaning of the preposition *'al* in the phrase *liṣbo' 'al har ṣiyôn wᵉ'al gib'ātāh*. It can mean "to fight *upon* Mount Zion and *upon* its hill" (to defend it) or the preposition can be translated "against" so that the understanding of *'al* determines whether this verse is intended in a threatening or a protective sense. Childs, *Isaiah and the Assyrian Crisis*, 58 f., is correct to claim that v. 4 originally was a threat, but his statement that v. 5 reinterprets v. 4 in a protective sense misses the irony in the verse. YHWH will indeed protect Jerusalem, like a vulture hovering over its prey!

will preside over Jerusalem after its repentance and restoration. Furthermore, these verses make it clear that at the reign of this king, the people's
understanding will return to them, unlike the situation which appeared in
chapter 28 and the following material. The second section of the unit, 32,
9 – 20, is demarcated by the feminine imperatives which address the women
of a city, presumably Jerusalem. This section instructs the women to mourn
for the city in its destruction until a time of justice when the "spirit is
poured out," presumably the previously mentioned restoration of Jerusalem
after its punishment. The lament for the dead in these verses serves as a
vehicle for the proclamation of peace in v. 15 – 20. As this section proclaims
the future restoration of Jerusalem, it may be labeled "Proclamation of
Jerusalem's Future Restoration." The structure is as follows:

Proclamation of Jerusalem's Future Restoration   32, 1 – 20

   I. Proclamation proper   32, 1 – 8

   II. Proclamation of Peace   32, 9 – 20

Having noted that the major problems set forth in chapters 28 ff.
are brought to resolution in chapter 32, it is somewhat surprising to
come upon another unit which begins with *hôy*. This formal similarity
suggests that the chapters should be considered a part of the unit in
chapters 28 – 32, but if the problems of the unit are brought to resolution
in chapter 32, what function would it serve? Indeed, this question applies
to chapters 34 – 35 as well, since there is a great deal of similarity in the
vocabulary of chapter 33 and chapters 34 – 35 which suggests some
relationship between them.[109] Chapters 33 – 35 share some of the motifs
found in chapter 32 which relate to the preceding chapters as well. There
is mention of a king who will rule in the time of deliverance in 33, 17
and 32, 1. Both 34, 16 and 32, 15 view the "Spirit" of YHWH as a
corrective or redeeming force that helps bring about the period of
redemption. Isa 35, 5 and 32, 3 – 8 are both concerned with the return
of understanding to the people (cf. 28, 9 – 13; 6, 9 – 10), especially
through the use of the blind and deaf images. Both 32 and 33 – 35 deal
with a period of restoration after a time of distress. Finally, 31, 8 – 9 and
chapters 33 – 35 announce the destruction of the enemies of Israel and
YHWH, whether they be Assyria, an unnamed destroyer, or Edom. Formally, chapter 33 is a prophetic liturgy[110] which relates the people's distress
over an unnamed destroyer, YHWH's decision to remove the threat, His
deliverance of the righteous, and His assumption of kingship in Zion.
Chapters 34 – 35 are demarcated from chapter 33 by the introductory
summons to hear directed to the nations. They announce YHWH's judgment against the nations, particularly Edom, and His redemption of Israel

---

[109] C. H. Cornill, ZAW 4 (1884), 100, cf. Fohrer, ALUOS 3 (1961), 22 f., esp. n. 26.

[110] H. Gunkel, ZAW 42 (1924), 177 ff., cf. Wildberger, Jesaja 28 – 39, 1284 f.

and restoration of Zion. Essentially, after YHWH acts and assumes kingship in chapter 33, His future plans for Israel and the world are announced. Chapters 33—35 provide the climax for chapters 28—32. Chapters 28—32 discuss judgment which leads to the time of restoration when the king will preside over a period of peace, justice, understanding, and restoration. Chapters 33—35, however, provide a dramatic effect with the liturgical setting of chapter 33 and the announcement that it is YHWH who will be king. This unit may be labeled, "Announcement of YHWH's Assumption of Kingship." The structure is as follows:

Announcement of YHWH's Assumption of Kingship	33, 1—35, 10
I. Prophetic Liturgy: YHWH's Assumption of Kingship	33, 1—24
II. YHWH's Plans for the World and Israel	34, 1—35, 10
A. The Nations: Judgment	34, 1—17
B. Israel/Zion: Restoration/Redemption	35, 1—10

This discussion has shown that chapters 28—35 are composed of seven interrelated units which start with a warning to the corrupt leaders of Jerusalem, continue with YHWH's decision to replace them and punish Jerusalem, and end with YHWH's assumption of kingship after restoring the proper state of affairs in the city. Thus, the unit may be labeled "Announcement of YHWH's Assumption of Kingship in Jerusalem" since His punishment of the city leads to His taking the throne. The structure of chapters 28—35 may be outlined as follows:

Announcement of YHWH's Assumption of Kingship in Jerusalem	28, 1—35, 10
I. Warning to the Leaders in Jerusalem	28, 1—29
II. Announcement of YHWH's Rendering the Leaders Incompetent	29, 1—14
III. Announcement of YHWH's Reversal of Knowledge	29, 15—24
IV. Announcement of Punishment for Jerusalem	30, 1—33
V. Appeal to Jerusalem to Return to YHWH	31, 1—9
VI. Proclamation of Jerusalem's Future Restoration	32, 1—20
VII. Announcement of YHWH's Assumption of Kingship Proper	33, 1—35, 10

6. Overview: Isaiah 2—35

This investigation of Isaiah 2—35 has identified the following blocks of material:

Prophetic Announcement concerning the Cleansing of Zion for its Role as the Locus for YHWH's Rule over the World	2—4
Announcement of YHWH's Judgment against Israel and Judah	5—12

It now remains to examine the relationships among these units in order to determine exactly what they are trying to say. A number of scholars have associated chapters 2 – 4 and 5 – 12 since both seem to have a common theme of Jerusalem and Judah.[111] Yet there are a number of reasons for holding that these units are separate. Among these are the emphasis in 2 – 4 on Jerusalem and Judah whereas in 5 – 12, the emphasis is on Judah and Israel. Likewise, in 2 – 4, the nations play a role as voluntary subjects to YHWH on Zion, whereas in 5 – 12, following the projected restoration of Judah and Israel, they are to be attacked and forced into submission. For these reasons, it seems best to retain the distinction between 2 – 4 and 5 – 12 and focus on other interrelationships among the units.

A number of scholars have suggested an association between 24 – 27 and 13 – 23.[112] This is certainly plausible since chapter 24 opens with an announcement of YHWH's intention to lay waste to the earth, an intention which certainly corresponds to the punishment against the nations announced in chapters 13 – 23. As shown in the discussion of chapters 24 – 27, the object of YHWH's punishment of the earth was to enable the nations to accept His rule on Zion (25, 6 – 12). But in chapters 26 – 27, Judah and Jacob (Israel) are to participate in this period of YHWH's rule, accepting it after the nations' submission. The discussion also noted the occurrence of a new vineyard song in 27, 2 – 6 which announces YHWH's satisfaction with His vineyard (i. e., Israel/Judah) and His intention to protect it from further harm. This song, of course, corresponds with the vineyard song in 5, 1 – 7 which announces YHWH's disappointment with His vineyard (i. e., Israel/Judah) and His intention to uproot it. It happens that the first vineyard song introduces the unit announcing the punishment of Judah/Israel and that the situation is apparently resolved with the second vineyard song near the end of 24 – 27. Thus, chapters 24 – 27 form a conclusion to both 5 – 12 and 13 – 23 since the announcement of the new world order resolves the problems of the punishment of Israel/Judah and the punishment of the nations by demonstrating the end to which the punishment is directed,

---

[111] Clements, Isaiah 1 – 39, 2, Skinner, Isaiah I – XXXIX, lxvii f., Duhm, Das Buch Jesaia, 10 ff., Barth, Die Jesaja-Worte, 297, Gray, Isaiah I – XXVII, xlvii, 1 f., Vermeylen, Du prophère Isaïe, I 35.

[112] Skinner, Isaiah I – XXXIX, lxviii f.; Clements, Isaiah 1 – 39, 196 f.; Wildberger, Jesaja 13 – 27, 892 f.; Vermeylen, Du prophète Isaïe, I 35.

YHWH's rule of Israel/Jacob and the nations from Zion. Therefore, Isa 5 – 27 forms a unit within Isa 2 – 35 which may be labeled, "YHWH's Chastisement of Israel/Judah and the Nations to Bring about the New World Order." The structure is as follows:

Announcement of YHWH's Chastisement of Israel/Judah and the Nations to Bring about the New World Order	5 – 27
I. Chastisement of Israel/Judah and the Nations	5 – 23
A. Israel/Judah	5 – 12
B. Nations	13 – 23
II. Announcement of the New World Order	24 – 27

Following this unit are chapters 28 – 35 which announce YHWH's assumption of kingship in Jerusalem. According to Isa 24 – 27, YHWH will exercise His rule over the new world order from Zion, but nothing is said about the preparation of Zion for this role. Chapters 28 – 35 deal specifically with this problem. The unit stresses the corruption of the leaders in Jerusalem which requires that YHWH remove them from power. With the corrupt leaders removed, YHWH will be able to establish His kingship in the newly cleansed city. It is apparent from these chapters that Jerusalem was in need of chastisement as were Israel/Judah and the nations, in order to properly prepare for the new world order. Therefore, chapters 28 – 35 and 5 – 27 together form a unit which describes in detail the process by which the world, including Israel/Judah, the nations, and Jerusalem, is made fit for YHWH's rule. Chapters 5 – 35 then elaborate on the announcement of the cleansing of Zion for its role as the locus of YHWH's rule in chapters 2 – 4. How is it that the nations will voluntarily submit to YHWH's rule?[113] How is it that Jacob will find a place in YHWH's new world order in response to the invitation in Isa 2, 5? How is it that Zion will be the location of YHWH's rule? In other words, Isa 5 – 35 explains how the plan in Isa 2 – 4 will be carried out. In the process of explaining the establishment of the new world order, chapters 2 – 35 explain the terrible disasters that befell Israel and the nations in the form of conquest by foreign powers. These conquests are explained as a cleansing process, carried out by YHWH, which brings about a period of peace and security. In explaining the conquests in this manner, Isa 2 – 35 asserts YHWH's world-wide power and ability to control the actions of nations so that they will bring about His own purposes. Since the basic purpose of the whole of Isa 2 – 35 is to announce YHWH's plan for a new world order, the entire unit may be labeled as such. The structure is as follows:

---

[113] On the relationship of Isa 13 – 23 to Isa 2 – 4, cf. Weis, The Genre Maśśā', 240 ff.

C. ANALYSIS OF ISAIAH 40 – 66

The last major division of the book of Isaiah is chapters 40 – 66. A number of studies have appeared which investigate the structure of these chapters, or portions thereof, but unfortunately, scholars have reached no consensus on this issue. For example, the majority of scholars see a basic division of these chapters into two parts, chapters 40 – 55 and 56 – 66, which correspond with Deutero- and Trito-Isaiah respectively.[114] But a significant number of scholars divide the chapters into 40 – 48, 49 – 57, and 58 – 66, claiming that chapters 56 – 57 are clearly related to what precedes.[115] Furthermore, the relationship between these parts is not clearly understood, whatever the division of the basic units. Thus, many scholars see chapters 56 – 66 as a collection of oracles added to a previously existing unit, chapters 40 – 55.[116] But some claim that the author of 56 – 66 organized 40 – 55 according to his own purposes and thus produced a coherent structure for all of chapters 40 – 66.[117] The situation is no better when one considers the sub-units of the larger portions. Within 40 – 55, for those who accept that division, a number of scholars claim that there are two basic portions, chapters 40 – 48, which deal primarily with Jacob/Israel, and chapters 49 – 55, which deal primarily with Jerusalem.[118] Others claim that the structure is much more complex since chapters 40 – 55 are formed from a larger number of units.[119] Those who agree that chapters 40 – 48 form a unit dispute its internal structure.[120] Very few attempts have been made to determine the structure of chapters 56 – 66 due to the diversity of material contained

---

[114] E.g., P.-E. Bonnard, Le Second Isaïe, Son Disciple et Leurs Éditeurs, Isaïe 40 – 66, 1972; C. Westermann, Isaiah 40 – 66: A Commentary, OTL, 1969.

[115] Delitzsch, The Prophecies of Isaiah, II 129; B. O. Banwell, ExpT 76 (1964 – 65), 166; Y. Kaufmann, The Babylonian Captivity and Deutero-Isaiah, 1970, 89 f.

[116] E.g., J. A. Soggin, Introduction to the Old Testament, 1976, 335.

[117] K. Elliger, Deuterojesaja in seinem Verhältnis zu Tritojesaja, BWANT 63, 1933, 219 ff.

[118] Kaiser, Introduction to the Old Testament, 262; Soggin, Introduction to the Old Testament, 313.

[119] Cf. R. Melugin, The Formation of Isaiah 40 – 55, BZAW 141, 1976; C. Westermann, Sprache und Struktur der Prophetie Deuterojesajas, CTM 11, 1981; H. C. Spykerboer, The Structure and Composition of Deutero-Isaiah, 1976.

[120] Cf. the following studies: Y. Gitay, Prophecy and Persuasion: A Study of Isaiah 40 – 48, FThL 14, 1981; M. Haran, The Literary Structure and Chronological Framework of the Prophecies of Isaiah XL-XLVIII, SVT 9 (1963), 127 – 155; R. P. Merendino, Der Erste und der Letzte: Eine Untersuchung von Jes 40 – 48, SVT 31, 1981.

therein. Those investigations which have been carried out generally see a symmetrical generic growth of the section, but do not interpret its message according to the final form of the unit.[121]

Since there is such diversity of opinion with respect to the structure of chapters 40 – 66, it seems best to proceed with the analysis of these chapters according to the method adopted for chapters 2 – 35. Smaller structural units will be identified and examined first in order to determine their structure and function within themselves. Afterwards, these units will be examined in relation to each other, in order to determine how they function together to form larger wholes. This should facilitate an assessment of the structure and function of Isaiah 40 – 66 as part of the book as a whole.

1. Isaiah 40, 1 – 11

The first sub-unit of these chapters is 40, 1 – 11. This unit is easily distinguished from the narrative concerning Hezekiah in chapters 36 – 39 by its poetic announcement style and the imperative verbs which introduce and appear throughout the unit. V. 12 begins a disputational questioning whereas v. 1 – 11 are concerned with announcing salvation. Furthermore, v. 1 – 11 begin and end by focusing on Jerusalem, a subject which does not appear again until Isa 44,26 ff.

Within 40, 1 – 11, v. 1 – 8 relate what was said when the prophet was commissioned in the divine council.[122] In v. 1 – 2, an unidentified speaker relates announcements by God that the people are to be comforted and that Jerusalem's punishment is fulfilled. In v. 3 – 5, another speaker[123] announces directions to an unspecified audience that preparations are to be made for YHWH's return and revelation to all flesh. V. 6 – 8 relate a dialogue[124] which begins with a voice's instructions to the prophet to cry out. The prophet objects to this instruction by metaphorically alluding to the transience of creation. He is reassured that although creation is transient, the word of God is not. The voices which speak in this section are evidently the heavenly beings which serve

---

[121] Westermann, Isaiah 40 – 66, 296 ff.; Bonnard, Le Second Isaïe, 315 ff.; K. Pauritsch, Die neue Gemeinde: Gott sammelt Ausgestoßene und Arme, AnBib 47, 1971, 241 ff.

[122] K. Elliger, Deuterojesaja 40, 1 – 45, 7, BKAT XI/1, 1978, 4 ff.; Melugin, The Formation of Isaiah 40 – 55, 82 ff.; J. Muilenburg, Isaiah 40 – 66, Introduction and Exegesis, IB, V 1956, 442 ff.

[123] If these verses were meant to be spoken by the same speaker as v. 1 – 2, there would be no need for an introductory qôl qôre'. They would simply continue v. 1 – 2.

[124] Elliger, Deuterojesaja, 9 f.

YHWH in the divine council. Their role here is to transmit the divine message to the prophet.

The second part of this unit, v. 9–11, is distinguished from the first by the feminine imperatives which introduce it. Here, the addressee is no longer the members of the heavenly council or the prophet, but Jerusalem. Jerusalem, which is identified as *mᵉbaśśæræt ṣîyôn*, "Herald of Good Tidings, Zion," is instructed to announce YHWH's return to the cities of Judah. These instructions are arranged so that they correspond to the instructions given in v. 1–8. Thus, v. 9, which instructs Jerusalem to make the announcement of salvation to the cities of Judah, corresponds to v. 1–2 in which instructions are given to comfort the people and announce deliverance to Jerusalem. Certainly, instructions to Jerusalem to announce YHWH's return would comfort the people and inform Jerusalem that her time of service was ended. V. 10–11 announce the return of YHWH. This would correspond to v. 3–5 which give instructions to make preparations for YHWH's return and revelation. Thus, v. 9–11 are a fulfillment of the instructions announced to the prophet in v. 1–8.[125]

A number of scholars have claimed that this unit is the prologue to Deutero-Isaiah (chapters 40–55).[126] This may be true but a decision on this matter must be postponed until the examination of the remaining material is complete. In the meantime, this section may be labeled, "Announcement of the Prophet's Commission," since it relates the call of the prophet to his commission and his carrying out that commission. The structure is as follows:

Announcement of the Prophet's Commission	40, 1–11
I. The Call of the Prophet	40, 1–8
II. The Prophet's Instructions to Jerusalem	40, 9–11

2. Isaiah 40, 12–31

The next sub-unit is 40, 12–31. This unit is syntactically unconnected to the preceding unit and is distinguished from the proclamatory character of v. 1–11 by its disputational orientation.[127] The disputation focuses on YHWH's role as creator throughout. This continues until

---

125 Elliger, Deuterojesaja, 34.

126 Melugin, The Formation of Isaiah 40–55, 82; Bonnard, Le Second Isaïe, 85; Spykerboer, The Structure and Composition of Deutero-Isaiah, 182 ff.; Muilenberg, IB, V 442 ff.; J. McKenzie, Second Isaiah, AB 20, 1968, 16 ff.

127 Westermann, Isaiah 40–66, 48 ff.; Sprache und Struktur, 44 ff.

41, 1 where there is a summons to trial directed to the coastlands. Isa 40, 12 – 31 is directed to Jacob (v. 27).

Isa 40, 12 – 31 is organized into three major sections, each of which begins with a question or a series of questions directed to Jacob, the prophet's disputant.[128]

The first section, v. 12 – 20, begins by asking who has measured creation and who taught YHWH the principles of knowledge, justice, and understanding which are the foundations of creation. The answer is obviously "nobody" since in v. 15 – 17, the nations are shown to be incomparable with YHWH. The section concludes with further questioning which is rhetorical in nature. Idols are obviously not to be compared with YHWH since they are created by craftsmen whereas YHWH has no creator, as seen in v. 12 – 14. Thus, the point is made that YHWH is the creator and nobody created Him.

The second section, v. 21 – 26, begins by questioning Jacob's knowledge. The point is made that Jacob should have known that YHWH is creator since this has been common knowledge from the beginning of creation.[129] This is supported by the control which YHWH exercises over the earth. Again, the section ends with a rhetorical question which emphasizes YHWH's ability to control creation and thus asserts that no power can be compared to Him since *only* YHWH controls creation.

The third section, v. 27 – 31, is the climax of the unit.[130] The introductory question drives right to the heart of the disputation, Jacob's contention that YHWH does not know what he (Jacob) does. The basis for this assertion has already been destroyed since if YHWH is the creator of the world and its master, He certainly would know of Jacob's actions. This point is further asserted in v. 28 – 31 which again question Jacob's knowledge. YHWH, as the everlasting God, is able to restore those who hope in Him. The implication for Jacob is that if he puts his trust in YHWH, who knows his situation, then YHWH will indeed deliver him.

Thus, 40, 12 – 31 emphasizes YHWH's role as the creator God and His ability as such to deliver His people from their present misery. The object is to convince the people of this.[131] The argument develops in three parts. In the first, YHWH's role as creator of the earth is emphasized. In the second, His role as master of the world is asserted and this leads to the next point, that He is therefore able to deliver His people if they will put their faith in Him. The structure is as follows:

---

[128] Cf. Bonnard, Le Second Isaïe, 96 f.

[129] Cf. Brownlee, The Meaning of the Qumran Scrolls, 171 f.

[130] Westermann, Isaiah 40 – 66, 48, 61.

[131] Cf. Gitay, Prophecy and Persuasion, 82.

Disputation: YHWH is the Master of Creation	40, 12 – 31
I. Assertion: YHWH is Creator	40, 12 – 20
II. Assertion: YHWH is Master of Creation	40, 21 – 26
III. Assertion: YHWH can deliver Jacob	40, 27 – 31

3. Isaiah 41, 1 – 42, 13

The next section of Isa 40 – 66 is 41, 1 – 42, 13.[132] Scholars generally agree that 41, 1 begins a new section since it introduces a trial scene with a summons to trial directed to the coastlands and the peoples.[133] The extent of the unit is often disputed, however. Some hold that the unit ends with 41, 29 which would exclude the first of the "servant songs" in 42, 1 – 4.[134] But the address to the servant in 41, 8 ff. suggests that the servant passage in 42, 1 – 4 should not be excluded from the larger unit. Muilenberg ends the unit with 42, 4,[135] but this would sever the servant song from the address to the servant in 42, 5 – 9. Others have focused on the hymn of praise to YHWH in 42, 10 – 13. Some claim that it should be joined with v. 14 – 17 so that it can conclude 41, 1 – 42, 9 or introduce the following section.[136] Both sections portray YHWH as warrior.[137] Furthermore. V. 14 – 17 are a quotation by YHWH and v. 13b, "He shouts, indeed He raises a war cry, He confronts His enemies," seems to introduce the quotation.[138] However, the verbs *rwᶜ* and *ṣrḥ* would be a strange introduction for a quotation since they never introduce quoted speech elsewhere in the Hebrew Bible.[139] Furthermore, v. 10 – 13 have strong connections with what follows. V. 10 – 13 repeat some of the terminology of what precedes in order to provide a response to the foregoing context.[140] Israel is instructed to sing a new song to

---

[132] Cf. Melugin, The Formation of Isaiah 40 – 55, 93 ff.

[133] Westermann, Isaiah 40 – 66, 63 f.; Muilenberg, IB, V 447 ff.; Bonnard, Le Second Isaïe, 107 f.

[134] Gitay, Prophecy and Persuasion, 98 ff.; J. Skinner, The Book of the Prophet Isaiah, Chapters XL – LXVI, CB, 1929², xi; Torrey, The Second Isaiah, 321 ff.; Marti, Jesaja, 285.

[135] Isaiah 40 – 66, 447.

[136] Spykerboer, The Structure and Composition of Deutero-Isaiah, 93 ff.; Bonnard, Le Second Isaïe, 120; McKenzie, Second Isaiah, 43 f.; Merendino, Der Erste und der Letzte, 256 f.; P. Volz, Jesaia II, KAT IX, 1932, 29.

[137] Spykerboer, Structure and Composition of Deutero-Isaiah, 95 f.

[138] Spykerboer, Structure and Composition of Deutero-Isaiah, 95.

[139] See especially 1 Sam 10, 24 where the verb *rwᶜ* is followed by a quote but the quote is introduced by *wayyoʾmᵉrû*.

[140] Westermann, Sprache und Struktur, 77.

YHWH who proclaims new things, to give praise to God who will not give praise to idols, to glorify YHWH who gives no glory to others, to declare praise to YHWH who declares the future.[141] V. 14−17 are a speech by YHWH and this speech is continued in v. 18−20. V. 14−17 emphasize the blind who are addressed in v. 18. V. 14−17 also announce YHWH's intention to lead the blind and following sections discuss the journey home by Jacob. Spykerboer is correct to see a transition between two sections in this material.[142] The transition is not formed solely by 42, 10−13 as he claims, but by 42, 10−13 in relation to 42, 14−17. There is, however, a division between v. 10−13 and 14−17 so that the former conclude 41, 1−42, 13 and the latter begin a new but related unit.[143]

Isa 41, 1 introduces the section with a summons to trial directed to the coastlands. The third person imperfect verbs in v. 1b indicate that a third party is addressed in addition to the coastlands, but this third party is not yet identified. V. 2−4 follow in which YHWH presents His contentions by means of self-answered rhetorical questions. He contends that He has directed political events, that He has brought Cyrus, the one from the east, who has enjoyed military success. YHWH argues that this is entirely His doing. V. 1−4 thus form a trial speech.[144]

V. 5−7 have often been included as part of the trial speech although they are not part of the form.[145] Their position here has therefore caused some confusion. V. 1−4 were addressed to the entire court, the coastlands, which are the other party to the legal proceeding, and the unnamed third party which presumably serves as witness. V. 5−7, on the other hand, speak about the coastlands in the third person which indicates that they are not addressed. Apparently, only the third party, the witness to the proceedings, is addressed although it is not clear who this third party is. The identity of the third party is made clear by the

---

[141] Melugin, The Formation of Isaiah 40−55, 101; cf. Gitay, Prophecy and Persuasion, 122 ff.

[142] Structure and Composition of Deutero-Isaiah, 96.

[143] Melugin, The Formation of Isaiah 40−55, 93. Isa 42, 1−13 is one of a number of hymns in Deutero-Isaiah which Westermann labels "Die (eschatologischen) Loblieder." According to him, these eschatological psalms of praise conclude major units in Deutero-Isaiah. For a detailed discussion of these hymns, see Sprache und Struktur, 157 ff.; The Praise of God in the Psalms, 1965, 142 ff. Melugin also adopts this structural principle (The Formation of Isaiah 40−55, 90).

[144] Westermann, Isaiah 40−66, 63 f.; cf. H. J. Boecker, Redeformen des Rechtslebens im alten Testament, WMANT 14, 1970², 69 f., who terms this Appellationsrede (Appeal Speech) since it involves the resolution of a civil question between two parties and does not seek to determine the guilt or innocence of someone accused of a crime.

[145] Cf. Boecker, Redeformen des Rechtslebens, 70, n. 1; Elliger, Deuterojesaja, 113 ff.

w^{e}'*attâ* in v. 8 which introduces an oracle of salvation for Israel in
v. 8 – 13.[146] Here, Israel is directly addressed and it becomes clear that
although the legal proceedings are directed against the coastlands, Israel
is the intended recipient of the message. The oracle of salvation in
v. 8 – 13, in which YHWH states His intent to help His "friend" and
"servant," Israel, contrasts directly with the portrayal of the coastlands
who put their trust in idols. There follows in v. 14 – 16 a proclamation
of salvation for Jacob, which reinforces the assurance of v. 8 – 13 by
emphasizing YHWH's power to save,[147] and a proclamation of salvation
for the poor in v. 17 – 20, which emphasizes YHWH's use of the elements
of creation to aid humans whom He chooses to aid. The entire section,
v. 5 – 20, is addressed to Israel and stresses YHWH's power in affecting
human events. The purpose is to convince Israel of this.

With the trial speech in v. 21 – 29, YHWH's address shifts away
from Israel and back to the other party in the legal proceeding. YHWH
challenges the gods of the coastlands in a direct second-person address
to refute His claim in v. 2 – 4 by demonstrating their power to declare
future events and explain past events. When they are unable to do so,
YHWH reasserts His claim that He has determined the world's events
and announces to the court that the gods are unable to challenge Him.
YHWH then presents His servant, Israel (cf. 41, 8), to the court in 42,
14,[148] claiming that the servant will bring justice to the earth. Since this
is accomplished because YHWH has put His spirit on the servant, the
servant acts as a surrogate ruler or representative for YHWH to the
world.

In v. 5 – 9, demarcated by the messenger formula and the hymn in
v. 10 – 13, YHWH commissions His servant.[149] He states His call of the
servant and the purpose for which he is called, to establish YHWH's
covenant with the world. By this means, YHWH asserts to the world
His role for Israel after all the suffering which he has caused her.

As noted above, the hymn in v. 10 – 13 concludes 41, 1 – 42, 9 by
acting as a response to the material which precedes.

The trial speeches of this section demonstrate YHWH's control of
world events for His own purposes. The intent of this section is not
only to demonstrate this mastery to Israel and to show Israel, the servant,
that she has a role in YHWH's plans for establishing justice in the
world. In effect, YHWH enters the courtroom to prove His power to
control human events and His purpose for doing so to Israel. Therefore,

---

[146] Melugin, The Formation of Isaiah 40–55, 94.

[147] Spykerboer, Structure and Composition of Deutero-Isaiah, 71.

[148] Cf. Melugin, The Formation of Isaiah 40–55, 67, who claims that 42, 1–4 displays
a style that is used to "announce the establishment of someone in a particular office."

[149] Melugin, The Formation of Isaiah 40–55, 67 ff.

this section is a trial, in which YHWH seeks to prove His mastery over human events. The structure is as follows:

Trial: YHWH is Master of Human Events	41, 1 – 42, 13
I. Address to Court (Trial Speech): YHWH's Contention that He is Master of Human Events	41, 1 – 4
A. Summons to trial: to coastlands	41, 1
B. YHWH's contention proper	41, 2 – 4
II. Address by YHWH to Israel: Contrast of Coastlands and Israel	41, 5 – 20
A. Coastlands: Reliance on YHWH	41, 5 – 7
B. Israel: Reliance on YHWH	41, 8 – 20
III. Address to Court	41, 21 – 42, 4
A. Trial Speech: YHWH's contention	41, 21 – 29
B. Presentation of Servant (Israel) to court	42, 1 – 4
IV. Address to Servant: Commission	42, 5 – 9
V. Concluding Hymn	42, 10 – 13

4. Isaiah 42, 14 – 44, 23

The next section of Isa 40 – 66 is 42, 14 – 44, 23.[150] The above discussion established 42, 14 – 17 as the beginning of a new sub-unit. The following discussion will show that 42, 18 – 44, 23 develops the point made in 42, 14 – 17. At the end of the unit is another hymn of praise similar to 42, 10 – 13 which concluded the preceding unit.[151] As the following discussion demonstrates, its praise of YHWH for redeeming Israel brings out the basic theme of this unit.

The proclamation of salvation in 42, 14 – 17 is a first person speech by YHWH in which He states His intention to deliver the blind Israel by leading them in new directions from darkness to light and from rough ground to smooth. He contrasts this deliverance with the fate of those who still worship idols. They shall not be included in this deliverance and will be put to shame. The point is elaborated in 42, 18 – 43, 7. Isa 42, 18 – 25 begins with a summons to hear in v. 18 which is syntactically unconnected to v. 14 – 17, but it is directed to the deaf and especially to the blind so that the connection with v. 14 – 17 is made thematically. V. 18 – 25 are a disputation speech as shown by the use of "who?" questioning similar to that of 40, 12 – 31.[152] The questioning first estab-

---

[150] Melugin, Formation of Isaiah 40 – 55, 90; Westermann, Isaiah 40 – 66, 142; cf. Elliger, Deuterojesaja, 450, who sees 42, 10 – 44, 23 as a redactional unit.

[151] Westermann, Sprache und Struktur, 78 f.; Isaiah 40 – 66, 142 ff.

[152] Westermann, Isaiah 40 – 66, 108 f.; Melugin, The Formation of Isaiah 40 – 55, 41 ff.

lishes that the blind party is YHWH's servant, previously identified as Israel in 41, 8, which suggests YHWH's good intentions. Second, the questioning establishes that YHWH was responsible for the present destitute state of the blind, here unmistakably identified as Israel and Jacob, but that this display of YHWH's anger was the result of Israel's sin and not of YHWH's malevolence or indifference. An oracle of salvation follows in 43, 1 – 7 which is connected to 42, 18 – 25 by an introductory $w^{e^c}att\hat{a}$.[153] In contrast to 42, 18 – 25, which discusses YHWH's punishment of the people, 43, 1 – 7 announces YHWH's coming redemption of Israel. Following the expanded YHWH speech formula, YHWH portrays Himself as the $g\hat{o}'el$, redeemer.[154] Thus, 42, 18 – 25 and 43, 1 – 7 together provide an elaboration of 42, 14 – 17. They explain that the misfortune of the blind Israel was YHWH's action to punish them for their transgression and that now YHWH will carry out the promise to deliver them made in 42, 14 – 17 because He is acting as their $g\hat{o}'el$, redeemer.

The next sub-unit, 43, 8 – 13, returns to a trial setting as indicated by the summons to trial in v. 8 – 9a. Here, both the blind Israel and the nations are called to trial. YHWH's claim in this trial speech is apparently directed against the nations who are challenged to bring witnesses that they are able to show the former things as YHWH claims He does. The blind here function as YHWH's witnesses, although the second person elements in this sub-unit, as well as in the other sub-units of 42, 14 – 44, 23, indicate that these proceedings are intended primarily to convince Israel of YHWH's claims rather than only the nations. Here, the point of contention is that YHWH has directed events and that it is He who saves Israel. Thus, YHWH is attempting to substantiate the claims He made in 42, 14 – 42, 7, that He is the redeemer of Israel.

The next sub-unit, 43, 14 – 15, is introduced by an expanded YHWH speech formula in v. 14a. Here, YHWH is identified as "your redeemer, the Holy One of Israel," which stresses the point argued in earlier sub-units of this section.[155] YHWH substantiates His claim by pointing out that He is the one who has initiated the overthrow of Babylonia.[156] He further underscores His relationship with Israel by identifying Himself as "your Holy One, the Creator of Israel, your King."

---

[153] Melugin, The Formation of Isaiah 40 – 55, 108.

[154] On the function of the $g\hat{o}'el$, see Ringgren, TDOT II 350 ff.

[155] Spykerboer, Structure and Composition of Deutero-Isaiah, 105.

[156] Note that in 43, 14 the verb $\check{s}illa\d{h}t\hat{i}$ is perfect which indicates that the process has begun, but $w^eh\hat{o}radt\hat{i}$ (with $mahpakh$ on the last syllable) is a converted perfect which indicates that the downfall is yet to come.

A proclamation of salvation for Israel follows in 43, 16 – 21.[157] It is introduced by an expanded YHWH speech formula in v. 16 – 17 which calls to mind YHWH's role as deliverer at the Exodus from Egypt. Here, YHWH announces that He is doing a "new thing" for Israel. By appealing to the old Exodus traditions, YHWH argues that He is bringing about a new Exodus in order to redeem His people anew. Isa 43, 22 – 44, 5, which is joined to 43, 16 – 21 by a connecting *waw* at the beginning of v. 22, elaborates on v. 16 – 21 in a manner similar to the elaboration of 42, 14 – 17 by 42, 18 – 43, 7. In the trial speech in v. 22 – 28, YHWH defends His punishment of Israel as justified by Israel's transgressions in not acknowledging YHWH as God.[158] But 44, 1 – 5 is an oracle of salvation in which YHWH announces His forgiveness for the people. This section is connected to 43, 22 – 28 by *we'attâ* at the beginning of v. 1 so that the oracle of salvation contrasts directly with the trial speech and its discussion of the punishment of Israel.[159] Furthermore, v. 5 makes it clear that the purpose of the punishment in 43, 22 – 28 is to bring Israel back to YHWH. Taken together, 43, 16 – 21, 43, 22 – 28, and 44, 1 – 5 function in a fashion very similar to 42, 14 – 43, 7, to announce YHWH's salvation and explain that the prior time of misery was YHWH's punishment for Israel's transgressions. There is a difference between the two units, however. The first is simply an announcement of YHWH's plans for the redemption of Israel. The second, 43, 16 – 44, 5, is spoken in a court of law (note the court setting in 43, 8 ff.) and serves as part of the evidence that YHWH has introduced to convince the court, Israel and the nations (cf. 43, 8 – 9a), that He is the redeemer of Israel.

The next section, 44, 6 – 8, opens with an expanded YHWH speech formula which emphasizes YHWH's role as King and Redeemer of Israel. This speech formula introduces another trial speech in which YHWH seeks to reiterate the point that He has been trying to make all along in this unit. He alone is God of Israel and no other can compare to Him. Functionally, this is a summary speech made before the court in which YHWH attempts to establish His claim.[160] The satire against

---

[157] Cf. Schoors, I am God your Saviour, SVT 24, 1973, 93; Westermann, Isaiah 40 – 66, 126 f.

[158] Cf. Boecker, Redeformen des Rechtslebens, 54 ff. Boecker follows Begrich in labeling this speech *Appellationsrede des Angeschuldigten* (appeal speech of the accused). He claims that this type of speech is used to justify actions that are the subject of legal accusation. The purpose is not to deny the specified action, but to show that it was legally warranted.

[159] On the connection of 43, 22 – 28 and 44, 1 – 5, see Elliger, Deuterojesaja, 364 ff.

[160] Boecker, Redeformen des Rechtslebens, 162 f., stresses that this is a public speech form (*Notarielle Redeform*) in which YHWH attempts to establish His claim by appealing to Jacob as witnesses.

idol worship in v. 9 – 20 emphasizes His point that there are no other gods beside Him.[161]

The exhortation in 44, 21 – 22, distinguished from the preceding descriptive material in v. 9 – 20 by its imperative form, concludes the trial scene begun in 43, 8. It is directed to Jacob/Israel and exhorts Israel to remember the points that YHWH made in the preceding material, that Jacob is YHWH's servant and that YHWH has forgiven Jacob's sins. It ends with an appeal to Jacob to return to YHWH, which has been the object of the legal proceedings of this unit, and the original announcement of YHWH's plan for Jacob's redemption in 42, 14 – 43, 7. YHWH has presented His arguments and it is now up to Israel to decide whether or not to believe them.

The section concludes with a hymn of praise in 44, 23. Because it is directed to the heavens and the earth, it must be distinguished from the trial scene which precedes. But as noted at the beginning of the discussion of 42, 14 – 44, 23, it sums up the main point of the unit, that YHWH is the redeemer of Israel.

This unit is an "Announcement of YHWH's Contention that He is the Redeemer of Israel" since this is the basic thrust of the section. The object is to convince Israel of this as indicated by the frequent addresses to Israel, and especially, the final exhortation in 44, 21 – 22. YHWH makes His point by announcing it and then going to court to prove it. In both the announcement and in the trial proceedings, YHWH states His case, that He is the Redeemer of Israel and then explains the past punitive actions which Israel might understand as proof that His relationship with them had ended. Instead, YHWH claims that these were only a temporary punishing measure and that once the punishment was completed, His relationship with Israel could be restored. The Concluding Hymn of Praise merely reiterates that YHWH is the Redeemer of Israel, and therefore Israel should glorify Him. The structure is as follows:

Announcement of YHWH's Contention that He is the Redeemer of Israel	42, 14 – 44, 23
I. Announcement of YHWH's Plan for the Redemption of Israel	42, 14 – 43, 7
A. Announcement proper	42, 14 – 17
B. Elaboration	42, 18 – 43, 7
1. disputation: punishment was from YHWH due to Jacob's sin	42, 18 – 25
2. oracle of salvation for Jacob: punishment is now over	43, 1 – 7

---

[161] Cf. Melugin, The Formation of Isaiah 40 – 55, 119 f.

II. Trial: YHWH Substantiates Claim in Court   43, 8 – 44, 22
    A. Trial speech: Challenge to opponents   43, 8 – 13
    B. Substantiation of YHWH's claim: Overthrow of Baby-
       lon   43, 14 – 15
    C. Presentation of YHWH's contention: He is redeemer
       of Israel   43, 16 – 44, 5
       1. proclamation of salvation to Israel   43, 16 – 21
       2. elaboration   43, 22 – 44, 5
          a. appeal of accused: YHWH justifies punitive ac-
             tions   43, 22 – 28
          b. oracle of salvation for Jacob   44, 1 – 5
    D. Summary statement by YHWH   44, 6 – 8
       1. summary statement proper   44, 6 – 8
       2. satire against idol worship   44, 9 – 20
    E. Final exhortation to Israel to return to YHWH   44, 21 – 22
III. Concluding Hymn of Praise   44, 23

5. Isaiah 44, 24 – 48, 22

The next major unit of Isa 40 – 66 is 44, 24 – 48, 22.[162] Following
the hymn which concluded the previous section, the present section
begins with an expanded YHWH speech formula. The speeches by
YHWH in this section all relate to YHWH's intention to use Cyrus as
His agent to restore Jerusalem and Judah and His arguments for this
decision.[163] The unit continues through 48, 20 – 21 (22)[164] which contains
a command (in hymnic form) to the Israelite exiles to leave Babylon.[165]
A speech by the servant, Israel, follows in 49, 1 – 6 which does not
directly relate to the specific concerns of the present unit. One might
argue that the unit should only extend to 45, 8 where there is another
concluding hymn.[166] But 45, 9 – 48, 22 contains a number of references
to Cyrus in 45, 13; 46, 10 – 11; and 48, 14 – 16. These references can not
be properly understood without the explicit mention of his name in 44,

---

[162] Westermann, Sprache und Struktur, 81; Merendino, Der Erste und der Letzte, 403;
Marti, Jesaja, 305.

[163] Westermann, Sprache und Struktur, 81; cf. Melugin, Formation of Isaiah 40 – 55, 126.

[164] V. 22 seems to be a marginal insertion from 57, 21 (cf. Westermann, Isaiah 40 – 66,
205). Some claim that it was intentionally placed here to provide a conclusion for one
of the major divisions of chapters 40 – 66 (Duhm, Das Buch Jesaia, 367; Muilenberg,
IB, V 563).

[165] Westermann, Isaiah 40 – 66, 204 f.

[166] Elliger, Deuterojesaja, 490 f. Westermann considers 44, 24 – 45, 8 to be a sub-unit of
44, 24 – 48, 22 (Sprache und Struktur, 82).

28 and 45, 1.[167] Furthermore, Melugin points to the focus on YHWH's "purpose" (*hæpæṣ*) which also ties this unit together.[168]

The unit opens in 44, 24–28 with a speech by YHWH introduced by an expanded YHWH speech formula. The speech is hymnic in style since it is composed of a series of participial phrases which qualify the self-predication by YHWH in v. 24b.[169] But closer examination of the contents of this speech reveal that its primary purpose is disputational. Although the qualifying phrases just mentioned are participial, each of them ends with an imperfect verb which announces action that YHWH takes or authorizes. Furthermore, the sequence of phrases starts with mention of YHWH's role as creator of the earth and master of the people within it. These are general propositions related to YHWH's role as cosmic overlord. But as the unit progresses, it focuses on more immediate issues, the rebuilding of Judah and Jerusalem and the use of Cyrus to accomplish this end.[170] Therefore, the passage is an argument that if YHWH is creator and master of the world, then He can use Cyrus, a non-Jew, to rebuild Jerusalem and His temple.[171] Thus, Melugin is correct to see 44, 24–28 as a self-contained disputation.[172] However, 44, 24–28 still introduces the next unit, 45, 1–7, even though it is not an integral part of it. The passages are linked by their common concern with Cyrus, but 45, 1–7 is a self-contained speech by YHWH to Cyrus introduced by a YHWH speech formula. YHWH's speech is a royal oracle to Cyrus in which he is commissioned as YHWH's anointed king.[173] Isa 44, 24–28 prepares the way for this oracle by providing the justification for a previously unheard of act, the use of a foreigner to build the temple of YHWH, an act formerly reserved for the king who

---

[167] Cf. Westermann, Sprache und Struktur, 81. Note the specific reference in 45, 13 to the building of Jerusalem in 44, 28.

[168] Isa 44, 28; 46, 10; and 48, 14. Melugin, The Formation of Isaiah 40–55, 126.

[169] Melugin, The Formation of Isaiah 40–55, 38 f.; Westermann, Sprache und Struktur, 61 ff.; Isaiah 40–66, 154 f.

[170] Note 1QIsaᵃ which reads that Jerusalem shall rebuild the temple (cf. Brownlee, The Meaning of the Qumran Scrolls, 224 f.).

[171] Cf. Gitay, Prophecy and Persuasion, 181 f.

[172] The Formation of Isaiah 40–55, 39. Westermann, Sprache und Struktur, 61 f., argued that 44, 24–28 could not stand alone since, as a series of appositions to a verbless clause, the unit was grammatically incomplete. These are hardly incomplete grammatically, since the participial statements all qualify the initial *'ānokî yhwh*, and therefore form a long continuous verbal sentence. (On the function of verbless sentences, see F. Andersen. The Hebrew Verbless Clause in the Pentaeuch, JBLMS 14, 1970.) Furthermore, the YHWH speech formula in 45, 1 indicates that 45, 1–7 is a separate unit as does the fact that the speech in 45, 2–7 is directed to Cyrus whereas the speech in 44, 24b–28 is directed to Israel.

[173] Melugin, The Formation of Isaiah 40–55, 123 f.

reigns in Jerusalem. Isa 45, 1 – 7 announces the fact, Cyrus will serve as YHWH's anointed king. Finally, the unit concludes with a hymn of praise which responds to the commission of Cyrus.

The next major sub-unit of 44,24 – 48, 22 is 45, 9 – 48, 19. As seen above, this section is concerned with Cyrus throughout but does not mention him by name. The unit is disputational in character in that it portrays another trial scene in which YHWH seeks to justify His use of Cyrus to restore Jerusalem. Again, the object is to convince Israel of the legitimacy of this act as indicated by the addresses to Israel in 45, 17 and 48, 1. The sub-unit does not include 48, 20 – 22 since these verses are not directly related to the trial proceedings.

The sub-unit begins in 45, 9 – 13 with a disputational speech by YHWH.[174] The disputation begins with two woe sayings which provide analogies to the dispute at hand, the right of that which is made to contend with its maker. Here, it is established rhetorically that clay has no right to question the potter about what he makes and children have no right to question their parents about what they beget. V. 11 – 13 contain the main point, the people have no right to question their maker. Hence, the people have no basis to challenge YHWH when He determines to use Cyrus (v. 13) to rebuild Jerusalem. V. 14 – 17 comprise a speech by YHWH, introduced by the messenger formula, which assures salvation to Israel.[175] This is followed by another speech by YHWH in v. 18 – 25 which is also introduced by an expanded YHWH speech formula but is connected to v. 14 – 17 by *kî*. These verses comprise a trial speech in which YHWH challenges His opponents to prove Him wrong and then appeals to the court to turn to Him when it is apparent that His position can not be challenged.[176] Both sections, v. 14 – 17 and 18 – 25, emphasize that there is no other God beside YHWH. Taken together, they emphasize the legitimacy of YHWH's position, since YHWH will bring salvation for His people which is something that no other god can do. Thus, the entire block, v. 9 – 25, focuses on the legitimacy of the legal case at hand. V. 9 – 13 dispute the right of the people to challenge YHWH in court, they were created by Him. V. 14 – 25 assert YHWH's right to act, since there is no other god beside Him who can challenge His power, leaving Him as the only one who can save His people, Israel. Thus, v. 9 – 25 are the preliminary arguments

---

[174] Westermann, Isaiah 40 – 66, 165.

[175] The genre of this pericope can not be satisfactorily ascertained since it does not correspond to the criteria for an oracle of salvation or a proclamation of salvation (Melugin, The Formation of Isaiah 40 – 55, 126 f.). Westermann, Isaiah 40 – 66, 169, claims that these verses are a combination of fragments.

[176] On the designation of this section as a trial speech, see A. Schoors, I am God your Saviour, SVT 24, 1973, 233 ff.

of the case since they focus on the legitimacy of the case rather than on the facts of the case.

In the next section, chapters 46–47, YHWH presents specific arguments for His case that He can use Cyrus if He so chooses. In chapter 46, the first sub-unit of this section,[177] YHWH compares Himself with the Babylonian gods. He notes how the idols of these gods must be carried and how they are a burden to those who carry them. He then notes that it is He who carries the house of Jacob. The point is obvious. Idols which must be carried have no power to deliver their people, but YHWH, who carries His people from their birth, has the power to save. There follows a disputation speech inviting the people to make the comparison themselves. Of course, it is clear that there is no comparison to YHWH. He then calls on the people to remember this and makes the point that He will do as He chooses. This includes using Cyrus, the foreigner, for His purposes. As the God of all creation, including Cyrus, who can challenge His decision? In chapter 47, which is also considered a unit by most scholars,[178] YHWH emphasizes His power. Here, He focuses on Babylon herself, demonstrating that she is powerless to resist Him. He portrays Babylon as a slave girl, fallen from her former glory as mistress of the nations. Because of her arrogance in abusing the nations which YHWH put under her charge, YHWH challenges Babylon to save herself through her own resources, but of course, this proves futile. Again, the point is made that there is no power capable of challenging YHWH. The powers that one might expect to challenge YHWH, the gods of Babylon, can help neither themselves nor their people.

Isa 48, 1–19 contains the summary speeches of the trial scene portrayed in 45, 9–48, 19.[179] The unit begins with a disputation speech (v. 1–11) in which YHWH challenges the people to review the evidence

---

[177] Most scholars consider chapter 46 to be a unit, Melugin, The Formation of Isaiah 40–55, 131 ff.; Westermann, Isaiah 40–66, 177 f.; Bonnard, Le Second Isaïe, 182 f.; Spykerboer, Structure and Composition of Deutero-Isaiah, 143 f.; Torrey, The Second Isaiah, 363 f.; Muilenberg, IB, V 535 f.; Marti, Jesaja, 315; Kissane, The Book of Isaiah, II 89; Skinner, Isaiah XL-LXVI, 75; Duhm, Das Buch Jesaia, 350; Delitzsch, The Prophecies of Isaiah, II 231 f.

[178] Melugin, The Formation of Isaiah 40–55, 135 f.; Bonnard, Le Second Isaïe, 191; Westermann, Isaiah 40–66, 186 ff.; Spykerboer, The Structure and Composition of Deutero-Isaiah, 152 ff.; Torrey, Second Isaiah, 367 f.; Muilenberg, IB, V 543 f.; Gitay, Prophecy and Persuasion, 206 f.; Marti, Jesaja, 317; Volz, Jesaia II, 82 ff.; Skinner, Isaiah XL-LXVI, 80 f.; Duhm, Das Buch Jesaia, 354; Delitzsch, The Prophecies of Isaiah, II 237.

[179] Melugin, The Formation of Isaiah 40–55, 141, notes the coherence of v. 1–19 by pointing out their focus on Israel's sinfulness, the name by which Israel is called, and language associated with Israel's being "cut off."

and arrive at the proper conclusion that He alone is the true power.[180] YHWH emphasized His ability to control past and future events and repeats the argument made in earlier units that He punished Israel because of her transgression. A trial speech follows in v. 12 – 16 in which YHWH challenges the court to produce any evidence that might refute His claim.[181] The issue of Cyrus appears again. YHWH reaffirms that He has chosen Cyrus for His own purposes and that Cyrus will act under His authority. Since no one is able to challenge His power, no one is able to challenge His decision to use Cyrus. Finally, in a speech introduced by an expanded YHWH speech formula (v. 17 – 19), YHWH concludes the trial scene by reasserting His role as Israel's leader expressing the wish that Israel had obeyed His commandments in the first place. Had she done so, none of the punishment would have been necessary.

The third major section is the hymn in 48, 20 – 21 (22) which concludes the unit.[182] Here, the exiles are told to leave Babylon and proclaim their redemption by YHWH.

Basically, the unit as a whole is an announcement by YHWH of His right to use Cyrus, a foreigner, to serve His purposes in redeeming Israel and rebuilding Jerusalem and the Temple. He does this by first announcing His decision publicly and then by defending His position in a court of law. He bases His defense on the premise that He is the all-powerful creator and hence master of the world. As such, no one has the right or the power to question or challenge His decision. Although His opponents in court may be the nations and their idols, this assertion is directed to Israel, to convince her that YHWH is still her God, that He still controls human events, and that His purpose is the ultimate welfare of His people who merely had to be punished. The structure is as follows:

Announcement by YHWH that He will use Cyrus for the Redemption and Restoration	44, 24 – 48, 22
I. Announcement of Plan to use Cyrus	44, 24 – 45, 8
A. To Israel: Disputation	44, 24 – 28
B. To Cyrus: Royal Commission	45, 1 – 7
C. Hymn of Praise	45, 8

---

[180] On the designation of these verses as a disputation speech, see Melugin, The Formation of Isaiah 40 – 55, 39 ff.; Westermann, Sprache und Struktur, 51; Schoors, I am God your Saviour, 291 f.

[181] Melugin, The Formation of Isaiah 40 – 55, 137. The position of v. 16 is uncertain. It is included with v. 12 – 15 because of its similar imperative formulation.

[182] Westermann, Sprache und Struktur, 78, 80.

6. Isaiah 49, 1 – 54, 17

The next major section of Isa 40 – 66 is 49, 1 – 54, 17. The unit is demarcated at the beginning by a summons to hear directed to the coastlands and peoples, which follows the concluding hymn of the previous section. One might argue, however, that the unit should extend only to 49, 13, since v. 13 contains one of the concluding hymns which close other major sections of Isa 40 – 66.[183] Furthermore, 49, 1 – 13 focuses on the servant of YHWH whereas the following section deals with Jerusalem, which is not mentioned in 49, 1 – 13. V. 14, however, opens with the *waw*-consecutive formation *watto'mær ṣîyôn* which suggests a connection with the preceding material. As Muilenberg points out, this "is hardly an appropriate beginning of a new unit."[184] Also, 49, 14 – 54, 17 contains two more of the "servant songs" in 50, 4 – 11 and 52, 13 – 53, 12, which would provide some connection with the servant song in 49, 1 – 6. The relationship of 49, 1 – 13 and 49, 14 – 54, 17 will require further study before any claim that these sub-sections form a unit can be made. As for the end of the section, most scholars

---

[183] Cf. Westermann, Sprache und Struktur, 79 f., but he is uncertain of exactly what 49, 13 concludes.

[184] Isaiah 40 – 66, 564; cf. C. R. North, The Second Isaiah, 1964, 193. Also note that Westermann's uncertainty over the concluding function of 49, 13 is caused in part by the relation of the following complex in 49, 14 – 26 (Sprache und Struktur, 79).

prefer to see chapter 55 as part of the unit.[185] Yet, there is an introductory
hôy in 55, 1 which sets the chapter off as a separate section. Chapter 55
also presupposes Jerusalem's restoration whereas the previous chapters
are concerned with announcing that restoration. Furthermore, as will
be seen below, chapter 55, with its appeal to join in the new eternal
covenant, has strong connections with the following material which
provides instruction on how to live under the covenant. While chapter
55 may at one time have functioned as the conclusion to chapters 40 – 55,
at present, it introduces chapters 56 – 66. In the present form of the
book, chapter 54, with its hymnic introduction and its concluding
summary appraisal, serves as an adequate conclusion to the preceding
material. It reviews the basic themes of chapters 49 – 53, the restoration
of Jerusalem, the renewal of its relationship with YHWH, and refers to
the servants of YHWH.

The first sub-unit of chapters 49 – 54 is 49, 1 – 13. This section is
demarcated by the summons to hear directed to the coastlands and
peoples at the beginning and the hymn which appears at the end.
Furthermore, the unit deals with the role of the servant in YHWH's
redemption of Israel and the earth throughout. The first part of this
unit is a speech by the servant to the peoples in 49, 1 – 6. These verses
are a report of the commissioning of the servant[186] in which he announces
to the peoples that his commission by YHWH requires him to not only
bring Israel back to YHWH, but to bring YHWH's salvation to them
as well. This contention is supported by YHWH's speech to the servant
in v. 7 – 12. Actually, there are two speeches by YHWH in this section,
each of which is introduced by a YHWH speech formula. The first, v. 7,
is a proclamation of salvation[187] to the servant which announces the
servant's coming recognition by the leaders of the nations. The second
speech, v. 8 – 12, elaborates on the first in that it provides some details
on how the servant will participate in YHWH's restoration of the
covenant to the people. The servant will help gather YHWH's people
from all the lands in which they are held captive and return them to
YHWH, presumably in their own land. The unit ends with a hymn of
praise concerning YHWH's comfort of His people.

---

[185] Isa 55, in whole or in part, is generally taken as the epilogue to Deutero-Isaiah. Cf.
Melugin, The Formation of Isaiah 40 – 55, 86 f.; Spykerboer, Structure and Composition
of Deutero-Isaiah, 184 f.; Muilenberg, IB, V 642; Westermann, Isaiah 40 – 66, 286 f.;
Sprache und Struktur, 81 f.; Bonnard, Le Second Isaïe, 300.

[186] Melugin, The Formation of Isaiah 40 – 55, 69 ff.

[187] Melugin, The Formation of Isaiah 40 – 55, 143. Note that Westermann, Isaiah 40 – 66,
213 f., and Schoors, I am God your Saviour, 97 ff., consider v. 7 – 12 as the proclamation
of salvation.

The next sub-unit of Isa 49 – 54 is 49, 14 – 52, 12. This section begins with a *waw*-consecutive construction which indicates some connection to the previous section. The unit focuses on Zion's restoration whereas 49, 1 – 13 focuses on the servant. The servant receives only a small amount of attention in 49, 14 – 52, 12 and, as later discussion will demonstrate, the mention of the servant relates to the predominating concern with the restoration of Zion. The unit ends with a concluding hymn of praise in 52, 9 – 10 followed by a command to the people to leave the city in v. 11 – 12.[188] Afterwards, the servant becomes the focus of attention again, not Zion. This section is divided into three parts, 49, 14 – 26; 50, 1 – 11; and 51, 1 – 52, 12.

Isa 49, 14 – 52, 12 opens in 49, 14 – 26 with YHWH's response to Zion's contention that He has abandoned and forgotten her. The response falls into two basic parts, each introduced with YHWH's quotation of a proverbial rhetorical question which emphasizes His point.[189] The first part of the response, v. 15 – 23, assures Zion that just as a mother can not forget her child, so YHWH can not forget Zion. He assures Zion that restoration is coming and that soon, He will raise His hand to the nations to signal the return of Zion's inhabitants to her. The second part of YHWH's response, v. 24 – 26, assures Zion that this restoration can be done. YHWH's power guarantees that He can take prey from the mighty and rescue Zion's captive inhabitants. Thus, the two sections of YHWH's answer deal with Zion's contention by asserting that YHWH intends to restore Zion. The section announces salvation for Zion but does so in a distinctly disputational manner since the object here is to refute Zion's contention and convince her of YHWH's intent and power to save.

In the second sub-unit of 49, 14 – 52, 12; 50, 1 – 11, YHWH sets forth some conditions for those who will benefit from His redemption of Zion. The unit is held together by its questioning style and its focus on trust in YHWH.[190] It begins with a trial speech[191] in which YHWH turns the tables on Zion and presents His contention to her that He never broke the covenant relationship, as might be inferred from 49,

---

[188] Westermann, Sprache und Struktur, 78, 81 f.

[189] Westermann, Isaiah 40 – 66, 218 f., argues that there are three sections in this unit, each of which begins by disputing an assertion made by Israel. But this division does not recognize that Zion's question in v. 21, with the following material in v. 22 – 23, functions as part of YHWH's answer to Zion which began in v. 15. V. 21 – 23 underscore the point made in v. 19 – 20 that Zion will be filled with inhabitants and therefore, YHWH has not forgotten her.

[190] Muilenberg, IB, V 578 ff.; cf. Melugin, Formation of Isaiah 40 – 55, 153 ff.

[191] Westermann, Isaiah 40 – 66, 223 f.; Schoors, I am God your Saviour, 197 ff.

14 – 26, but that the people themselves broke it by their transgressions.[192] This is followed by a psalm of confidence, spoken by the servant, which YHWH presents to serve as a model for the behavior of His people.[193] Finally, in v. 10 – 11, YHWH questions the people as to who is righteous, stating that those who are shall trust in Him. Those who prefer to trust their own resources rather than YHWH shall be tormented. Thus, only those who are righteous, i. e., who trust in YHWH, will be eligible for inclusion in the restoration of YHWH's relationship with His people.

Isa 51, 1 – 52, 12 actually proclaims the restoration of Zion as the location from which YHWH will rule. The unit is demarcated at the beginning by its summons to hear directed to the righteous. There is a hymn of praise at the end followed by a command to leave the city. The unit is concerned throughout with proclaiming salvation for Jerusalem. The unit is composed of two sections. The first, 51, 1 – 8, contains three sections, each of which is introduced by its own summons to hear. Scholars have pointed to the disputational character of these sections as well as their function to proclaim salvation.[194] In their present context preceding the section which announces YHWH's return to Zion, they function not just to proclaim salvation or prove YHWH's fidelity to His people, but to draw attention to what is to come. In this respect, the summons to hear at the beginning of each sub-section (v. 1 – 3, 4 – 6, and 7 – 8) plays an important role. The announcements of salvation which follow the summons each provide a reason for hearing so that the three sections in 51, 1 – 8 serve as exhortations to hear. These verses attempt to convince the people to pay attention by briefly alluding to the salvation which is to come. This salvation is described in the second section of 51, 1 – 52, 12. Isa 51, 9 – 52, 12 combines a series of units which together describe the process of deliverance in which YHWH is roused to come to the aid of Zion and eventually returns there to reestablish His rule. The first of these sub-units, 51, 9 – 16, is an answered lament in which an appeal by the people for YHWH's deliverance is quoted and followed by a salvation speech in which YHWH assures the people that He will act.[195] The second sub-section, 51, 17 – 23, begins like the preceding section with an arousal command. This time, however, it is directed to Jerusalem in order to introduce a speech of salvation which declares to Jerusalem that her suffering is over.[196] The third

[192] Muilenberg, IB, V 579, 580.
[193] Melugin, The Formation of Isaiah 40 – 55, 71 f., 153.
[194] Melugin, The Formation of Isaiah 40 – 55, 156 f.; Schoors, I am God your Saviour, 154 ff.
[195] Westermann, Isaiah 40 – 66, 240; Melugin, The Formation of Isaiah 40 – 55, 159 f.
[196] Cf. Melugin, The Formation of Isaiah 40 – 55, 24 f., 161. This speech employs language used to comfort mourners.

section, again introduced by an arousal command which is directed to Zion, is 52, 1–6. This section begins in v. 1–2 with an exhortation of comfort for Zion.[197] A section connected by *kî* in v. 3–6 explains that the reason for the comfort to Zion is YHWH's redemption of the people so that they will recognize His name. V. 3–6 relate to Deut 26, 5–11 which describe YHWH's deliverance of His people from Egypt. Apparently, these verses are intended to suggest a new relationship for the people of Israel and YHWH in analogy to the relationship created at the first Exodus from Egypt. The fourth section, 52, 7–10, a vision of the herald of good tidings,[198] announces the return of YHWH to Zion to establish His rule. The last section of 51, 9–52, 12 is v. 11–12, which are a command to the people to go out and join YHWH in His journey through the wilderness to Zion.

An overview of 49, 14–52, 12 shows that the entire unit is designed to lead toward the restoration of Zion. The first section, 49, 14–26, is a disputational proclamation of salvation in which YHWH refutes Zion's contention that He has abandoned her. The second section, 50, 1–11, is a trial scene in which YHWH contends that the people broke the covenant and that they will have to adhere to His conditions in order to be included in the redemption. The third section, 51, 1–52, 12, announces the restoration of Zion and YHWH's return there to establish His rule. The whole section may therefore be labeled, "Announcement by YHWH of the Restoration of Zion."

The third major section of Isa 49–54 is 52, 13–53, 12. This unit stands out from the context due to its focus on the servant of YHWH. It has been widely discussed in the literature and there is no need to go into the details here since adequate summaries of the discussion exist elsewhere.[199] For the present, it will suffice to note that the purpose of this unit is to announce the exaltation of the servant of YHWH. In doing so, it focuses on the servant's suffering on behalf of the people and their recognition of this. Because of his extreme suffering, YHWH promises that he will be rewarded with a portion among the great as well as general prosperity and well-being. The placement of this section after the section announcing the restoration of Zion shows that the servant, Israel, will be redeemed after YHWH's return to the restored Zion.

The fourth major section of Isa 49–54 is 54, 1–17. It is demarcated at the beginning by its hymnic introduction which calls upon Zion to

---

[197] Melugin, The Formation of Isaiah 40–55, 162.

[198] Melugin, The Formation of Isaiah 40–55, 162.

[199] See esp. C. R. North, The Suffering Servant in Deutero-Isaiah: An Historical and Critical Study, 1956; Westermann, Isaiah 40–66, 253 ff.; Melugin, The Formation of Isaiah 40–55, 37 f., 167 ff.

rejoice and at the end by the summary appraisal which sums up the
unit as the vindication of the servants of the Lord and their heritage.
Furthermore, the unit is concerned throughout with proclaiming the
restoration of the eternal covenant relationship between YHWH and
Zion.[200] This chapter serves as both climax and summary of chapters
49 – 54. It is the climax in that the unit has been directed toward
convincing the people that YHWH is still God and that He will resume
His rule on Zion when the people return to Him. It is a summary in
that it reiterates a number of themes mentioned previously in chapters
49 – 54.[201] V. 1 – 3 focus on the large number of children which the
formerly barren Zion will have which fulfills the promises made by
YHWH to Zion in 49, 19 – 23. The promise in 54, 3, that Zion's
descendants will possess the nations, might be taken to refer to the
servant's commission to spread YHWH's salvation to the ends of the
earth. The reference to Zion as the restored bride of YHWH contrasts
sharply with the image of Zion as the divorced mother of the inhabitants
of Zion in 50, 1 – 3. Again, the reference to YHWH as God of all the
earth in 54, 5 can refer to the servant's mission to the nations and their
realization of YHWH's power (52, 14 – 15). The reference to YHWH's
temporary forsaking of Zion in 54, 7 – 8 would refer to YHWH's
punishment of Zion for the transgression of her people in 50, 1 – 3 and
the suffering of the servant in 52, 13 – 53, 12. The reference to the
covenant with Noah in 54, 9 – 10 calls to mind the reference to the
covenant with Abraham in 51, 2. The promises of riches and protection
for Zion in 54, 11 – 17 can refer back to the exaltation of the servant
who will prosper (52, 12; 53, 12) and the promise of protection for Zion
in 51, 12 – 16. Finally, the mention of the servants of YHWH in 54, 17
underscores the point that the servant of YHWH refers to the righteous
who will trust in YHWH, i. e., Israel, in 49, 1 – 6; 50, 4 – 9; and 52,
13 – 53, 12.

Because the restoration of the covenant between YHWH and Zion
is the goal of this section, it may be labeled, "Announcement of the
Restoration of YHWH's Relationship with Zion." One may also note
the alternation in focus on the servant of YHWH (Israel) and Zion,
which indicates their interrelationship in the restoration of YHWH's
rule. The servant is YHWH's agent for demonstrating YHWH's power
to the whole earth and Zion is the seat of YHWH's rule. Together, the
servant (Israel) and Zion serve as the starting point for YHWH's rule
over the entire earth. The structure of this section is as follows:

---

[200] On the proclamatory nature of this material, see Westermann, Isaiah 40 – 66, 270.
[201] Cf. Bonnard, Le Second Isaïe, 288, who points out a number of connections between
    Isa 54 and 52, 13 – 53, 12.

7. Isaiah 55 – 66

The last section of Isa 40 – 66 is chapters 55 – 66. Isa 55 or 55, 6 – 13 is generally considered as the epilogue for the prophecies of Deutero-Isaiah in chapters 40 – 55. This is due to the chapter's concern with the eternal covenant which is also the subject of Isa 54, its correspondence to the prologue in 40, 1 – 11,[202] and its general characteristics as a concluding speech.[203] Yet, a number of scholars have noted connections between chapter 55 and the following material, primarily by means of similarity in vocabulary and the notion of an everlasting covenant in

---

[202] Cf. Melugin, The Formation of Isaiah 40 – 55, 86 f., 172 ff.

[203] See esp. Y. Kaufmann, The Babylonian Captivity and Deutero-Isaiah, 84 ff. See also Delitzsch, The Prophecies of Isaiah, II 360; Torrey, The Second Isaiah, 426 ff. Note that 1QIsa^a connects chapter 56 to chapter 55 with ky'.

56, 4 – 5.[204] In this connection, the concept of covenant or eternal covenant appears again in 59, 21 and 61, 8. Isa 55 differs formally from the preceding material in that it begins with an introductory *hôy* following the summary appraisal form which concludes chapter 54. This *hôy* is not intended to refer to a woe speech but serves as an exclamation to attract the attention of the listener or reader. In any case, it serves as the introduction for a new formal unit. Furthermore, Isa 55 is distinguished from the preceding material by its use of masculine plural imperatives whereas Isa 54 uses feminine singular imperatives to address Zion. Isa 55 does not address Zion, but like chapter 56, which also uses masculine plural imperatives, it addresses the people who are eligible to participate in the eternal covenant. The chapter falls into two parts. The first part, v. 1 – 5, is an invitation by personified Wisdom to be a guest at her table.[205] It is, of course, used metaphorically here to invite the people to join in YHWH's eternal covenant. The second part, v. 6 – 13, is an exhortation to the people to follow YHWH in that it provides the positive benefits of doing so. Together, these sections form an exhortation to the people to join in YHWH's eternal covenant. They exhort the people to hear YHWH (v. 2 – 3), seek and call on Him (v. 6), and return to Him (v. 7). In other words, they exhort the people to adhere to YHWH's conditions for participation in the covenant. This is in contrast to the preceding material which only announces the establishment of the new covenant. Chapters 55 – 66 begin and end with speeches which discuss YHWH's criteria for selecting those who fulfill His conditions for participation in the covenant. This is because these chapters are primarily concerned with discussing the nature of the new covenant community, the selection of those who will be a part of it, and the rejection of those who will not. This is not to deny the observations of scholars who see this chapter as the epilogue to chapters 40 – 54. There are certainly many strong connections between chapters 55 and the preceding material. But while it is likely that chapter 55 was originally composed as the conclusion for chapters 40 – 55, in its present context it serves as an introduction to chapters 56 – 66, forming a "bridge" between chapters 40 – 54 and 56 – 66. Isa 55 – 66 would then serve as the conclusion to Isa 40 – 66.

Chapters 56 – 66 are united by their focus on the nature of the reconstituted covenant community and the requirements for those who will participate in it. The materials contained within this section are of

---

[204] Muilenberg, IB, V 643; W. Janzen, Mourning Cry and Woe Oracle, BZAW 125, 1972, 20, n. 69.

[205] J. Begrich, Studien zu Deuterojesaja, ThB 20, 1969, 59 ff.; Westermann, Isaiah 40 – 66, 281 ff.

a rather diverse nature.[206] However, on broad thematic grounds and to a lesser extent on formal grounds, one can identify three major blocks of material within these chapters: 56–59; 60–62; and 63–66.[207]

The first sub-unit of Isa 56–66 is chapters 56–59, which focus on the behavior expected of those who will be members of the new covenant community. The unit begins with a YHWH speech formula in 56, 1 which sets it off from the preceding material in chapter 55. The summary appraisal in 59, 21 ends this section with its summation of YHWH's covenant, a theme which introduces the unit (Isa 56, 4–5, 6). The first sub-unit of this section is 56, 1–8, which is demarcated by its introductory YHWH speech formula and its closing oracular formula.[208] The unit employs a combination of exhortation and instruction language[209] which sets forth some of YHWH's most basic expectations for those who will be part of the covenant community; doing justice and righteousness, keeping the Sabbath, and refraining from doing evil. The unit strengthens its point, that admission to the covenant community is determined by fidelity to YHWH's requirements, by stating that persons who were previously denied admission to the covenant community, foreigners and eunuchs, would be admitted if they kept its basic stipulations. The next section is 56, 9–57, 21. This section is demarcated by its direct address to the wicked, portrayed as devouring beasts, after the concluding oracular formula in 56, 8 and the concluding statement by God that there is no peace for the wicked which precedes the introductory imperatives of the following unit.[210] The unit is often divided into two or more units

---

[206] The question of the unified authorship of these chapters is not settled. Cf. Kaiser, Introduction to the Old Testament, 268 f.

[207] Westermann, Isaiah 40–66, 296 ff., presents an analysis of the structure of Trito-Isaiah which claims that chapters 60–62 and some other materials form the core of the work. According to him, the rest of the book grew gradually from this core to its present form in several stages. Westermann is followed in his basic thesis by Bonnard, Le Second Isaïe, 315 ff., and Pauritsch, Die neue Gemeinde, 241 ff. Westermann's discussion of the structure is more helpful for understanding the process of composition of the book than for determining how a reader of these chapters will follow the development of ideas within them or how they might be arranged to set forth a message. Pauritsch overcomes this to some extent by claiming that 56, 1–8 is the "motto" of the collection, 56, 9–65, 24 is the "corpus of the book," and 66 is the conclusion (Die neue Gemeinde, 243 f.). The structure analysis here is not intended to argue for a process of composition but to show how these chapters, in their present form, develop the themes that are contained within them and how the individual units work together to present a coherent message.

[208] Pauritsch, Die neue Gemeinde, 31; cf. Muilenberg, IB, V 653.

[209] Westermann, Isaiah 40–66, 305.

[210] Cf. Bonnard, Le Second Isaïe, 353 ff.

such as 56, 9 – 57, 13, a collection of judgment oracles,[211] and 57, 14 – 21, a proclamation of salvation.[212] However, these units are connected at 57, 14 by the conjunction *waw* so that the themes of judgment and salvation form the constituent parts of a single message.[213] Together, these units emphasize YHWH's willingness to forgive wrongdoing. However, the concluding v. 20 – 21 make it clear that those who choose to remain wicked will not be delivered. The third sub-unit of chapters 56 – 59 is chapter 58. It is demarcated at the beginning by its introductory imperatives and the concluding YHWH speech formula in 58, 14bβ. Its character throughout is that of a speech by YHWH whereas in the preceding unit, the prophet quotes YHWH and in the following unit, the prophet addresses the people. This unit is an admonition or warning in which YHWH points out the wrongdoing of His people and contrasts that with specific examples of the behavior which He expects.[214] The specific requirements include social and religious responsibilities, including the care of the poor, the prevention of false accusation, and the keeping of the Sabbath. The last section of chapters 56 – 59 is chapter 59. It is formally distinguished by its introductory exclamation, its concluding summary appraisal, and its character as a speech by the prophet. This unit takes the form of a lament[215] and reiterates that the people's lack of salvation is the result of their own wrongdoing. The concluding verses make it clear that YHWH will redeem His people. The unit stresses YHWH's intent and ability to deliver His people. It also stresses that the people must turn to YHWH before He will redeem them (v. 20). Thus, chapters 56 – 59 set forth YHWH's requirements for covenant membership and stress that the people must turn to Him in order to receive His deliverance.

The second major unit of Isa 56 – 66 is chapters 60 – 62. These chapters are distinguished formally by their second person feminine singular address and substantially by their consistent theme of salvation for Jerusalem and her people. The entire unit is a proclamation of salvation which describes Zion's primary position among the nations, YHWH's eternal covenant with Zion, and His protection of the city.[216] The position of these chapters after the preceding chapters shows what those who accept YHWH's covenant, and do what He desires, can

---

211 Westermann, Isaiah 40 – 66, 301 f.; Vermeylen, Du prophète Isaïe, II 458.
212 Pauritsch, Die neue Gemeinde, 72 f.; Westermann, Isaiah 40 – 66, 302 f.
213 Muilenburg, IB, V 670.
214 Westermann, Isaiah 40 – 66, 303.
215 Westermann, Isaiah 40 – 66, 300 f.
216 On the unity and genre of this section, see Westermann, Isaiah 40 – 66, 296 ff., 352 f.
    Cf. Pauritsch, Die neue Gemeinde, 103 ff., 221 f.; Bonnard, Le Second Isaïe, 327, 400.

expect. The unit therefore serves as a motivation for the people to accept YHWH's stipulations and participate in His covenant.

The final section of Isa 56 – 66 is chapters 63 – 66. This section is demarcated thematically from the proclamation of salvation which precedes by its focus on the process of selecting those who will participate in the new covenant and those who will perish. The unit opens in 63, 1 – 6, which is distinguished formally by its dual question and answer format. The questions are those put by a sentry at the gate to someone who approaches dressed for battle and covered with blood.[217] The first answer indicates that it is YHWH who comes as the divine warrior, speaking with righteousness and mighty to save. The second answer relates how He has been among the peoples, slaughtering them in His vengeance. Thus, YHWH, the warrior, is portrayed as a deliverer and a threat. The next sub-unit emphasizes the element of threat since it takes the form of a lament.[218] The unit is distinguished by its first person orientation and extends from 63, 7 to 64, 12. The purpose of this unit in its present setting is to portray the people as appealing for mercy to the approaching warrior, YHWH. Apparently, the speaker wishes to be sure that he is reckoned among those for whom YHWH is fighting and not against them. The last sub-unit is chapters 65 – 66 which in their present position, serve as YHWH's answer to the people's lament.[219] This section is composed of several different units which relate speeches by YHWH together with some framework material such as speech formulae. These chapters focus on the contrast of the fates of those who will be spared to enjoy YHWH's covenant and those who will die because they do not meet YHWH's criteria for participation. YHWH makes it clear that only those who are righteous will live and those who are not will be slaughtered. He also portrays the restored Jerusalem as a mother giving birth to a nation and depicts the happiness of the people who live there. He announces His rule and stresses that a new heaven and a new earth are being created for His new world order. Finally, YHWH emphasizes that His rule will include the entire world and that the people who make up His new covenant community will include foreigners so that all flesh will worship Him, a fitting conclusion to the book of Isaiah.

The unit is designed throughout to convince the people that they should want to be a part of YHWH's new covenant community by stating the conditions and benefits of joining as well as the consequences

---

[217] Westermann, Isaiah 40 – 66, 380 f.
[218] Westermann, Isaiah 40 – 66, 300 f.; Fohrer, Das Buch Jesaja, III, 1964, 246 f.
[219] Bonnard, Le Second Isaïe, 462; Torrey, The Second Isaiah, 466 f. On these sections as a unit, see Westermann, Isaiah 40 – 66, 462 f.; D. R. Jones, Isaiah 56 – 66 and Joel, TB, 1964, 104 f.; cf. Marti, Jesaja, 400.

for not joining. The label for this section should therefore be, "Exhortation to Join the New Covenant Community." The structure of this unit is as follows:

Exhortation to Join the New Covenant Community	55, 1 – 66, 24
I. Exhortation Proper	55, 1 – 13
A. Invitation to Join	55, 1 – 5
B. Exhortation to follow YHWH	55, 6 – 13
II. Portrayal of the New Covenant Community	56, 1 – 66, 24
A. Instruction concerning proper observance of the covenant	56, 1 – 59, 21
1. basic instruction/exhortation	56, 1 – 8
2. concerning YHWH's willingness to forgive repenters	56, 9 – 57, 21
3. admonition to repent: specific criteria for covenant expectations	58, 1 – 14
4. lament: YHWH's intent and ability to deliver those who repent	59, 1 – 21
B. Proclamation of Salvation: What to expect in the new covenant community	60, 1 – 62, 12
C. Concerning the Process of Selection	63, 1 – 66, 24
1. YHWH's approach as the Divine Warrior	63, 1 – 6
2. the people's lament: appeal for mercy	63, 7 – 64, 11
3. YHWH's answer: salvation for the righteous and death for the wicked	65, 1 – 66, 24

8. Overview: Isaiah 40 – 66

The above discussion has identified seven major units within Isa 40 – 66:

1) Announcement of the Prophet's Commission	40, 1 – 11
2) Disputation: YHWH is the Master of Creation	40, 12 – 31
3) Trial: YHWH is Master of Human Events	41, 1 – 42, 13
4) Announcement of YHWH's Contention that He is the Redeemer of Israel	42, 14 – 44, 23
5) Announcement by YHWH that He will use Cyrus for the Redemption and Restoration	44, 24 – 48, 22
6) Announcement of the Restoration of YHWH's Relationship with Zion	49, 1 – 54, 17
7) Exhortation to Join the New Covenant Community	55, 1 – 66, 24

When examined together, units 2 through 6 display common elements. Each of these units make extensive use of trial and disputation language in order to argue for the point which it is trying to make. The object here is to override the objections of the audience to the point at issue and convince the audience of the legitimacy of that position.[220] The case is generally presented as follows: YHWH presents His arguments to the court which demonstrate that He is able to perform the task or fill the role in question. He then appeals to His courtroom opponents, the gods and idols of the nations, to present their arguments that they are able to perform the task or fill the role in question. When no challenger is able to present such an argument, YHWH's case is made and His point is proven. At this time, the audience, generally the nations and Israel, must come to the conclusion that YHWH performs the task or fills the role in question. Furthermore, when the arguments of units 2 through 6 are examined together, one sees a series of arguments which begin with a very broad, general premise, that YHWH is the Master of all creation, and then work progressively through more specific arguments. The first unit of the series, 40, 12 – 31, argues that YHWH is the Master of all creation. The second unit, 41, 1 – 42, 13, argues that YHWH is the Master of all human events, a somewhat more specific sphere than all creation. The third unit argues that YHWH is the redeemer of Israel, Israel being one component of all that comprises human events. The fourth unit seeks to legitimate YHWH's use of Cyrus, a foreigner, to bring about the redemption and restoration. The fifth and last unit of the series, 49, 1 – 54, 17, argues that YHWH has restored His covenant relationship with Zion, through which all of Israel is redeemed. By moving from very broad assertions to progressively more specific and focused assertions, the audience is led to accept the next argument in the series. If YHWH controls creation, if He controls human events, if He is the redeemer of Israel, if He can use Cyrus for redemption, then He certainly must be restoring His covenant relationship with Zion.

It is in relation to the last unit of the series in units 2 – 6 that the first unit, 40, 1 – 11, gains its significance in the whole. Isa 40, 1 – 11 relates the commission of the prophet. It has a number of connections with the following materials so that it is generally considered the "prologue" of Second Isaiah.[221] Yet, it does not function on quite the same level as units 2 – 6 in that it does not present arguments to substantiate points of contention as these units do. Rather, the main purpose here is to announce the prophet's commission, how he got it (v. 1 – 8) and what

---

[220] Cf. Gitay, Prophecy and Persuasion, who attempts to show how chapters 40 – 48 are designed to convince an audience of a given point.

[221] Bonnard, Le Second Isaïe, 85; Melugin, The Formation of Isaiah 40 – 55, 82 ff.; Muilenberg, IB, V 422 ff.; Spykerboer, Structure and Composition of Deutero-Isaiah, 182 ff.; Westermann, Isaiah 40 – 66, 32 f.

it is (v. 9 – 11). It is at this point that one should note that the prophet's commission is to proclaim salvation to Jerusalem so that she in turn may proclaim salvation to Judah. The prophet announces to Jerusalem that YHWH is returning and that He means to restore the city. In the aftermath of the destruction of Jerusalem by Babylonia and the deportation of the leading elements of Judean society, such an assertion would certainly be open to question. YHWH was defeated by the Babylonian gods. How could He possibly redeem His shattered Zion when He could not even protect it in the first place? The answer to such a question is given in units 2 through 6. YHWH controls events. The destruction was part of His plan for a better covenant community and He has the power to carry out His plan. Thus, units 2 through 6; 40, 12 – 54, 17, act as the substantiation for the assertion in unit 1; 40, 1 – 11. An audience might not be prepared to accept the initial assertion of the prophetic commission that YHWH was returning to redeem Zion. But after being led through the arguments which finally demonstrate that YHWH is restoring His covenant relationship with Zion, the audience would accept the initial assertion. Units 1 and 2 – 6 together form a larger unit, assertion followed by substantiation.

Unit 7; 55, 1 – 66, 24, also gains its significance in relation to the final argument of units 2 – 6, that YHWH is reestablishing His covenant with Zion. Unit 7 is an exhortation so that, like units 2 – 6, it seeks to convince. However, it does not use disputational, trial-oriented language to gain its ends. It does not even seek to substantiate an assertion and therefore, can not be considered a part of the previous section. It presupposes the argument of units 1 – 6. But the purpose of unit 7 is to convince the audience to become a part of that reestablished covenant by meeting YHWH's criteria for participation. The fact of the reestablished covenant is proven. The people must now be persuaded to join it and this is the ultimate goal of chapters 40 – 66. Once the people are certain that YHWH is still the all-powerful God who rules on Zion, they will be more likely to accept that rule.

Thus, there are two main units in Isa 40 – 66. The first unit, Isa 40 – 54, is an announcement that YHWH is reestablishing His covenant with Zion. It consists of two parts. The first, 40, 1 – 11, is the announcement proper, the prophet's commission which announces the return of YHWH to Jerusalem. The second part, 40, 12 – 54, 17, provides substantiation for this announcement by proving that YHWH has renewed His covenant with Zion. The second major unit, Isa 55 – 66, exhorts the people to join the new covenant community. Since this is the ultimate goal of the entire section, Isa 40 – 66 should be labeled "Exhortation to Participate in YHWH's Renewed Covenant." The structure of this unit is as follows:

D. STRUCTURAL OVERVIEW: THE BOOK AS A WHOLE

The discussion may now turn to the structure of the book as a whole. The above discussion has concluded that chapters 2 – 35, 36 – 39, and 40 – 66 form a larger unit, 2 – 66, which is introduced by a prologue in chapter 1. However, there has been no explanation of how these units work together to present a coherent message.

The investigation of the first unit of chapters 2 – 66 showed that chapters 2 – 35 are an announcement of YHWH's plan for a new world order.[222] Essentially, this section presents a theological explanation for the Assyrian empire's takeover of the Syro-Palestinian region and its repressive overlordship of the countries in that area, particularly Israel and Judah. This was explained as a necessary component of YHWH's plan to establish world dominion based in Zion. This plan, announced in chapters 2 – 4 and spelled out in detail in chapters 5 – 35, posited that the punishment of Israel, Judah, and the nations was required because of the people's lack of faith in YHWH. The Assyrian overlordship was brought on the people by YHWH to punish them and demonstrate His power. When Assyria overstepped its bounds by oppressing the people beyond call and by claiming to have obtained success without recognizing YHWH's role in that success, YHWH decided that the people had been punished enough. Accordingly, an announcement was made that the overthrow of Assyria was imminent, after which YHWH would establish His rule over the world at Zion.

Earlier discussion concluded that chapters 36 – 39 provide a transition between chapters 2 – 35, which deal with the Assyrian period of oppression, and chapters 40 – 60, which deal with the end of the Babylonian period. As such, chapters 36 – 39 explain why YHWH's plan was not realized at the end of the period of Assyrian oppression. Certainly the historical events of the late 7th – early 6th centuries would have required such an explanation. The end of Assyrian domination did not bring a time of redemption as promised in chapters 2 – 35. Instead, they brought another oppressor, the Babylonian empire, which was worse for Judah than Assyria since the Babylonians destroyed Jerusalem and the Temple. According to chapters 36 – 39, Jerusalem was spared destruction by the Assyrians because of King Hezekiah's piety. But this resulted only in a temporary reprieve for Jerusalem. The punishment was not

---

[222] On YHWH's plan in Isaiah, see J. Fichtner, ZAW 63 (1951), 16 ff.

cancelled, only postponed. Since Jerusalem played such an important role in YHWH's plan for world dominion, the postponement of punishment and the cleansing of Jerusalem meant the postponement of the implementation of YHWH's plan for world dominion.

The investigation of Isa 40 – 66 showed that these chapters are an exhortation to the people of Jerusalem and Judah to participate in YHWH's eternal covenant with Zion. The unit accomplishes this end by first announcing YHWH's return to Jerusalem to bring salvation to the city. This is followed by a long section which substantiates this claim of redemption in disputational trial language, proving that YHWH is in control of all worldly and cosmic events, including those directly related to Jerusalem. As in chapters 2 – 35, the punishment received by YHWH's people was brought about by YHWH because of the people's transgression. This section also argues that YHWH uses foreigners, not only for punishment, but for salvation as well. This argument is designed to convince the people that YHWH is using Cyrus, the king of Persia, as His agent in the restoration of Jerusalem. This restoration leads to the reestablishment of YHWH's eternal covenant with Zion. Chapters 55 – 66 then exhort the people to participate in this renewed covenant by accepting YHWH's conditions for participation. Essentially, these conditions mean accepting YHWH as God. This final section includes a description of the new world order which YHWH is establishing and announces that only those who accept YHWH will be part of the new world order. Thus, chapters 40 – 66 are essentially an exhortation to the people of Jerusalem and Judah to play their role in YHWH's new world order. The plan would be void otherwise, since Jerusalem is to be the seat of YHWH's rule.

All three units of Isa 2 – 66 emphasize that YHWH controls human events to accomplish His purpose, the establishment of His rule over all the world. The role of Jerusalem is especially stressed in the plan for YHWH's rule since it will serve as His capital. But like the rest of the world, Jerusalem was in need of punishment before the new world order could be established. Jerusalem had to be rendered fit for its role and this had to be accomplished by a punishment which cleansed the city of the transgression of its people. This theme of punishment for Jerusalem, which cleanses the city and leads to its eventual redemption, is also the main concern of Isa 1. Isa 1 begins with a condemnation of the people in the form of a lawsuit. The people are accused of not recognizing YHWH as their true God which has resulted in the devastation of Judah. Instead of purishing the city in its entirety, YHWH offers the people a second chance. If they will turn from their wickedness and accept YHWH as their God, they will be forgiven and redeemed with the city. If they refuse, they will perish. Thus, Isa 1 is an exhortation which intends to provoke a change in the people's behavior so that they will return to

YHWH.[223] Likewise, Isa 2 – 66 leads to the eventual redemption of Jerusalem, the restoration of those who return to YHWH, and the destruction of those who do not. Isa 2 – 66 goes beyond Isa 1, however, since it not only deals with the process of punishment and restoration of Jerusalem, but also shows how this punishment and restoration fits into YHWH's larger plans for the entire world. Thus, Isa 2 – 66 elaborates and expands on the theme of Isa 1 by spelling out the implications of Jerusalem's punishment and restoration for the whole world. In this sense, Isa 1, with its limited perspective on the fate of Jerusalem, serves as a fitting prologue for the rest of the book. The entire book should therefore be labeled, "Exhortation to the People of Jerusalem/Judah to Return to YHWH as their God." The structure of the book is as follows:

Exhortation to the People of Jerusalem/Judah to Return to YHWH as their God	1 – 66
I. Prologue: Exhortation: YHWH's Offer of Redemption to the People	1
II. Elaboration: Exhortation to People to Participate in YHWH's Plan for New World Order	2 – 66
A. Announcement of YHWH's plan for New World Order centered in Zion	2 – 35
1. Announcement concerning the cleansing of Zion for its role	2 – 4
2. Elaboration on implementation of plan to achieve new world order under YHWH	5 – 35
a. chastisement of Israel/Judah and the nations	5 – 27
b. announcement of YHWH's assumption of kingship in Zion	28 – 35
B. Transition: Narrative Explanation for Delay in Implementation of Plan	36 – 39
C. Exhortation to Participate in YHWH's Renewed Covenant	40 – 66
1. Announcement that YHWH is reestablishing His covenant with Zion	40 – 54
a. announcement proper: prophet's commission to announce YHWH's return to Zion	40,1 – 11
b. substantiation: YHWH is renewing His covenant with Zion	40, 12 – 54, 17
2. Exhortation proper to join covenant	55 – 66

The entire book emphasizes YHWH's control of human events to bring about His own rule of the world, even if this means disaster for His own people. As such, the book is an argument that YHWH is all-powerful, that He controls the entire world as well as His own people.

---

[223] On the definition of exhortation, see Kaiser, Introduction to the Old Testament, 294 f.; Fohrer, Introduction to the Old Testament, 355.

Such an argument would be particularly important to a people who had been defeated in war and carried off into exile as the people of Jerusalem and Judah had been in the 6th century. They would have believed that YHWH was powerless since He was unable to stop the disasters which befell them. The book of Isaiah is designed to counter such a belief. It maintains that YHWH is still God, not only of Judah but of the entire world. In order to establish His rule over the world, YHWH brought punishment to His own people. Such punishment was necessary in order to cleanse them so that they would be fit to populate His capital, Zion. But the book does not only attempt to convince the people of YHWH's power. Its ultimate goal is to motivate the people to turn from their present disbelief and accept YHWH as their God. To do this, they must accept YHWH's conditions for participation in His covenant which are spelled out in chapters 56 – 59 as well as in chapter 1. The book demands a decision from its readers or hearers to alter their behavior. It uses a variety of literary types to accomplish this end; disputations, announcements of salvation and judgment, narrations, etc., but the ultimate purpose overrides these types so that the book as a whole must be characterized as exhortation. Such an exhortation would best serve the needs of the late 5th century Jewish community in Jerusalem. At that time, exiles were returning, Jerusalem was being rebuilt, and the reforms of Ezra and Nehemiah were underway in an attempt to convince the people to return to YHWH and His Torah. The book of Isaiah provides a theoretical basis for the restoration of Judah's religion. YHWH is still God, therefore His people must acknowledge Him as such.[224]

---

[224] In addition to the generic character of Isaiah as an exhortation to return to YHWH and the commonly accepted 5th century dating for Trito-Isaiah, other factors support a late 5th century dating for the book. First, the book presupposes the period of Persian rule. Isa 13, 17 and 21, 2 indicate that the Medes are responsible for the overthrow of Babylon and 44, 28 and 45, 1 indicate that Cyrus is YHWH's annointed ruler. Furthermore, neither Persia nor Media are condemned in the oracles against the nations (Isa 13 – 23) and there is no indication in the book that they are to be judged. Likewise, Greece is not recognized as a major world power in Isaiah (cf. Zach 9, 13; Dan 8, 21). These considerations would be problematic if the book was dated to the Hellenistic age. Second, the references to "Torah" in the book never presuppose that the Torah refers to the Five Books of Moses or any specific body of teaching. As J. Jensen has shown (The Use of *tôrâ* by Isaiah: His Debate with the Wisdom Tradition, CBQMS 3, 1973), *tôrâ* functions in a much more generalized sense as "wise instruction" in First Isaiah (p. 120) or as "instruction" or "revelation" in Second Isaiah (p. 23 f.). In contrast, Torah takes on a much more specific meaning in the period following Ezra's reform. Finally, the distinction between the righteous and the wicked (Isa 1; 65 – 66) together with the question of membership in the covenant community (Isa 56, 1 – 8; 66, 18 – 21) were crucial issues at the end of the 5th century. The willingness to accept foreigners, eunuchs, etc., indicates that the final redaction of the book of Isaiah may have been an alternative or challenge to the program of Ezra.

Chapter IV
Analysis of Isaiah 1 and Isaiah 2 – 4

1. Demarcation of the Unit

The previous chapter has already noted the basic formal features which mark the boundaries of this unit. The beginning of the unit, Isa 1, 1, is a superscription which has a double-duty function in that it can introduce the entire book of Isaiah or only chapter 1. The superscription in 2, 1 marks the beginning of a new unit so that the initial unit of the book comprises Isa 1, 1 – 31.

As noted above, scholars have observed that 1, 1 – 31 rehearses the major themes of the book of Isaiah and therefore serves as the "prologue" of the book.[1] In order to fully understand the role of Isa 1 as the "prologue" for the book of Isaiah, it must be examined form critically in order to ascertain its structure, genre, setting and intention. Once this is complete, the redactional formation of the unit can then be examined.

It can not be assumed that Isa 1 is a self-contained unit since this is what must be proved. Therefore, the analysis can not begin with an examination of the structure of the whole unit. Rather, it must begin with the identification and examination of the constituent parts of the chapter, first individually and then in relation to one another. This will aid in determining whether the various sub-units which appear in this chapter function together to produce a coherent larger unit. Once this is done, the structure of the whole may be analyzed.

2. Isaiah 1, 1

This verse is a superscription which introduces the following material. As such, it stands apart from the material which it introduces as a separate unit in the structure of the larger text.

---

[1] See esp. Fohrer, BZAW 99, 1967, 147 ff.; Becker, Isaias – Der Prophet und sein Buch, 45 ff. Cf. Clements, Isaiah 1 – 39, 28 f.; Skinner, Isaiah I – XXXIX, 2 f.; Delitzsch, The Prophecies of Isaiah, I 72; Procksch, Jesaia I, 20.

3. Isaiah 1, 2 – 3

V. 2aα opens with a proclamation formula which introduces the unit. This proclamation formula together with the prophetic citation formula in v. 2aβ are spoken by the prophet to call attention to the speech by YHWH which follows in v. 2b – 3. V. 4 opens with a "woe" formula which generally introduces a new sub-unit. Furthermore, v. 4 opens a speech by the prophet whereas in v. 2 – 3, the prophet quotes a speech by YHWH. Therefore, the present unit comprises only v. 2 – 3.[2]

The basic sub-division of this unit is between v. 2a, a speech by the prophet which introduces the speech by YHWH, and v. 2b – 3, which comprise the speech by YHWH.[3] This division is indicated by the imperative style of the verbs, *šimᵉʿû* and *wᵉhᵃʾazînî*, as well as the third person references to YHWH in v. 2a whereas v. 2b – 3 are first person singular, indicating direct speech. That this is a speech by YHWH is evident from the prophetic citation formula in v. 2aβ.

V. 2a consists of two parts. V. 2aα is a proclamation formula or call to attention which summons the Heavens and the Earth to hear what is about to be said.[4] This is followed by a prophetic citation formula in v. 2aβ[5] which identifies what is about to be said as a speech by YHWH and therefore motivates the addressees to listen.[6] Thus, v. 2a is the prophet's introduction to a speech by YHWH summoning Heaven and Earth as witnesses to what YHWH has to say.

The speech by YHWH in v. 2b – 3 consists of two parts. The first part, v. 2b, is identified by its focus on children whereas the following material focuses on animals. V. 2b is a speech by a father concerning the behavior of his children.[7] In v. 2bα, the father describes what he has done for his children, i. e., raised them. V. 2bβ describes the negative reaction of the sons to their father's care. Instead of showing gratitude, v. 2bβ states that the children have rebelled against the father. Thus, the father's speech in v. 2b serves as an accusation concerning his children's

---

[2] Cf. Wildberger, Jesaja 1 – 12, 8; Kaiser, Isaiah 1 – 12, 10; Clements, Isaiah 1 – 39, 30; Whedbee, Isaiah and Wisdom, 28, Fohrer, BZAW 99, 151; Das Buch Jesaja, I 24 f. Other scholars see these verses as parts of larger units, e. g., v. 2 – 20 (Vermeylen, Du prophète Isaïe, I 42 ff.; Y. Gitay, VT 33 (1983), 207 ff.; Kissane, The Book of Isaiah, I 3, 8; Roberts, PSB 3 (1982), 293 ff.; Skinner, Isaiah I – XXXIX, 3, 4; J. Willis, VT 34 (1984), 63 ff.; Duhm, Das Buch Jesaia, 23; Marti, Jesaja, 2); v. 1 – 9 (Procksch, Jesaia I, 27, 29).

[3] Cf. Wildberger, Jesaja 1 – 12, 11; Kaiser, Isaiah 1 – 12, 10.

[4] Wildberger, Jesaja 1 – 12, 9.

[5] Kaiser, Isaiah 1 – 12, 10.

[6] Whedbee, Isaiah and Wisdom, 28.

[7] Kaiser, Isaiah 1 – 12, 13; Whedbee, Isaiah and Wisdom, 36.

improper behavior.[8] A parable follows in v. 3. V. 3a describes the behavior of animals, in this case, an ox (v. 3aα) and an ass (v. 3aβ), who know their place and the source of their livelihood. This is an obvious contrast with the children of v. 2b who do not. The parable continues in v. 3b with the two-fold statement that Israel does not know (v. 3bα) nor do YHWH's people understand (v. 3bβ).[9] Here, the intent of the parable is clear. Israel does not even know what animals understand, i. e., who their master is and who provides for their welfare. With the identification of "Israel" and "My people" in v. 3b as the ones who do not know who provides for them, it is clear that the children referred to in v. 2b were also Israel. YHWH is charging His people with rebellion. The parable, a typical wisdom device,[10] reinforces YHWH's case that His children's (Israel's) behavior is indefensible.

Thus, v. 2b–3 is an accusation speech by YHWH against Israel, albeit expressed in part as a parable.[11] Such a speech would have been used in a courtroom by a plaintiff who brought a charge against a defendant in a legal case. Because YHWH's accusation speech is introduced by the prophet and quoted by him, the whole of v. 2–3 may be defined as a "Prophetic announcement of YHWH's accusation against Israel." The structure may be outlined as follows:

Prophetic Announcement of YHWH's Accusation against Israel	1, 2–3
I. Prophet's Introduction: Summons of Witnesses	2a
A. Call to attention to Heaven and Earth	2aα
B. Motivation: Prophetic citation formula	2aβ
II. Accusation speech by YHWH against Israel	2b–3
A. Father speech: complaint against children for improper behavior	2b
1. concerning father's beneficial actions for children	2bα
2. concerning children's improper response	2bβ
B. Wisdom parable: consequence from complaint	3
1. analogy of animals	3a
a. ox	3aα
b. ass	3aβ
2. application to Israel	3b
a. Israel does not know	3bα
b. people do not understand	3bβ

---

[8] For the understanding of this statement (*Anklage*), cf. Wildberger, Jesaja 1–12, 12; Kaiser, Isaiah 1–12, 11; Fohrer, BZAW 99, 151; Boecker, Redeformen des Rechtslebens, 84.

[9] Note the deliberate contrast of Israel with the ox by the repetition of *yāda'*.

[10] Wildberger, Jesaja 1–12, 14 f.; Whedbee, Isaiah and Wisdom, 39 ff.

[11] That v. 3 is a parable, the background of which is found in wisdom circles, does not undermine the legal character of v. 2b–3. Here, the parable is a device used by the prophet to further his legal aim, the lodging of an accusation against the people of Israel. On the overlapping of complaint and accusation, see Whedbee, Isaiah and Wisdom, 35 f.

4. Isaiah 1, 4−9

The unit begins with a "woe" formula which often introduces prophetic oracles. V. 10 contains another call to attention which introduces a new unit so that the present unit comprises v. 4−9.[12] Furthermore, in v. 4−9, the prophet delivers his own speech to the people instead of quoting a speech by YHWH as in v. 2−3. This speech is addressed to the people of Israel as indicated by the vocative address in v. 4a and the second person perspective of v. 5−9. The first person plural style of v. 9 in no way undermines the character of this speech as an address to the people. Here, the prophet uses the first person plural style as a rhetorical device to include himself among those whom he addresses. In this way, he identifies with his audience and assures himself of their sympathy with his message.

The passage begins with a woe oracle in v. 4 as indicated by the introductory *hôy*.[13] The first part of this oracle, v. 4a, is a woe address which uses four different vocative appellations to address the party to which the oracle is directed. Each of these appellatives characterizes the nature of the people. Thus, in v. 4aα[1], the people are called "sinning nation," in v. 4aα[2], "people heavy with guilt," in v. 4aβ, "wicked offspring", and in v. 4aγ, "corrupt sons." Furthermore, the sequence of these appellations corresponds to a progression of social relationships. Thus, *gôy* refers to a national entity, *'am* to a tribal or ethnic group, *zæra'* to family descendants in general, and *bānîm* to the closest family descendants. Such a progression, from the most distant to the closest of social relationships, leads the listener or reader to consider the corruption of this people in progressively more personal terms. This is not simply a matter of a sinful nation, it involves the corruption of children. Presenting the matter in this perspective leads to a more intense emotional response in the listener or reader since it will inevitably lead him to consider how he would react if his own children were of similar character. The second part of the woe oracle, v. 4b, contains three statements which are formulated with third person plural perfect verbs.[14]

---

[12] Cf. Wildberger, Jesaja 1−12, 20; Kaiser, Isaiah 1−12, 17; Clements, Isaiah 1−39, 30 f.; Fohrer, BZAW 99, 149, 150 f., 153.

[13] Wildberger, Jesaja 1−12, 20; Kaiser, Isaiah 1−12, 17.

[14] Although these statements are formulated with third person plural perfect verbs, they must still be understood as part of the vocative address begun in v. 4a. Cf. Roberts, PSB 3 (1982), 296 ff., and D. R. Hillers, Hôy and Hôy-Oracles: A Neglected Syntactic Aspect, The Word of the Lord Shall Go Forth: Essays in Honor of David Noel Freedman in Celebration of His Sixtieth Birthday, ed. by C. L. Meyers and M. O'Conner, 1983, 185 ff., who discuss the syntax of woe oracles beginning with *hôy* and demonstrate that they should be understood as second person addresses to capture the intention of

These state three accusations against the people which substantiate their negative characterization in the first part of the woe oracle. Thus, the entire woe oracle is accusatory in nature.

The second part of this passage begins in v. 5a with a rhetorical question addressed to the people asking them why they would be stricken again. Naturally, the people would not want to be stricken again but the second part of the question in v. 5aβ makes it clear that their continued apostasy will lead to just such a result. V. 5b − 9 do not answer the rhetorical question in v. 5a but they relate directly to it in that they demonstrate how much the people have suffered already.[15] Apparently, this oracle was uttered after some catastrophe from which the people did not draw the lesson that their own behavior caused YHWH to bring it about. V. 5b − 9 provide the basis from which the question in v. 5a proceeds, the present suffering of the people. The suffering of the people described in these verses would suggest that the people should feel that they have had enough. In the prophet's view, this suffering was brought about by the people's apostasizing behavior. Therefore, the description of suffering in v. 5b − 9 serves as a motivation for the people to end their wrongdoing and consequently, their suffering.

V. 5b − 9 include four parts, each of which focuses on a different aspect of the people's suffering presupposed in v. 5a. V. 5b − 6 focus on the sickness of the people. These verses constitute a figurative speech which uses the language of physical sickness to describe the present misery of the people. V. 5b − 6a describe the sickness itself, beginning with a general statement that both head and heart are ill (v. 5b) followed by a description of the extent and nature of the disease (v. 6a). V. 6b consists of three statements which claim that the disease is left untreated. In v. 7, the language changes from the descriptive language of v. 5b − 6 to second person plural address. This verse discusses the desolation of the land. V. 7a brings up the desolation of the land itself in two parts including both land and cities. V. 7b, with its introductory statement that "your land is before you," deals with the people's inability to prevent their land's destruction by foreigners. This provides a parallel to the untreated sickness of v. 5b − 6. V. 8 returns to descriptive language focusing on the isolation of Jerusalem with the use of three similes. The first two express Jerusalem's isolation in agricultural terms, comparing the city to the temporary shelters used by the farmers in their fields (v. 8a, 8bα). The third simile in v. 8bβ relates the actual situation, that

---

the *hôy* construction. V. 4bγ appears to be a marginal gloss. It's stylistic deviance from v. 4bα + β, use of the root *zwr* from v. 6b, and its anticlimatic character suggest that this is an interpretative comment added by someone who drew out the implications of forsaking YHWH and rejecting the Holy One of Israel.

[15] Cf. Vermeylen, Du prophète Isaïe, I 50.

Jerusalem is a besieged city.[16] Finally, v. 9 concentrates on the small remnant of the people, presumably those who have survived the desolation of the land by foreigners and who have secured refuge within the besieged Jerusalem. This verse employs first person plural language which refers to both the speaker and the audience which it addresses, the survivors of the people who are left in Jerusalem. In this way, the speaker includes himself as one of those addressed and thus gains the sympathy of the audience for his position. In v. 9a, the prophet negatively states a condition, that YHWH had allowed a small remnant to remain. The results of this condition, which had not been met, then follow in v. 9b in two parts, that the people would have been like Sodom and resembled Gomorrah. Such a comparison to Sodom and Gomorrah brings home two points: 1) the near extinction of the people, like Sodom and Gomorrah, and 2) the wickedness of the people, again, like Sodom and Gomorrah.[17]

The reference to Sodom and Gomorrah, with its allusion to the guilt of the people, and the question concerning apostasy in v. 5a indicate that the sickness of the people refers to more than only their present state of misery following the invasion of their land. This suggests that the illness of the people is a symptom of their moral, religious, and social corruption.[18] Thus, the sequence of the four parts of v. 5b−9 suggests an element of cause and effect. The moral sickness of the people (v. 5b−6) leads to the desolation of the land by foreign invaders (v. 7), which leads to the isolation of Jerusalem (v. 8), which contains the small remnant of the people who survive in the besieged city. The effect of the whole is to place the blame for the suffering of the people directly on their own shoulders since their apostasy led to an invasion of their land and its consequences. Hence, v. 5b−9 relate to the rhetorical question of v. 5a and suggest an answer to the question. The people should have had enough of suffering. V. 5a suggests a threat of continued suffering if the people do not cease their apostasy. Therefore, v. 5−9

---

[16] There is no need to change n^eṣûrâ to n^eṣôrâ in order to match the MT to the LXX's understanding of the passage as BHS suggests. The word n^eṣûrâ is a feminine passive participle from the root nṣr which means "watch," "guard," or "keep." This may be understood from the perspective of the inhabitants of the city in which case, the phrase would be understood as "a guarded city" or "a defended city." If it is understood from the viewpoint of attackers, however, "a guarded city" can be understood as a "besieged city." The latter would, of course, normally use the root ṣûr instead of nṣr, but the LXX would have understood n^eṣûrâ in the former sense to translate the phrase as *hos polis poliorkoumene*.

[17] Cf. Vermeylen, Du prophète Isaïe, I 50.

[18] Cf. Deut 28, 20−24 which states that YHWH will bring various diseases upon the people should they disobey Him.

serve as a motivation to the people to stop their apostasizing behavior. Apostasy is precisely the crime of which the woe oracle in v. 4 accuses the people. V. 4 and 5 – 9 function together as an admonition to the people to discontinue their apostasy against YHWH.[19] The structure is as follows:

Prophetic Admonition Speech to the People concerning their Continued Apostasy	1, 4 – 9
I. Woe Oracle: Accusation of Apostasy	4
A. Woe address: Characterization	4a
1. to sinning nation	4aα¹
2. to people heavy with guilt	4aα²
3. to wicked offspring	4aβ
4. to corrupt sons	4aγ
B. Substantiation of Characterization	4b
1. forsaking YHWH	4bα
2. rejecting Holy One of Israel	4bβ
3. apostasy	4bγ
II. Motivation to Cease Apostasy: Threat concerning Continued Apostasy	5 – 9
A. Rhetorical question	5a
1. question proper	5aα
2. implications	5aβ
B. Basis for question	5b – 9
1. concerning sickness of people	5b – 6
a. concerning sickness	5b – 6a
1) basic statement of sickness	5b
a) in head	5bα
b) in heart	5bβ
2) extent and nature of sickness	6a
a) extent	6aα
b) nature	6aβ
i. wound	6aβ¹
ii. stripe	6aβ²
iii. oozing sore	6aβ³
b. concerning lack of treatment	6b
1) no pressing	6bα¹
2) no binding	6bα²
3) no softening with oil	6bβ
2. concerning desolation of land	7
a. basically stated	7a
1) for land	7aα
2) for cities	7aβ
b. concerning inability to defend	7b

---

[19] Cf. Wildberger, Jesaja 1 – 12, 20, who considers v. 4 – 9 as a *"Scheltwort"* (rebuke) which passes over into a *"Mahnrede"* (admonition). He is correct to note both elements of rebuke and admonition, but the primary function of this passage is admonishment so that the people do not continue their past mistake.

5. Isaiah 1, 10 – 17

Although this unit begins with a first person plural perspective which would correspond to that of v. 9, it must be considered a new unit due to the introductory call to attention in v. 10.[20] This call to attention, or more specifically, call to instruction,[21] is spoken by the prophet to introduce a speech by YHWH in v. 11 – 17 whereas in v. 4 – 9, only the prophet's words are recorded. V. 18 – 20 also contain a quotation of a speech by YHWH by the prophet but these verses may not be considered a part of the present unit since they contain their own speech formula in v. 18 which marks them off as a distinct unit.[22] Furthermore, v. 10 – 17 are concerned with instruction throughout whereas v. 18 – 20 are concerned with legal matters. Likewise, the admonition in v. 4 – 9 is not generically related to the instruction of v. 10 – 17.[23]

The unit begins with a specialized form of the call to attention known as the call to instruction. Such a call generally includes two commands to hear using imperative verbs such as $šim^{e^c}\hat{u}$, $haqšîbû$, or $ha^{\,\flat}azînû$.[24] The purpose is to direct the addressee's attention to the instruction which is to follow. In v. 10 are two parallel statements introduced by the imperative verbs $šim^{e^c}\hat{u}$ and $ha^{\,\flat}azînû$ respectively. As indicated by the reference to $tôrat$ $^{\,\flat}ælohênû$ in v. 10b, their purpose is specifically to call the addressee's attention to the instruction of God which the prophet quotes in v. 11 – 17. Here, the addressees are called

---

[20] Wildberger, Jesaja 1 – 12, 34; Kaiser, Isaiah 1 – 12, 24; Gray, Isaiah I – XXVII, 16.
[21] Cf. H. W. Wolff, Hosea, Herm, 1974, 97; Jensen, The Use of tôrâ by Isaiah, 68 ff.
[22] Wildberger, Jesaja 1 – 12, 34; Kaiser, Isaiah 1 – 12, 25.
[23] Other scholars who see v. 10 – 17 as a unit include Clements, Isaiah 1 – 39, 32; Vermeylen, Du prophète Isaïe, I 57 (but it is part of the larger unit, v. 2 – 20); Gray, Isaiah I – XXVII, 16; Duhm, Das Buch Jesaia, 23; Skinner, Isaiah I – XXXIX, 2; Fohrer, BZAW 99, 149; Das Buch Jesaja, I 32 f.; Scott, IB V, 170; Marti, Jesaja, 9.
[24] For a discussion of this form, see Wolff, Hosea, 97.

"rulers of Sodom" and the "people of Gomorrah." By this means, the prophet insures that all of society is addressed, both rulers and people, so that the blame for the people's wrongdoing can not be passed off from group to another. The reference to Sodom and Gomorrah figuratively indicates the disaster that will come if the people do not mend their ways.

V. 11 – 17 are a prophetic quotation of a YHWH speech as indicated by the YHWH speech formula in v. 11aα², and the first person singular perspective of the speech itself which refers to YHWH. Within these verses are two rhetorical questions in v. 11 and 12 concerning the legitimacy of present cultic practice. Neither question is answered directly. Instead, v. 13 – 17 follow with instructions concerning proper service to YHWH. A closer analysis of v. 11 – 12 and v. 13 – 17 will clarify their respective functions and the relationship between them.

The first part of v. 11 is v. 11a which is YHWH's interrogation of the people. This consists of the question itself in v. 11aα¹ and the YHWH speech formula in v. 11aα². The question, "Why do you multiply sacrifices to Me?" is rhetorical because no satisfactory answer can be given. Here, the authority who would require such sacrifices questions their legitimacy. Consequently, there is no reason to offer them. The statement which follows the question in v. 11aβ + b, which is distinguished by its use of the first person verbs, *śābaʿtî* and *ḥāpāsṭî*, makes this quite clear. First, in v. 11aβ, YHWH states that He is sated with the offerings, that is, He has no need for them. Second, in v. 11b, He states that He has no desire for such offerings. Since YHWH neither needs nor desires the sacrifices, there is obviously no reason to make them. The question in v. 12 is structured somewhat differently from the question in v. 11. The first part of the question in v. 12a is a conditional clause which states the circumstances presupposed by the question proper in v. 12b. In this case, the circumstances or situation is that of public worship of YHWH. The question relates directly to this situation of worship so that YHWH questions the manner in which such public worship is conducted. The "trampling of courts" refers to the public services held at the temple when people and animals filled the courtyards for sacrifices to YHWH. As in v. 11, YHWH questions the legitimacy of such a form of worship. This time, however, the question does not focus on YHWH's need for sacrifice. Instead, the question asks who requests such a form of worship. Again, the question is rhetorical. Who but YHWH would request such sacrifice? Because YHWH asks the question, obviously He did not request it. As in v. 11, there is no legitimate answer. Together, v. 11 – 12 point out that the behavior of the people is misguided in that v. 11 denies the need for sacrificial worship and v. 12 denies that it was requested. Such misguided behavior requires correction and this is what follows in the instruction material in

v. 13 – 17. V. 11 – 12 prepare the way for v. 13 – 17 which instruct the people in the alternatives to the sacrificial system so that they may serve YHWH in the manner which He desires. Thus, v. 11 – 12 serve as the basis for the instruction in v. 13 – 17 in that they establish the need for instruction.[25]

V. 13 – 17 provide instructions for the proper service of YHWH. These instructions are formulated in two parts, negative (v. 13 – 15) and positive (v. 16 – 17) so that the answer specifies both what should not be done and what should be done.

The negative instruction in v. 13 – 15 contains only one prohibition which is in v. 13aα. V. 13aβ – 15 provide reasons for this prohibition which are organized into three sections. The first section, v. 13aβ – 14, contains four statements which deal with YHWH's unwillingness to endure the people's cultic observances. The second section, v. 15a, contains two statements concerning YHWH's refusal to respond to the people's prayer. In the first statement (v. 15aα), YHWH states that when the people spread their hands to Him in prayer, He will hide His eyes. In the second statement (v. 15aβ), He states that when the people pray, He will not listen. The third section (v. 15b) simply states the people's guilt in one sentence.[26] This last section not only serves as part of the explanation for the negative instruction in v. 13aα, it also serves as the explanation for YHWH's unwillingness to endure the people's cultic practices and His refusal to acknowledge their prayer.

The positive instruction in v. 16 – 17 contains nine instructions for the proper service of YHWH, each indicated by an imperative verb. There is a progression of concepts in these instructions. Thus, washing (v. 16aα[1]) leads to purification (v. 16aα[2]) which, of course, means the removal of evil (v. 16aβ) and this allows one to stop doing evil (v. 16b). Once one ceases doing evil, he may begin to learn good (v. 17aα). This naturally leads to the general goals of seeking justice (v. 17aβ) and

---

[25] Such rhetorical questions are often found in the accusation of a legal proceeding where they aid in establishing the plaintiff's case against the defendant (cf. Jer 2, 5; Mic 6, 3; Job 38, 1 – 40:2). Such a question is asked of a defendant by a plaintiff who expects no satisfactory reply, thus providing the basis for the legal proceeding. In this text, however, no further accusation or judgment appears which one might expect in a legal proceeding. Instead, instruction follows which demonstrates that the prophet has adapted a legal form, the accusatory rhetorical question, to an instruction context. Jensen, The Use of tôrâ by Isaiah, 72 f., also notes the use of the rhetorical question in the wisdom tradition where it is used in a similar fashion to aid in establishing the speaker's contention.

[26] Note the dual meaning of the blood imagery employed here. Not only are the people's hands full of blood from carrying out the sacrifices which YHWH does not want, they are also full of blood as a sign of their guilt.

correcting oppression (v. 17aγ) as well as the more specific goals of judging the orphan (v. 17bα) and pleading for the widow (v. 17bβ).

Thus, the two rhetorical questions in v. 11 – 12 establish the need for cultic instruction which follows in v. 13 – 17. In many respects, these verses resemble the priestly Torah or instruction form but there are some differences.[27] In the priestly instruction, one finds a Torah question followed by a Torah answer. The question is usually one seeking information on the correct procedure for a given cultic act. In Isa 1, 10 – 17, however, this is not the case. There are questions, but they are not formulated to directly request information on cultic procedure. They are asked by God and request information on the legitimacy of the cultic process itself. Because the questions are rhetorical and asked by the Supreme Cultic Authority, they indicate that the cultic process is not legitimate. The instruction which follows does not deal with correct cultic practice as one might expect in a priestly Torah. Rather, it provides an alternative to the cultic process which emphasizes moral considerations over ceremonial procedure, thus instructing the people in what YHWH really wants. Consequently, this is a modified priestly Torah or instruction speech since it is similar to the standard form but deviates from it in purpose.[28] The purpose is not to clarify cultic procedure but to argue for moralistic observance. Because v. 11 – 17 are the prophet's quotation of an instruction speech by YHWH, these verses should be labeled as such and the unit should be called a "Prophetic Torah Speech."[29] Its structure is as follows:

Prophetic Torah Speech Concerning Proper Service to YHWH	1, 10 – 17
I. Call to Instruction	10
A. To the "Rulers of Sodom"	10a
B. To the "People of Gomorrah"	10b
II. Quotation of a YHWH Torah Speech	11 – 17
A. Concerning the need for instruction	11 – 12
1. concerning the necessity for sacrifice	11
a. interrogation by YHWH	11aα
1) question	11aα^1
2) YHWH speech formula	11aα^2
b. basis for interrogation	11aβ + b
1) YHWH does not need	11aβ
b) YHWH does not want	11b
2. Concerning the request for sacrifice	12
a. case-circumstance	12a
b. question proper	12b

---

[27] For a full discussion of the priestly Torah, see J. Begrich, BZAW 66, 1936, 63 ff.

[28] Cf. Clements, Isaiah 1 – 39, 32.

[29] So Wildberger, Jesaja 1 – 12, 36; Fohrer, BZAW 99, 156; C. Westermann, Basic Forms of Prophetic Speech, 1967, 203 ff.

B. Prophetic instruction	13 – 17
1. expressed negatively	13 – 15
a. prohibition	13aα
b. reasons for prohibition	13aβ – 15
1) YHWH's unwillingness to endure cult	13aβ – 14
a) concerning incense	13aβ
b) concerning false cult	13b
c) concerning hatred for festival	14aα
d) concerning inability to bear	14aβ + b
2) YHWH's refusal to respond	15a
a) will not look	15aα
i. case	15aα¹
ii. response	15aα²
b) will not listen	15aβ
i. case	15aβ¹
ii. response	15aβ²
2. expressed positively	16 – 17
a. wash yourselves	16aα¹
b. purify yourselves	16aα²
c. remove evil	16aβ
d. cease doing evil	16b
e. learn doing good	17aα
f. seek justice	17aβ
g. correct oppression	17aγ
h. judge the orphan	17bα
i. plead for the widow	17bβ

6. Isaiah 1, 18 – 20

Although this unit is still a speech by YHWH which would indicate some connection with the speech in v. 11 – 17, the YHWH speech formula in v. 18aβ marks off v. 18 as the beginning of a new unit. Furthermore, the unit beginning at v. 18 is no longer a part of the prophetic Torah which precedes. Instead, it is a legal form. The unit extends through v. 20 which closes with the formula, *kî pî yhwh dibber*, indicating the end of the speech by YHWH. V. 21 begins a speech by the prophet which does not continue his quotation of YHWH. Furthermore, v. 21 begins with *'êkâ*, which indicates the beginning of a dirge, a genre different from the trial genre of v. 18 – 20.[30]

---

[30] On the demarcation of this unit, cf. Wildberger, Jesaja 1 – 12, 50; Kaiser, Isaiah 1 – 12, 36 f.; Vermeylen, Du prophète Isaïe, I 57; Clements, Isaiah 1 – 39, 34; Skinner, Isaiah I – XXXIX, 2; Gray, Isaiah I – XXVII, 26; Duhm, Das Buch Jesaia, 31 f.; Marti, Jesaja, 15; Scott, IB V, 174 f.

The unit begins in v. 18a with an invitation to arbitration. It is formulated with an imperative and a first person plural (cohortative) verb which sets it apart from the third and second person plural statements which follow beginning in v. 18b. Furthermore, v. 18a consists of two parts, the invitation to arbitration proper in v. 18aα and the YHWH speech formula in v. 18aβ which also sets off the invitation from the following material.

V. 18b – 20 consist of two parts. V. 18b – 20bα contain four conditional statements, each beginning with the particle 'im. They provide incentive to the people to enter into arbitration with YHWH as suggested in v. 18a. V. 20bβ is a YHWH authorization formula which guarantees that the preceding promises are a word of YHWH and that they will come to pass under the stated conditions.

The four conditional statements of v. 18b – 20b may be arranged in two pairs.[31] In v. 18b, the two paired statements, v. 18bα and v. 18bβ, belong together because of their parallel content and construction. Each states a condition referring to the present sinful state of the people and each follows with a possible result of forgiveness of those sins which the people can expect if they enter into arbitration with YHWH.[32] In v. 19 – 20bα, the two paired statements are linked by *waw*-conjunctive. They are not parallel but contain similarly constructed contrasting statements which make it clear that the people have alternative courses of action from which to choose and alternative consequences which they can expect from their choice. Thus, according to v. 19, if the people obey YHWH, they can expect prosperity. But, according to v. 20a + bα, if the people do not obey YHWH, they can expect disaster. These verses also build on the attempt to provide incentive to the people as in v. 18b. But they can also make it clear that not only is there a positive result from cooperation with YHWH, there is a negative result from lack of cooperation. Thus, the people are warned that they have a responsibility to act in accordance with YHWH's wishes in order to receive the

---

[31] Cf. the discussion by Scott, IB V, 174 f.

[32] The view that these statements must be translated as questions presupposes that this unit can in no way be associated with YHWH's forgiveness of the people (e. g., Fohrer, BZAW 99, 160). Such a view completely misses the point of this unit, especially in relation to v. 10 – 17. V. 10 – 17 provide instruction in the proper worship of YHWH, i. e., they presuppose that the people have a chance to reform. Such a presupposition is also operative in v. 19 – 20. Yet, Fohrer chooses to eliminate v. 19 – 20 as secondary additions. While they may be secondary, they only serve to emphasize the point made in v. 18, that YHWH's forgiveness is available even though the people have sinned. The purpose of this passage is not to condemn the people utterly, but to motivate them to reform. [Cf. J. Willis, JSOT 25 (1983), 35 ff., who sees v. 18 as an offer of divine forgiveness.]

beneficence offered in v. 18b. The strategy here is to emphasize the good results of arbitration with YHWH in v. 18b in order to draw the people into accepting YHWH's offer. The verse clearly states the conditions of the offer so that the people will be aware that they must earn their land in the future if they are to retain it. Here, the people get a second chance to obey YHWH.

Because the prophet quotes YHWH's appeal to begin a legal proceeding, the unit may be labeled as a "Prophetic Announcement of YHWH's Appeal to begin a Legal Proceeding."[33] Its structure is as follows:

Prophetic Announcement of YHWH's Appeal to Begin a Legal Proceeding	1, 18 – 20
I. Invitation to Arbitration	18a
A. Invitation proper	18aα
B. YHWH speech formula	18aβ
II. Incentive for Entering into Arbitration	18b – 20
A. Statements of incentive	18b – 20bα
1. YHWH's offer of vindication	18b
a. first statement	18bα
1) case	18bα^1
2) projected result	18bα^2
b. second statement	18bβ
1) case	18bβ^1
2) projected result	18bβ^2
2. YHWH's statement of His conditions	19 – 20bα
a. positive statement	19
1) case: people obedient	19a
2) positive result	19b
b. negative statement	20a + bα
1) case: people disobedient	20a
2) negative result	20bα
B. YHWH authorization formula	20bβ

7. Isaiah 1, 21 – 26

V. 21 introduces a marked change of subject. Whereas the previous unit held out some hope of forgiveness for the people, v. 21 introduces a dirge, indicated by the initial 'êkâ, which suggests the coming punishment of the people. The unit extends through v. 26, as indicated by the appearance of qiryâ næ'æmānâ which, together with the other occur-

---

[33] On this form, see Boecker, Redeformen des Rechtslebens, 68 ff. Cf. Wildberger, Jesaja 1 – 12, 51; Kaiser, Isaiah 1 – 12, 36 f.; Clements, Isaiah 1 – 39, 34.

rence of this designation in v. 21, provides an inclusion for the passage.[34] Within the unit, no speaker is specifically indicated for v. 21 – 23, but one may assume that the prophet speaks here as suggested by the oracle formula in v. 24a.[35] V. 24 – 26 contain the prophet's quotation of a speech by YHWH which relates directly to v. 21 – 23 by its use of metal smelting imagery. Thus, the entire unit is a speech by the prophet. Furthermore, the following analysis will show that these verses are generically distinct in that they are a modified form of a prophetic judgment speech.[36]

The unit consists of two major portions as indicated by the oracle formula at the beginning of v. 24. In v. 21 – 23, the prophet describes the corrupt state of the city (Jerusalem), using both metaphorical and specific language to make his point. These verses therefore serve as the indictment of the city.[37] V. 24 – 26 contain the prophet's quotation of a speech by YHWH in which YHWH describes what He intends to do about this situation as well as the expected results.

Within v. 21 – 23, v. 21 speaks of Jerusalem in the third person and discusses the general corruption of the city. V. 21a contains a dirge in 3/2 meter introduced by 'êkâ.[38] V. 21b explains the circumstances which prompted the dirge by referring to the city's former state of righteousness in v. 21bα + β and her present state of corruption as indicated by the presence of murderers within her (v. 21bγ). V. 22 – 23 are addressed directly to the city as indicated by the use of the second person feminine singular pronouns. These verbs state specific accusations against the city which support the charge of corruption. V. 22 provides specific evidence of corruption in that it points out the use of impure silver in v. 22a and watered down wine in v. 22b so that people are cheated in the market place. V. 23 focuses on the leaders of the people and in doing so, suggests a reason for the corruption of the city. V. 23aα discusses the general character of the leaders, stating that they are both perverse and friends of thieves. V. 23aβ states that they are open to influence in that they love bribes and pursue gifts. V. 23b states that justice is corrupt in that

---

[34] Vermeylen, Du prophète Isaïe, I 71; Procksch, Jesaia I, 45. Other scholars have noted the chiastic construction of these verses (e. g., Whedbee, Isaiah and Wisdom, 34).

[35] Wildberger, Jesaja 1 – 12, 57.

[36] Other scholars who see v. 21 – 26 as a unit include Wildberger, Jesaja 1 – 12, 56 f.; Vermeylen, Du prophète Isaïe, I 71; Whedbee, Isaiah and Wisdom, 139; Fohrer, BZAW 99, 149, 163, n. 26; Marti, Jesaja, 17 f.; Y. Gitay, JQR 75 (1984), 162 ff. Many scholars include v. 27 – 28 as part of the unit but consider them as later additions: Clements, Isaiah 1 – 39, 36 f.; Fohrer, Das Buch Jesaja, I 42; Gray, Isaiah I – XXVII, 31, 37; Duhm, Das Buch Jesaia, 32, 35; Procksch, Jesaia I, 45, 49.

[37] Wildberger, Jesaja 1 – 12, 56.

[38] Wildberger, Jesaja 1 – 12, 57.

orphans are not judged correctly and the cases of widows are not considered in court.[39] There is a progression in these three sections concerning the leaders. Their general corruption (v. 23aα) leads to their being influenced by bribes (v. 23aβ) which results in the corruption of justice (v. 23b). Thus, the blame for Jerusalem's corruption is placed squarely on the leaders of the city, whose practices lead to the corruption of the entire city. Criminals are not checked because those who would stop them are themselves criminals.

V. 24 – 26 contain an expanded oracular formula in v. 24a followed by the speech by YHWH in v. 24b – 26. Within this speech is a woe statement in v. 24b – 26a in which YHWH states what He intends to do about the present situation of the city. The woe statement is constructed with six sentences constituted with first person singular imperfect verbs and linked together by *waw*-conjunctives. The two statements in v. 24b discuss YHWH's vengeance in general terms. The three statements in v. 25 metaphorically discuss the removal of corrupt leaders by using metal refining language. Finally, the statement in v. 26a announces the restoration of proper leadership. Following the woe statement in v. 24b – 26a is v. 26b, a second person feminine singular statement addressed to Jerusalem, which states the expected results of YHWH's proposed action, the reestablishment of Jerusalem as a righteous city. Thus, the YHWH speech resembles an announcement of judgment in that it announces judgment against the corrupt leaders of the city.[40] But the goal of the speech is not simply to announce punishment as an end in itself. Rather, its purpose is to cleanse the city of its corrupt elements so that the city may be restored to its proper state of righteousness. Therefore, the speech by YHWH in v. 24b – 26 must be considered as an announcement of cleansing judgment and v. 24 – 26 as a whole are a prophetic announcement of cleansing judgment or rehabilitation.

This assessment of v. 24 – 26 influences the generic identification of the entire unit. As noted above, v. 21 – 23 are an indictment speech against the city of Jerusalem and v. 24 – 26 are very similar to a prophetic announcement of judgment. This suggests that the whole unit is similar to a prophetic judgment speech since it contains the two major components of such a genre, indictment and announcement of judgment. Yet, the assessment of v. 24 – 26 indicates that the purpose of this oracle is not simply judgment, but cleansing and thus, rehabilitation. V. 21 – 26 are therefore a prophetic rehabilitation speech which is based on the prophetic judgment speech. The structure is as follows:

---

[39] Note that the members of each of the three pairs of statements in v. 23aα¹, 23aα², and 23b are joined by *waw*.

[40] Cf. Wildberger, Jesaja 1 – 12, 56, who claims that this is a *Gerichtsankündigung*.

Prophetic Announcement of the Cleansing of Jerusalem: Pro-	
phetic Rehabilitation Speech	1,21 – 26
I. Indictment of Jerusalem	21 – 23
A. Dirge concerning the Corrupt State of the City	21
1. dirge proper	21a
2. explanation of dirge	21b
a. former state of righteousness	21bα + β
b. present state of corruption	21bγ
B. Specific accusations	22 – 23
1. evidence of corruption	22
a. impure silver	22a
b. watered down wine	22b
2. reason for corruption: leaders	23
a. their general character	23
1) perversc	23aα^1
2) friends of thieves	23aα^2
b. open to influence	23aβ
1) love bribes	23aβ^1
2) pursue gifts	23aβ^2
c. result: corrupt justice	23b
1) orphans not judged	23bα
2) widows' cases not heard	23bβ
II. Prophetic Announcement of Cleansing Judgment	24 – 26
A. Expanded oracle formula	24a
B. Announcement of cleansing judgment: Speech by	
YHWH	24b – 26
1. woe speech: YHWH's proposed actions	24b – 26a
a. concerning YHWH's vengeance	24b
1) satisfaction from opponents	24bα
2) vengeance from enemies	24bβ
b. removal of corrupt leaders	25
1) hand against you	25aα
2) smelt your dross	25aβ
3) remove your dregs	25b
c. restoration of proper leaders	26a
2. result of YHWH's proposed actions: Jerusalem's	
character reestablished	26b

8. Isaiah 1, 27 – 31

Following the prophetic rehabilitation speech in v. 21 – 26 are v. 27 – 31. Their character as a distinct unit is somewhat questionable since they are often seen as supplements to the preceding material.[41] For

---

[41] Fohrer, BZAW 99, 163, n. 26; Skinner, Isaiah I – XXXIX, 2; Scott, IB V, 179; Marti, Jesaja, 22 f. For the view that v. 29 – 31 are a fragment, see Wildberger, Jesaja 1 – 12,

the present, however, they will be considered separately due to the generic consistency of v. 21 — 26. V. 27 clearly is not a speech by YHWH addressing Jerusalem as were the verses which preceded. Instead, v. 27 — 28 speak of Jerusalem with a third person perspective. Furthermore, the mention of YHWH in v. 28 indicates that the prophet is the speaker here. Although v. 29 — 31 are a second person masculine plural address, the third person plural verb *yeboŝû* and the connecting *kî* indicate that these verses were originally independent and were deliberately attached to v. 27 — 28.[42] This was done so that v. 29 — 31 could refer to groups of repenters and transgressors mentioned in v. 27 — 28. Finally, the superscription in Isa 2, 1 marks the beginning of an entirely new unit and thus indicates the end of the present unit.

There are two basic sections in v. 27 — 31. V. 27 — 28 are a third person statement concerning Zion's redemption and the destruction of the corrupt people who had been in her midst. V. 29 — 31 are primarily a second person address to the corrupt people mentioned in v. 27 — 28. As noted above, they are connected to v. 27 — 28 by an introductory *kî* and the change of the initial verb to *yeboŝû*.

Within v. 27 — 28 are two parts. V. 27 announces the redemption of Zion (v. 27a) and those of her people who choose to repent (v. 27b). V. 28 announces the annihilation of the corrupt people of the city by stating that those who forsake YHWH shall come to an end (v. 28b).

In v. 29 — 31, v. 29 states that the people will be ashamed of their wrongdoing. This is done in two parts. First, they shall be ashamed of the oaks in which they delighted (v. 29a). Second, they shall be ashamed of the gardens which they chose (v. 29b). Both oaks and gardens are symbols of a fertility cult so that the people's transgression is understood in terms of cultic apostasy.[43] V. 30 — 31, connected to v. 29 by *kî*, announce the consequences of such apostasy in the form of a simile. The simile is stated in two parts in v. 30. As a result of their apostasy, the people will become like a rotten oak (v. 30a) and like a dry garden (v. 30b). Thus, by the use of the simile, the prophet describes the corruption caused by apostasy. V. 31 describes the results that the people can expect from their corruption by apostasy, again stated figuratively in reference to the simile of v. 30. The strength shall become weak so that its product (leaves) becomes tinder (v. 31a), i. e., they will deteriorate.[44]

70; Kaiser, Isaiah 1 — 12, 46; Clements, Isaiah 1 — 39, 37; Gray, Isaiah I — XXVII, 37; Duhm, Das Buch Jesaia, 35; Procksch, Jesaia I, 50; Marti, Jesaja, 21.

[42] Wildberger, Jesaja 1 — 12, 69.

[43] Cf. Clements, Isaiah 1 — 39, 37.

[44] The term, *upoᶜalô* "his work," refers to the product (leaves) of the tree since the suffix "his" can refer grammatically only to *hæḥāson* "the strength" or generative power of the tree.

Deterioration results in destruction (v. 31b) which is described figuratively as a burning plant with no one to quench the fire. Thus, v. 29 – 31 elaborate on the fate of the transgressors mentioned in v. 27 – 28.

Essentially, v. 27 – 31 contain a basic statement of an announcement of redemption for Zion and annihilation of her corrupt people as well as an elaboration on this statement.[45] Therefore, the whole unit is an announcement of the redemption of Zion and annihilation of her sinners. The structure is as follows:

Announcement of the Redemption of Zion and the Annihilation of Her Sinners	1, 27 – 31
I. Basically Stated	27 – 28
A. Redemption of Zion and her Repenters	27
1. Zion	27a
2. Repenters	27b
B. Annihilation of Sinners	28
1. Breaking of rebels and sinners	28a
2. End of forsakers of YHWH	28b
II. Elaboration Concerning the Fate of the Sinners	29 – 31
A. Concerning the shame of the sinners	29
1. due to oaks	29a
2. due to gardens	29b
B. Consequences of their sin	30 – 31
2. statement of simile	30
a. like a rotten oak	30a
b. like a dry garden	30b
2. expectation for the future	31
a. deterioration	31a
1) of oak	$31a\alpha$
2) of garden	$31a\beta$
b. destruction	31b
1) burning	$31b\alpha$
2) no quenching	$31b\beta$

9. Structural Overview: Isaiah 1, 1 – 31

This study has identified seven units in Isa 1. These include the superscription in v. 1; a Prophetic Announcement of YHWH's Accusation against Israel in v. 2 – 3; a Prophetic Admonition Speech to the People concerning Continued Apostasy in v. 4 – 9; a Prophetic Torah speech in v. 10 – 17; a Prophetic Announcement of an Appeal to Begin

---

[45] Wildberger, Jesaja 1 – 12, 69, correctly labels v. 29 – 31 as *Gerichtsankündigung* but notes that it is fragmentary.

a Legal Proceeding in v. 18−20; a Prophetic Rehabilitation Speech in
v. 21−26; and an Announcement of the Redemption of Zion and the
annihilation of her Sinners in v. 27−31. While some scholars view this
chapter as a collection of independent units,[46] there is evidence that the
units contained in this chapter have some relation among themselves.
Other scholars have noted catchword connections between some of
the units of this chapter,[47] generic patterns,[48] thematic relations,[49] and
evidence of unified compositions.[50]

The first case to consider is that of the four units in v. 2−20.
Harvey and others have already noted that these verses are demarcated
by the rhetorical device of *inclusio* in that the phrase, *kî yhwh dibber*,
occurs in v. 2aβ and a similar phrase, *kî pî yhwh dibber*, occurs at
v. 20bβ.[51] Furthermore, there are catchwords which link the four units
of these verses.[52] Thus, v. 2−3 are linked to v. 4−9 by the occurrence
of *bānîm* in v. 2 and *bānîm mašḥîtîm* in v. 4. V. 4−9 are linked to
v. 10−17 by the mention of Sodom and Gomorrah in v. 9 as well as in
v. 10. Other catchword links include *tôsîpû sārâ* in v. 5 and *lo' tôsîpû
hābî' minḥat šāw'* in v. 13 as well as the mention of *zæraʿ mᵉreʿîm* in
v. 4 and *hidlû hāreᶜᵃ* in v. 16. V. 10−17 are linked to v. 18−20 not by
catchwords but by imagery. Thus, the lawsuit imagery of v. 18−20
connects to the specific legal terminology of v. 17. Furthermore, both
v. 18−20 and 10−17 share the notion of purification through the mention of *raḥᵃṣû hizzakkû* in v. 16 and the cleansing of sin in v. 18. The
imagery of the red blood of the sacrificial cult is evident in both passages.
In v. 15, the people are charged with having hands full of blood and in
v. 18, the people are offered the opportunity to cleanse the redness of
their sins from themselves so that they will become white. Finally, while
major portions of these units contain speeches by YHWH, they are
always introduced by the prophet so that all four units are styled as
speeches by the prophet.

When viewed as parts of a whole, it is evident that the four units
in v. 2−20 work together as a coherent larger unit. V. 2−3 contain
YHWH's basic accusation against the people of Israel, the setting of
which is a court of law. Witnesses are called and the charges are stated.
At this point, the charges are very general, informing the court of the

[46] E.g., Gray, Isaiah I−XXVII, 3 f.

[47] J. Harvey, Le plaidoyer prophétique contre Israël après la rupture de l'alliance, 1967,
38; Fohrer, BZAW 99, 149; Wildberger, Jesaja 1−12, 73.

[48] Harvey, Le plaidoyer prophétique, 36 ff.; Vermeylen, Du prophète Isaïe, I 44 f.

[49] Fohrer, BZAW 99, 149.

[50] S. Niditch, Bibl 61 (1980), 509 ff.

[51] Harvey, Le plaidoyer prophétique, 37; Vermeylen, Du prophète Isaïe, I 42 f.

[52] Most of the following are taken from Fohrer, BZAW 99, 149.

basic purpose of the proceeding. V. 4 – 9 provide evidence to substantiate the initial charge of v. 2 – 3. The land is desolate so the people must be guilty of something. But the purpose of this evidence goes beyond merely supporting YHWH's initial charge. The question, "Why would you be smitten again that you continue apostasy?" in v. 5 suggests that the purpose of this unit is also to convince the people to end their apostasy in order to end the punishment.[53] The passage presupposes that punishment has already come, but it also implies that more punishment will come if the people do not correct their behavior. In v. 10 – 17, YHWH questions the people to determine the basis for their actions. The rhetorical questions establish that there is no legitimate reason for their actions since YHWH neither needs nor wants their cultic observances. After establishing the people's wrongdoing through these questions, YHWH takes the opportunity to instruct the people in what He does need and want: moral behavior and social justice. The presupposition here is that the people have sinned out of ignorance. That situation is corrected by YHWH's instruction so that the people may correct their own behavior, presumably to end the punishment mentioned in v. 4 – 9.[54] Finally, in v. 18 – 20, YHWH specifically invites the people to arbitration so that they can purify themselves.[55] He offers to forgive them if they repent. There is no opportunity for the people to defend their actions here since YHWH has already established in the previous sections that the people are guilty and that their actions are indefensible. Instead, the people have the opportunity to correct themselves now that they know they are wrong. Generically, the legal background of much of the material in v. 2 – 20 and their accusational character suggest that these verses are a speech of an accuser in court. However, they go beyond the purpose of accusation in that they are designed to motivate the people to repent of their wrongdoings and live as YHWH requires. Thus, this speech of the accuser functions as an exhortation to repent.

The discussion of v. 27 – 31 noted that a number of scholars see a relationship between these verses and v. 21 – 26. Both units are characterized as speeches by the prophet although v. 21 – 26 contain a quotation by the prophet of YHWH. There is also a catchword connection between v. 21 and 27, which both mention *mišpāṭ*, as well as *ṣædæq* in v. 21 and *ṣᵉdāqâ* in v. 27. The use of these words in v. 27 suggests a restoration

---

[53] Cf. H. W. Hoffmann, Die Intention der Verkündigung Jesajas, BZAW 136, 1974, 85. He claims that the purpose of v. 2 – 3 is to warn the people to repent while there is still time.

[54] Cf. Hoffmann, Die Intention der Verkündigung Jesajas, 96, who claims that the purpose of v. 10 – 17 is to motivate the people to repent by offering them forgiveness.

[55] Hoffmann, Die Intention der Verkündigung Jesajas, 105, labels v. 18 – 20 as *"Appel zur Umkehr."*

of the former state of righteousness which the city had lost as mentioned
in v. 21. The imagery of the nature cult in v. 29–31 and the mention of
the people's shame over this cult contrasts directly with v. 21, which
calls the city a harlot, a term often employed for the female prostitutes
of the fertility cults. Finally, the redemption of Zion in v. 27 and the
annihilation of the sinners in v. 28 continues the theme of v. 21–26
which were concerned with cleansing undesirable elements from the city.
V. 27–31 make it clear that the cleansing of the city means the elimination of the sinners so that v. 27–31 serve as an explanation for the
metal refining metaphor introduced in v. 21–26. Thus, v. 21–26 are a
prophetic announcement of the cleansing of Jerusalem and v. 27–31 are
an explication which makes clear the meaning of v. 21–26. V. 21–31
as a whole are a prophetic announcement of Zion's redemption.

V. 21–31 also have a number of catchword connections with
v. 2–20. Thus, $m^e le^{\,a} t\hat{\imath}$ $mi\check{s}p\bar{a}\underline{t}$ contrasts with $y^e d\hat{e}k\,\!\!\!\!\!æm$ $d\bar{a}m\hat{\imath}m$ $m\bar{a}le^{\,}\hat{u}$
in v. 15. Also, the mention of $mi\check{s}p\bar{a}\underline{t}$ in v. 21 connects not only with
v. 27, but with $dir\check{s}\hat{u}$ $mi\check{s}p\bar{a}\underline{t}$ in v. 17 as well. The accusation against the
leaders of the city, that they do not judge the orphan or hear the case
of the widow, contrasts directly with the instructions to do so in v. 17.
The mention of $po\check{s}^{e^c}\hat{\imath}m$ in v. 28 recalls the statement w^ehem $p\bar{a}\check{s}^{e^c}\hat{u}$ $b\hat{\imath}$
of v. 2. The $w^eha\underline{t}\underline{t}\bar{a}\,{}^{\,}\hat{\imath}m$ of v. 28 relates to $g\hat{o}y$ $ho\underline{t}e^{\,}$ of v. 4 and the
$w^{e^c}oz^eb\hat{e}$ $yhwh$ of v. 28 relates to ${}^{\,}\bar{a}z^eb\hat{u}$ ${}^{\,}æt$ $yhwh$ of v. 4.

In v. 21–31, YHWH announces His intention to separate the
righteous from the wicked, redeeming the righteous and destroying the
wicked. This is particularly important when these verses are considered
together with v. 2–20. As noted above, v. 2–20 are a speech of an
accuser in court. In v. 21–31, YHWH speaks as a judge, the One who
decides who is righteous and who is not. Thus, generally speaking,
v. 21–31 are a speech by the judge in court. Together, the speech of the
accuser in court and the speech of the judge in court are two elements
of the trial genres (*Gerichtsreden* or *rîb*-pattern).[56] Normally, one would
expect a defense speech by the accused,[57] but as mentioned earlier,
YHWH has already established that the accused has no defense so that
such a speech is not necessary. While v. 2–31 constitute a trial genre,
their purpose goes beyond merely accusing, convicting, and sentencing
a guilty party. They are also designed to motivate the people to repent,

---

[56] See esp. Harvey, Le plaidoyer prophétique, 36 ff.; B. Gemser, The RIB- or Controversy
Pattern in Hebrew Mentality, SVT 3 (1955), 120 ff.; H. Huffmon, JBL 78 (1959),
285 ff.; E. von Waldow, Der traditionsgeschichtliche Hintergrund der prophetischen
Gerichtsreden, BZAW 85, 1963; Vermeylen, Du prophète Isaïe, I 44 f.

[57] Cf. the categories outlined by von Waldow, Prophetischen Gerichtsreden, 6 ff. (*An-
klagereden, Verteidigungsreden, Urteile und Urteilsfolgebestimmungen*) and Boecker,
Redeformen des Rechtslebens, 71, 94, 122.

to leave the ranks of the guilty by obtaining YHWH's forgiveness and living a proper life. This is accomplished by threat, since those who do not repent will be destroyed in YHWH's judgment of the guilty, but those whom YHWH judges as righteous, including those forgiven by Him, will live in the redeemed Jerusalem. Thus, v. 2 – 31 are not only a trial genre, they function as an exhortation to the people to repent.

Finally, the superscription in 1, 1 introduces both v. 2 – 31 and the whole book of Isaiah. The structure of Isa 1 is as follows:

Exhortation to Repent	1, 1 – 31
I. Superscription	1
II. Exhortation Proper: Trial Genre	2 – 31
A. Speech of the accuser	2 – 20
1. announcement of YHWH's accusation against Israel	2 – 3
2. Admonition concerning continued wrongdoing	4 – 9
3. Prophetic Torah on proper service of YHWH	10 – 17
4. Appeal to begin legal proceeding	18 – 20
B. Speech of the Judge: Announcement of Zion's redemption	21 – 31
1. concerning the cleansing of Jerusalem: rehabilitation speech	21 – 26
2. explication: redemption for Zion's righteous and annihilation for her sinners	27 – 31

10. Redaction Analysis: Isaiah 1, 1 – 31

The above discussion has demonstrated that Isa 1 has a coherent structure and intent. The chapter is an exhortation to the people of Israel to repent, return to YHWH, and live their lives according to His requirements. Furthermore, the present form of the chapter in the context of the book as a whole, dates to the latter part of the fifth century and serves as the prologue to the book of Isaiah.[58] However, the questions of literary integrity and the time of composition still need to be addressed.

---

[58] There are a number of indications that this chapter addresses the situation of the post-exilic period. Certainly, the countryside was devastated and Jerusalem had been a besieged city (v. 7 – 8). Also, the people who survived could be described as a remnant (v. 9). There was some controversy over the resumption of the sacrificial cult and v. 10 – 17 would certainly address that problem. V. 27 refers to the redemption of Jerusalem which was taking place at that time with the cooperation of the Persian authorities. Also, $w^e\check{s}\bar{a}b\hat{e}h\bar{a}$ of v. 27 could certainly be taken to refer to the returning exiles (cf. LXX and TJ). Finally, the implication that cultic apostasy in the form of fertility cult worship led to the people's downfall corresponds to the explanation given by Jeremiah and the Deuteronomistic History, which were promulgated at this time.

Was the chapter written at the time and for the purposes identified above or was it written at some earlier time and for some other purpose? Was it written as a whole or is it a combination of elements, some older and reapplied to a new context, some specifically composed for their present literary setting?

There are a number of tensions and inconsistencies in this material which require explanation. Thus, v. 4 – 9 presuppose that a disaster has stricken the country. The land is desolate, the cities are burned, and foreigners are ravaging the countryside. V. 10 – 17 presuppose a prosperous, stable existence where the sacrificial cult operates to full capacity undisturbed. The people can hardly be expected to offer the sacrifices mentioned in these verses under the circumstances described in v. 4 – 9.[59] Indeed, the threat in v. 20 that the people may be devoured by the sword is really quite pointless when read together with v. 4 – 9.[60] Another point of discrepancy between these two sections is their understanding of Sodom and Gomorrah. In v. 9, the cities are mentioned in order to refer to their destruction but in v. 10, the reference is meant to call to mind their wickedness.[61] Furthermore, the reference to Sodom and Gomorrah in v. 10 is phrased so that both the leaders and the people of Israel are addressed and compared to these wicked cities. But v. 21 – 26, which correspond to v. 10 – 17 by presuming a stable political and economic situation, blame only the leaders for wrongdoing. All the people are addressed in v. 2 – 3 and 4 – 9. The oracle in v. 29 – 31 is a particularly obvious clue. It is concerned with cultic apostasy as a crime which the people have committed, yet it is clear throughout the rest of the passage that the prophet is concerned with social justice and moral behavior. Nowhere else in this chapter is he explicitly concerned with the people's participation in a fertility cult. In fact, these verses are somewhat of a surprise in chapter 1.

These tensions and inconsistencies suggest that Isa 1 was not entirely written or spoken at one time and for a single purpose. Rather, they indicate that the chapter is a composite work, including material from various times and written or spoken for various purposes. The next task will be to identify the various independent or authorial units of material

---

Note also that the rejection of cultic sacrifice and festival observance (v. 10 – 17) is an important part of the restoration program in Trito-Isaiah (Isa 65, 1 – 7; 66, 1 – 4).

[59] Willis argues that v. 10 – 17 can be understood in relation to the Assyrian invasion of 701 B.C.E. since ancient peoples increased their ritual practices in times of crisis in order to appease a deity [VT 34 (1984), 76]. This view is undermined, however, by the mention of new moons, Sabbaths, and festival assemblies in v. 13 f. These observances indicate a routine ritual program, not a time of crisis.

[60] Cf. J. Milgrom, VT 14 (1964), 174.

[61] Cf. Milgrom, VT 14 (1964), 174 f.

as well as the redactional material which was composed to fit the independent units into their present context. Furthermore, the dating of the materials, the situations for which they were created, and their intentions must be identified. In order to accomplish this, each sub-unit identified above must be studied in order to determine its date, setting, intention, and whether it was ever independent from the present context. This data will then be used to reconstruct the process and circumstances of the formation of this chapter.

a. Isa 1, 2 – 3

The above discussion noted the legal character of this unit, defining it as an accusation speech. Such a conclusion is supported by the call to Heaven and Earth, which usually serve as witnesses to a legal proceeding between YHWH and His people. It is also supported by its accusational nature, which would find its setting in a court of law.[62] There are wisdom elements in the unit, however. These include the use of father-son imagery, the comparison of the people's behavior with that of animals, and the introductory call to attention, which in many respects is similar to a call to instruction.[63] Nevertheless, this unit cannot be considered a wisdom speech. It uses wisdom elements, but only to further its legal purposes, i. e., placing an accusation against the people in a court of law.[64]

There is no reason to deny this passage to Isaiah. The use of parabolic imagery is one of his trademarks[65] as is his comparison of people with children.[66] Unfortunately, the passage provides practically no indication of the time of its composition. The crime of the people mentioned here, rebellion, is often considered as a political term as well as religious and could refer to the attempts to form a political alliance, either with the Assyrians against the Syro-Ephraimitic coalition or with the Egyptians against the Assyrians.[67] Both of these alliances were the objects of Isaiah's cirticism elsewhere.[68]

---

[62] Cf. Huffmon, JBL 78 (1959), 285 ff.

[63] On the father-son relationship, see Whedbee, Isaiah and Wisdom, 36 ff. On the parable, see Whedbee, Isaiah and Wisdom, 39 ff. On the call to instruction, see Wolff, Hosea, 97, but note Whedbee's warning that the wide use of this formula does not restrict it to wisdom settings (Isaiah and Wisdom, 29, n. 14).

[64] Note Deut 21, 18 – 21 in which a rebellious son can be taken to court by his father (Whedbee, Isaiah and Wisdom, 29).

[65] Cf. Isa 5, 1 – 7; 28, 23 – 29.

[66] Cf. Isa 29, 23; 30, 1; 30, 9.

[67] On the meaning of pš' as a political act of rebellion, see 2 Reg 8, 20.

[68] Cf. Isa 7 – 8; 18 – 19; 30, 1 – 7.

Determining whether the unit was at one time independent is problematic. Its purpose is clearly to announce to the people that they have committed a crime of rebellion, but it does not specify the rebellion. If this oracle was originally independent, the people who heard or read this oracle in its original setting would have little basis for understanding Isaiah's reference to rebellion. Because such a reference is not evident, the oracle was probably not independent. Instead, it is likely that it was composed in relation to another text, the most likely candidate being 1, 4 ff. Although v. 2 – 3 appear to have little explicit connection with the major concerns of v. 4 – 9, the two texts are associated by a number of underlying considerations. Both focus on "sons" and "offspring" in v. 2 and 4 as well as the general theme of ignorance which is explicitly mentioned in v. 3 and implied in v. 5. Furthermore, the theme of rebellion in v. 2 appears to be the underlying cause of the people's suffering according to v. 5. Finally, v. 3 indicates that YHWH is master of the people and v. 4 and 9 indicate that YHWH is master of the people in that their rejection of Him brought about their suffering. Consequently, 1, 2 – 3 appears to have been composed as an introduction to 1, 4 – 9. The date and circumstances of their composition must be determined in relation to v. 4 – 9.

b. Isa 1, 4 – 9

As noted above, this unit is a prophetic admonition which warns the people against continued rejection of YHWH. The prophet points to the destruction of the land which the people have already suffered to indicate to them that they should feel as if they have had enough. The prophet assumes in this unit that it is YHWH who has brought about this destruction. This connection is made in v. 5a in which the prophet ties together apostasy against YHWH with punishment. Part of his purpose would therefore be to make it clear to the people that the destruction is an act of YHWH meant to punish the people for forsaking Him.

The destruction described here corresponds to the circumstances that one would expect from Sennacherib's invasion of Judah and siege of Jerusalem in 701 B. C. E.[69] Sennacherib states in his report of this campaign that he ravaged the land of Judah, destroying forty-six cities as well as smaller villages. Furthermore, although he states that he laid siege to Jerusalem, he does not claim to have destroyed the city.[70] These claims correspond to the picture of v. 7 – 8 in which the countryside and its cities are desolate and Jerusalem is besieged, but not destroyed. The

---

[69] Cf. Wildberger, Jesaja 1 – 12, 20 f.; Clements, Isaiah 1 – 39, 30 f.

[70] ANET, 288.

original form of this oracle may therefore be dated to the aftermath of
Sennacherib's campaign in 701 B. C. E. The people apparently do not
believe that YHWH brought about the attack. Isaiah seeks to overcome
this disbelief in order to convince the people to return to YHWH. Such
a concern would correspond with v. 2 – 3 which stress the people's lack
of understanding.

A number of scholars have pointed out problems with v. 9 which
have led them to claim that it is a later redactional addition designed
to link v. 4 – 9 with v. 10 – 17.[71] The verse is styled as a first person
plural statement which is striking in a context that uses a second person
address. However, as noted above, the use of the first person plural is
a rhetorical device used by the prophet to include himself with the
audience and thus gain their sympathy. Furthermore, the progression
from land (v. 7) to Jerusalem (v. 8) to the people themselves (v. 9) focuses
the people's attention on their own suffering. This helps to support the
prophet's contention that they should accept YHWH and thus stop their
suffering. The prophet's use of the second person plural form of address
in previous verses of this unit is also understandable. By this means, he
focuses on the people's role in bringing about the disaster. He places
the blame squarely on them but in v. 9, he points out that he also suffers.
The use of the term *śārîd*, "remnant," to refer to the people left in the
city is generally taken as a reference to the survivors of the Babylonian
destruction of Jerusalem and therefore is used as another indication of
the verse's later date. Yet, such a position ignores the deaths that would
have occurred in the Assyrian assault and the captives that were taken
away to Nineveh. The entire countryside was destroyed and most of it
was stripped from Judah when it was made an Assyrian province. Only
Jerusalem and a small amount of territory remained. After the Assyrian
onslaught, the taking of captives, and the political reorganization, the
use of the term *śārîd* to refer to the people left in Jerusalem after 701
B. C. E. would be quite appropriate. Finally, the reference to Sodom and
Gomorrah was a common ploy used not only by Isaiah, but by Amos
and Hosea before him.[72] Furthermore, a different emphasis on the
Sodom/Gomorrah tradition does not entail different authorship. It was
common knowledge in ancient Israel that these cities were destroyed on
account of their wickedness so that both these themes, wickedness and
destruction, were closely linked in the Sodom/Gomorrah traditions. The
emphasis of one or the other merely serves the immediate purposes of
the author. Therefore, v. 9 was a part of the original oracle in v. 4 – 9.

---

[71] F. Crüsemann, Studien zur Formgeschichte von Hymnus und Danklied in Israel,
WMANT 32, 1969, 163 ff.; Barth, Die Jesaja-Worte, 190 f.

[72] Isa 1, 10; Am 4, 11; Hos 11, 18.

In making this claim, however, it must be recognized that the verse was subject to reinterpretation in light of the Babylonian destruction of Jerusalem. Furthermore, the mention of Sodom and Gomorrah lent itself to redactional combination with v. 10−17,[73] which certainly was written at another time and for another purpose.

c. Isa 1, 10−17

As noted above, the purpose of the prophetic Torah in v. 10−17 is to point out to the people the correct way to serve YHWH. YHWH neither requires nor requests cultic sacrifice and false festival observance. Instead, He requires righteousness and justice in the people.

The passage seems to presuppose a stable political situation and prosperous economic climate in which the cult could function regularly without interruption. Furthermore, there is no hint here that the country is in danger. The passage does emphasize the hypocrisy of the cultic observance, however, which suggests that the sacrifice is made for other purposes than the service of YHWH. Such a situation fits well with the early years of Hezekiah's reign when he instituted his cultic reforms.[74] It is evident from the later course of events that Hezekiah's reforms were not done simply for the sake of cultic service. Rather, they were the focal point of a nationalistic revival which served as the ideological basis for Hezekiah's revolt against Assyria. Isaiah was opposed to such a revolt and would have criticized the cultic reforms because their true purpose was to serve Hezekiah's plans for political rebellion.[75] Therefore, the original form of this passage dates to 715−701.

d. Isa 1, 18−20

As noted above, v. 18−20 are an appeal to begin a legal proceeding in which YHWH offers to forgive the transgressions of the people if they will repent.

There are some problems with the literary integrity of this passage. The structure analysis of this passage indicated two pairs of statements beginning with 'im in v. 18b and 19−20bα. These pairs, however, are

---

[73] Cf. Becker, Isaias, Der Prophet und sein Buch, 46; Jones, ZAW 67 (1955), 238 f. Both of these scholars assume a later date when claiming that the verse was created to serve the purposes of the redactor. However, the redactor does not need to write the verse in order to use it to link v. 4−9 to the following passage.

[74] On Hezekiah's reforms and his motivations for carrying them out, see the remarks by H. Donner in Israelite and Judaean History, ed. by J. Hayes and J. M. Miller, 1977, 442 ff.

[75] Cf. Isa 30, 1−7 which condemns the alliance between Judah and Egypt against the Assyrians.

not constructed similarly. The two statements in v. 18b both begin with *'im* and are parallel in content. The statements in v. 19 − 20bα also begin with *'im* but are connected by *waw*-conjunctive. Furthermore, they are antithetical statements.⁷⁶ In other words, these verses are formally different from the pair in v. 18b. Scholars have also noted the connections of v. 19 − 20bα with Deuteronomistic thought in that they specifically tie faithfulness to YHWH with reward and rebellion with punishment.⁷⁷ Likewise, the reward and punishment are expressed in terms of the people's enjoyment of the land, a typical Deuteronomistic theme. Finally, the statements of v. 19 − 20bα appear in a very similar form in Deut 1, 26 and 1 Sam 12, 14 − 15, both of which are included in the framework speeches which tie the Deuteronomistic History together. V. 19 − 20bα are therefore additions made by someone who was strongly influenced by the Deuteronomistic school.⁷⁸

V. 18 does not present such a problem, however. There is no reason to deny it to Isaiah.⁷⁹ However, it would be difficult to see this verse as an independent oracle. As noted above, it has connections with the preceding section. V. 18 focuses on the redness of sins and proposes that if the people arbitrate with YHWH, their sins will be forgiven. The image of red relates well with the imagery of sacrifice in v. 10 − 17, in that the blood of the sacrificial animals was red. Furthermore, in v. 15, the people are charged with having hands full of blood and in v. 18, YHWH offers to cleanse the redness of sins away. This offer is particularly significant when one considers that a major function of sacrifice was to cleanse a person of sin. When v. 18 is taken together with v. 10 − 17, it is clear that YHWH is offering an alternative to the people. He will cleanse them of their sins since the sacrifices will not do the job.⁸⁰ His conditions for doing so are stated in v. 16 − 17. Consequently, v. 18 must have originally belonged together with the Prophetic Torah of v. 10 − 17. V. 18 enables the prophet to drive home his point that only

---

⁷⁶ Scott, IB V, 174.
⁷⁷ Kaiser, Isaiah 1 − 12, 37; Vermeylen, Du prophète Isaïe, I 60 ff.
⁷⁸ Vermeylen, Du prophète Isaïe, I 60, n. 5, notes that the formula *kî pî yhwh dibber* is frequently used in Deuteronomistic literature.
⁷⁹ Vermeylen's word statistics can not be accepted as proof that Isaiah did not utter or write these words. (Cf. Du prophète Isaïe, I 58 ff.) Such a view presupposes a highly limited use of language within the various groups of ancient Israel.
⁸⁰ Note the sacrificial background of much of the terminology use here:
šānî/tôlā': Ex 25, 4; 26, 1, 31, 36; 27, 16; 28, 5, 6, 8, 15, 33; 35, 6, 23, 25, 35; 36, 8, 35, 37; 38, 18, 23; 39, 1, 2, 3, 5, 8, 24, 29; Lev 14, 4, 6, 49, 51, 52; Num 4, 8, 19, 16.
lbn: Ps 51, 9; Dan 11, 35; 12, 10.
'dm: Ex 25, 5; 26, 14; 35, 7, 23; 36, 19; 39, 34; *krt* 11, 62, 156.

reliance on YHWH will benefit the people. False cultic acts are a waste of time. This is consistent with Isaiah's political views that alliances will not save the country. Only reliance on YHWH will accomplish that.

e. Isa 1, 21 – 31

As noted above, v. 21 – 31 are an announcement of the redemption of Zion. However, in making this announcement, this unit makes it clear that the redemption of Zion will be accomplished only after the undesirable elements, those who forsake YHWH, are removed.

This is clearly a composite unit. The structure analysis of the passage noted that v. 29 – 31 do not have the same concerns as the rest of the unit. These verses emphasize that the sin of the people was cultic apostasy, specifically, their participation in a fertility cult which used oaks and gardens as symbols. The rest of the passage focuses on the people's practice of social injustice. Furthermore, the appearance of *yebošû* in v. 29 is the result of the redactional combination of these verses with the rest of the passage. The word should originally have read *tebošû* which would correspond with the second person style of the rest of the passage. But it was changed to the third person plural form *yebošû* so that it could refer to the parties mentioned in v. 27 – 28.[81] This oracle is not the work of Isaiah. He was concerned with political and social problems but not with cultic apostasy in and of itself. Rather, the concern with the people's apostasy in the practice of fertility cults was much more the concern of Jeremiah. While no specific prophet can be proved to be the author of this oracle, its concern with fertility cults does correspond well with Deuteronomistic ideology. It appears that the oracle stems from the late pre-exilic or exilic period and that it was written by an author with ties to Deuteronomistic ideology.

The structure analysis also noted that v. 21 – 26 are a self-contained oracle which is defined by the *inclusio*, *qiryâ næ'æmānâ*, in v. 21 and 26 as well as its chiastic pattern. There is no reason to deny this passage to Isaiah. The use of parabolic language (i. e., the foundry imagery) and the concern with corrupt leaders are typical of the prophet. The intention of the oracle was to condemn the leaders of the city for their corruption and announce that the city would be restored to its former state of righteousness after their removal. Such an oracle, with its charges of marketplace cheating, presupposes a time of peace and prosperity in which trade could be conducted without restriction. This situation fits

---

[81] Both LXX and TJ modify the person of verbs in this to eliminate the inconsistency. The appearance of *ky' ybwšw* in 1QIsa[a], however, indicates that the MT preserves the correct, but not the original, text.

the period after the fall of Samaria in 722 and before Hezekiah's revolt in 701.

This leaves v. 27 – 28. The structure analysis of this passage noted that these verses draw out the implications of the oracle in v. 21 – 26, but they are not an original part of the oracle due to its well-defined construction. Furthermore, the focus of these verses on the redemption of Zion is an indication of their post-exilic origin since this presupposes that the city had been cast away by YHWH and that redemption was a viable expectation. The reference to the "returners," whether they are understood as "repenters" or those returning from exile, calls to mind a typically Deuteronomistic theme.[82] Likewise, the reward of the righteous and the destruction of the wicked are typically Deuteronomistic. Consequently, these verses were written in the post-exilic period by an author heavily influenced by Deuteronomistic thought.

f. Redactional reconstruction: Isa 1, 1 – 31

The redactional analysis has thus far identified the following units, their authorship, and the dates of the their composition:

v. 2 – 9:   Isaiah, 701 B. C. E. or later
v. 10 – 18: Isaiah, 715 – 701 B. C. E.
v. 19 – 20: Deuteronomistic orientation, post-exilic period
v. 21 – 26: Isaiah, 722 – 701 B. C. E.
v. 27 – 28: Deuteronomistic orientation, post-exilic period
v. 29 – 31: Anonymous, late pre-exilic or exilic

It is striking that the various units of chapter 1 were written by Isaiah, an anonymous writer, or by a writer with a Deuteronomistic orientation. This suggests that the Deuteronomistically influenced writer was responsible for presenting this chapter in its present form. In order to determine the role of such a Deuteronomistically influenced writer in the formation of this chapter, the study must turn to the relationship of this writer's sections with those of Isaiah.

V. 19 – 20 appear at the end of a major unit of this chapter, the speech of the accuser in v. 2 – 20.[83] These verses draw out the theme of

---

[82] Cf. H. W. Wolff, The Kerygma of the Deuteronomic Historical Work, The Vitality of Old Testament Traditions, by W. Brueggemann and H. W. Wolff, 1976, 83 ff.

[83] W. Werner's view that 1, 2 – 3 and 1, 18 – 20 were composed as the redactional framework for 1, 2 – 20 must be rejected (Eschatologische Texte in Jesaja 1 – 39: Messias, Heiliger Rest, Völker. FZB 46, 1982, 128 ff.). Although both passages have a legal character and provide the boundaries of the speech of the accuser in 1, 2 – 20, there are no explicit literary or thematic indications that they were composed by the same hand. The phrase *kî pî yhwh dibber* in v. 20 appears to be modeled on *kî yhwh*

v. 18 by making sure that only those who accept YHWH will be forgiven of their transgressions. Those who do not, will suffer the consequences. Since v. 18 presupposes v. 10 – 17, it is clear that obedience or rejection in v. 19 – 20 is defined in terms of the instruction offered in v. 10 – 18. If the people obey YHWH's instructions in these verses, they will be forgiven, if not, they will suffer. It is interesting how the consequences of obedience or rejection are expressed, that is, in terms of eating. Thus, if the people obey, they will eat the good of the land. If they reject, they will be eaten by the sword. Such statements call to mind the picture of destruction in v. 4 – 9 in which foreigners were described as eating the land. As mentioned above, such a threat would hardly be useful in Isaiah's time since it had already taken place, but from the perspective of Deuteronomistic theology, the picture of destruction in v. 4 – 9 serves as a model by which to judge the people's disobedience to YHWH. If the people rebel, this is what will happen to them. In this manner, the statements in v. 19 – 20 serve as an explanation for the destruction portrayed in v. 4 – 9 which would be understood in reference to the Babylonian invasion. The people suffered because they rejected YHWH.[84] But the text also offers prosperity and good life to the people if they will obey YHWH. The question in v. 5, "Why would you be smitten again, that you continue apostasy?" allows for this offer. The offer of this alternative indicates that the Deuteronomistically oriented writer believed that the people had another chance. They could either repeat their former mistakes and suffer the consequences again, or they could reform themselves and live in peace. In this view, the people's second chance would have been their return to Jerusalem in the post-exilic period. Isaiah's oracles are used to warn the people of what might happen to them if they forsake YHWH again and instruct them in how to serve YHWH properly. The rest is up to them.

V. 27 – 28 follow the announcement of the cleansing of Jerusalem in v. 21 – 26. As noted above, they draw out the implications of v. 21 – 26 by stating that Jerusalem and her repentant people would be redeemed but that the wicked would be destroyed. These verses link v. 29 – 31 with v. 21 – 26 so that those who abandon YHWH are characterized as cultic apostates, a typical Deuteronomistic concern. Also noted were the connections of v. 27 – 28 with earlier parts of the chapter, especially v. 2 and 4. Using these links, v. 27 – 28 draw out the themes of earlier parts of the chapter. Zion, which was left alone and besieged (v. 8), will be redeemed when the people repent, i. e., when they take up YHWH's

---

dibber in v. 2 by the Deuteronomistically influenced writer of v. 19 – 20 who used this convention to bring vv. 2 – 9 and 10 – 18 together.

[84] This corresponds to the Deuteronomistic explanation for the fall of Jerusalem.

offer of forgiveness (v. 18 – 20) by fulfilling His conditions as stated in v. 10 – 17. The unrighteous, i. e., the rebels and forsakers of YHWH who do not take advantage of His instruction, will perish.

Finally, the superscription in 1, 1 appears to have some Deuteronomistic connections. Certainly, the mention of "Judah and Jerusalem" rather than the Isaianic order of Jerusalem/Judah is an indication of this verse's post-exilic origin. As Jones notes, this post-exilic formula for the Jerusalem-based Jewish community was favored in the Deuteronomistic History.[85] This and the concern with the kings of Judah in the verse have led a number of scholars to posit a Deuteronomistic origin for this verse.[86] Isa 1, 1 therefore belongs to the Deuteronomistically oriented redaction of chapter 1.

Thus, v. 27 – 28, with the aid of v. 19 – 20, tie the entire chapter together to form an exhortation to the people. By this means, the Deuteronomistically oriented writer related the oracles of Isaiah to the situation of the post-exilic period when the exiles were returning to rebuild Jerusalem. By claiming that Jerusalem and her repenters would be redeemed, the text encourages the people to make sure that they are among the righteous and not among the wicked who will perish. The oracles of Isaiah facilitated this by providing instruction in the proper way of returning to YHWH, i. e., how to be righteous, as well as examples of what will happen to the wicked. The result is an exhortation to the people to choose righteousness which now stands at the beginning of the book of Isaiah.

---

[85] ZAW 67 (1955), 239 f.
[86] Tucker, Prophetic Superscriptions, 69 f.; Kaiser, Isaiah 1 – 12, 1 f.; Vermeylen, Du prophète Isaïe, I 41 f.

B. ISAIAH 2−4

1. Demarcation of the Unit

Since the demarcation of Isa 2−4 has already been discussed in relation to the structure of the book as a whole, only a summary of those arguments need be presented here. The unit begins in 2, 1 with a superscription which identifies the following material as "the word which Isaiah ben Amoz saw concerning Judah and Jerusalem."[87] Chapters 2, 3, and 4 are all ultimately concerned with Judah and Jerusalem and, as will be seen from a structure analysis of these chapters, discuss the cleansing and restoration of Jerusalem and Judah so that Zion can serve as YHWH's capital for ruling the entire world. While the parable of the vineyard in 5, 1−7 refers to the men of Judah and Jerusalem, it is ultimately concerned with Judah and Israel (cf. Isa 5, 7). These considerations lead to the conclusion that chapters 2−4 form a self-contained unit, but final determination of this point depends on demonstrating that these chapters have a coherent structure and intent. Again, analysis must begin with the identification and analysis of the sub-units of chapters 2−4. Afterwards, they will be considered in relation to each other to determine whether they function together to create a coherent structure and intent for all of Isa 2−4.[88]

---

[87] On the basis of thematic similarities and a presupposition that oracles of promise should be appended to the various sub-collections of the book of Isaiah, Fohrer has suggested that 2, 1−5 actually forms the conclusion to Isa 1 [ALUOS 3 (1961), 365 f.]. This is unlikely, however, due to the superscription which occurs at 2, 1. According to standard Biblical and Near-eastern practice, such a superscription should appear at the beginning of a collection of materials, not within it (cf. Tucker, Prophetic Superscriptions, 57 f.). Ackroyd has attempted to eliminate this superscription by claiming that it is an insertion by a later hand who, noting the other occurrence of the following oracle (Isa 2, 2−4) in Mic 4, 1−4, attempted to claim Isaianic authorship for that oracle [ZAW 75 (1963), 320 f.; Cf. SVT 29 (1978), 32 ff.]. However, if 2, 1 was inserted specifically to refer to 2, 2−4, there would be no reason to claim that it is "the word which Isaiah ben Amoz saw concerning *Judah* and Jerusalem," since v. 2−4 have nothing to do with Judah. Rather, 2, 1 introduces a new unit, separate from chapter 1.

[88] By employing modern theories of linguistic text interpretation, B. Wiklander has already attempted to determine the structure, genre, setting, and intent of Isa 2−4 (Prophecy as Literature: A Text-Linguistic and Rhetorical Approach to Isaiah 2−4. CBOTS 22. 1984). He argues that Isa 2−4 is a "restoration of the covenant by means

2. Isaiah 2, 1

This verse is a superscription which stands apart from the material which it introduces.[89] As noted above, it mentions Judah and Jerusalem which indicates that it does not relate solely to the Jerusalem-oriented unit in v. 2 – 4 but to the following material as well. Isa 2, 1 therefore constitutes the first sub-unit of Isa 2, 1 – 4, 6.

3. Isaiah 2, 2 – 4

Scholars generally agree that v. 2 – 4 belong together but they disagree on the relation of v. 5 to this unit. Some favor ending the unit with v. 4 and view v. 5 as an editorial link with the oracle beginning in v. 6.[90] Others see v. 5 as an editorial link with v. 6 ff. but end the unit with v. 5.[91] Still others see v. 2 – 5 as a distinct unit unto itself.[92] Finally, at least one scholar views chapter 2 as a unified composition and avoids dividing it into units.[93]

Isa 2, 5 seems to have been formed with v. 3 as a model which might indicate that it belongs with v. 2 – 4 as a unit.[94] There is a similar

of prophetic revelation" (p. 219). The text was composed ca. 734 – 622 B. C. E. by an author who attempted to convince his audience to give up a vassal relationship with a foreign power in order to return to the covenant of YHWH (p. 181 ff.). Although Wiklander's approach is theoretically sound, the execution of his study suffers from his assumption that "covenant" and "treaty" operate as the underlying concepts of this text (p. 112). According to Wiklander, these concepts were often metaphorically expressed by the author. This assumption leads him to a number of questionable semantic, generic, and historical conclusions which are often forced to fit this covenant concept.

[89] Tucker, Prophetic Superscriptions, 57 f.

[90] Duhm, Das Buch Jesaia, 36, 39; Gray, Isaiah I – XXVII, 40 f.; K. Budde, ZAW 49 (1931), 182 ff., 188; R. B. Y. Scott, The Literary Structure of Isaiah's Oracles, Studies in Old Testament Prophecy, ed. H. H. Rowley, 1957, 183; Skinner, Isaiah I – XXXIX, 13 – 15, 17.

[91] H. Junker, Sancta Civitas, Jerusalem Nova, Ekklesia: Festschrift für Bischof Dr. Matthias Wehr, TThS 15, 1962, 19 ff., 25; Wildberger, Jesaja 1 – 12, 77 f.; Kaiser, Isaiah 1 – 12, 52, 56.

[92] Scott, IB V, 180, 182; Fohrer, Das Buch Jesaja, I 47 f.; Vermeylen, Du prophète Isaïe, I 131 (he sees v. 5 as a late addition); Clements, Isaiah 1 – 39, 39 f., 42 (v. 5 is late); Procksch, Jesaia I, 61 f., 63; Marti, Jesaja, 24, 27 (v. 5 is late); H. Cazelles, VT 30 (1980), 409 ff.

[93] Kissane, The Book of Isaiah, I 21 f. He seems to assume that v. 2 – 5 are a sub-section of the chapter [cf. p. 22, section b)].

[94] Cf. Vermeylen, Du prophète Isaïe, I 131. Scott, IB V, 182, claims that it is a textual variant of v. 3.

syntactic arrangement of imperative verb, *waw*-consecutive, and first person plural imperfect verb in v. 3 and 5 (i. e., *lᵉkû wᵉna'ᵃlæh* in v. 3 and *lᵉkû wᵉnelᵉkâ* in v. 5). Furthermore, there is a correspondence in that *lᵉkû* occurs in both v. 3 and 5 as does *wᵉnelᵉkâ*. The verbs *lᵉkû* and *wᵉnelᵉkâ*, which are the first and last verbs spoken by the nations in v. 3, enclose their proposal to go to Zion. The occurrence of these verbs at the beginning of v. 5 in a statement directed to the House of Jacob implies that Israel (i. e., the House of Jacob) should go and do like the nations mentioned in v. 3.

In spite of the modeling of v. 5 on v. 3, there are a number of reasons for considering v. 5 to be structurally separate from v. 2 − 4. First, there is no syntactic connection between v. 4 and 5. Second, the verbs in v. 5 indicate a perspective different from that of v. 2 − 4. The verb *lᵉkû* in v. 5 is imperative and addresses the House of Jacob. Likewise, *wᵉnelᵉkâ* specifically addresses the House of Jacob. The constitutive verbs of v. 2 − 4, on the other hand, are imperfects or converted perfects which report actions and do not presuppose any particular audience. Finally, v. 6 begins with *kî*, which syntactically links v. 5 and 6 together. Thus, Isa 2, 2 − 4 must be a unit separate from v. 5 since, syntactically, v. 5 belongs with v. 6 ff. and since v. 2 − 4 have a perspective different from that of v. 5.[95]

The first main unit of v. 2 − 4 is v. 2 − 3a whose governing verbs constitute a *waw*-consecutive verbal formation. Syntactically, *nākôn yihyæh* is the basis from which the converted perfect verbs, *wᵉniśśā'*, *wᵉnāhᵃrû*, *wᵉhālᵉkû*, and *wᵉ'āmᵉrû* proceed.[96] All other statements or phrases in v. 2 − 3a are in some manner subordinate to this *waw*-consecutive formation. Thus, v. 2aα¹ is a temporal clause subordinate to the statement in v. 2aα². Likewise, the statements in v. 3aα²ᵇ⁻ᶠ+β+γ constitute the speech made by the nations and as such, are all subordinate to *wᵉ'āmᵉrû* in v. 3aα²ᵃ.

Within v. 2 − 3a is a basic division among its governing verbs. Thus, *nākôn yihyæh* and *wᵉniśśā'* are third person masculine singular and have *har bêt yhwh* as their subject so that v. 2aα and 2aβ are two statements

---

[95] The Masoretes also recognized a distinction between v. 2 − 4 and v. 5 in that they placed a *petuḥah* after v. 4. The *petuḥah*, "open section," indicates a paragraph division in Scripture which begins with a new indented line. This is in contrast to a *setumah*, "closed section," which indicates a Scripture paragraph separated from the preceding section by a vacant space in the same line (cf. C. D. Ginsberg, Introduction to the Massoretico − Critical Edition of the Hebrew Bible, 1966, 9 ff.). The closed sections indicate divisions that are of lesser importance than those indicated by the open sections.

[96] Cf. Gesenius, Kautzsch, Cowley, Gesenius' Hebrew Grammar, 1974, sec. 112a; A. B. Davidson, Hebrew Syntax, 1976, sec. 72.

which describe the elevation of Zion. The governing verbs of v. 2b – 3a, $w^e n\bar{a}h^a r\hat{u}$, $w^e h\bar{a}l^e k\hat{u}$, and $w^e {}^{\,\flat} \bar{a}m^e r\hat{u}$, are all third person plural with either $k\dot{a}l\ hagg\acute{o}yim$ or ${}^{\flat}amm\hat{i}m\ rabb\hat{i}m$ as their subjects. Thus, the statements in v. 2b – 3a describe actions on the part of the nations who react to the elevation of Zion.

Within v. 2b – 3a are two parallel statements in v. 2b and $3a\alpha^1$ which state that the nations come to Zion. V. $3a\alpha^{2+3}+\beta+\gamma$, on the other hand, states what the nations say in reaction to Zion's elevation. Following the speaking formula, $w^e {}^{\,\flat} \bar{a}m^e r\hat{u}$, in v. $3a\alpha^{2a}$, is their speech in v. $3a\alpha^{2b-f+3}+\beta+\gamma$. The speech contains a proposal to go up to the mountain, Zion, in v. $3a\alpha^{2b-f+3}$ as well as the purpose for going up in v. $3a\beta+\gamma$. The purpose is so that YHWH will teach the people His ways (v. $3a\beta$) with the result that the people will learn them (v. $3a\gamma$). Thus, v. 2 – 3a describe Zion's future establishment as the locus of YHWH's rule over the world in both its cosmological dimensions (v. 2a, elevation of Zion) and its social/political dimensions (v. 2b – 3a, the nations' pilgrimage to Zion).

The second major division of v. 2 – 4 begins with v. 3b which is not a part of the *waw*-consecutive sequence of verbs observed in v. 2 – 3a. Instead, it includes the simple imperfect verb, $te\d{s}e^{\flat}$, and is introduced by a causal $k\hat{i}$.[97] This $k\hat{i}$ indicates a syntactic connection with the material which precedes. V. 3b, however, is not a part of the nations' speech. The speech has first person plural perspective which is not evident in v. 3b. Rather, the $k\hat{i}$ provides the connection with v. 2 – 3a as a whole, indicating that v. 3b provides a basis or explanation for the establishment of Zion and the pilgrimage of the peoples described in v. 2 – 3a. Furthermore, v. 4 follows logically from v. 3b and not from v. 2 – 3a in that YHWH's judgment and arbitration stem not from the elevation of Zion or the peoples' coming there, but from His instruction or Torah which is mentioned in v. 3b. This instruction provides the principles of judgment and arbitration presupposed by the statements of v. 4. Thus, v. 3b – 4 consist of two parts. V. 3b states the basic reason for Zion's establishment as the location of YHWH's world rule, so that His Torah and His word may go forth from Jerusalem. V. 4 discusses the consequences or results of YHWH's Torah going out from Zion. V. 4a describes YHWH's actions of judgment (v. $4a\alpha$) and arbitration (v. $4a\beta$) which are based in His Torah. V. $4b\alpha$ discusses the peoples' reaction to YHWH's judgment and arbitration, they will convert their weapons to agricultural tools. The result of this disarmament appears in v. $4b\beta$. The nations will not attack each other (v. $4b\beta^1$) nor will they learn the art of war (v. $4b\beta^2$). Thus, v. 3b – 4 provide the reason for Zion's establishment

---

[97] Gesenius, sec. 158 b.

which was mentioned in v. 2 – 3a as well as the consequences or results which could be expected from that establishment.

Generically, these verses may be labeled as a prophecy of salvation[98] or more specifically, a prophetic announcement concerning the future establishment of Zion as the location of YHWH's world rule. The structure is as follows:

Prophetic Announcement Concerning the Future Establishment of Zion as the Locus for YHWH's World Rule	2, 2 – 4
I. Concerning the Fact of Zion's Establishment	2 – 3a
A. Cosmological dimension: Elevation of Zion	2a
1. first statement	$2a\alpha$
a. time of elevation: latter days	$2a\alpha^1$
b. statement proper	$2a\alpha^2$
2. second statement	$2a\beta$
B. Social/Political dimension: Nations' pilgrimage to Zion	2b – 3a
1. they come	$2b – 3a\alpha^1$
a. nations	2b
b. many peoples	$3a\alpha^1$
2. they speak	$3a\alpha^{2+3}+\beta+\gamma$
a. speaking formula	$3a\alpha^{2a}$
b. speech by nations	$3a\alpha^{2b-f+3}+\beta+\gamma$
1) proposal to go up to Zion	$3a\alpha^{2b-f+3}$
2) purpose of proposal	$3a\beta+\gamma$
a) YHWH's instruction	$3a\beta$
b) nations' learning	$3a\gamma$
II. Concerning the Reason for Zion's Establishment	3b – 4
A. Reason proper: YHWH's Torah	3b
1. Torah	$3b\alpha$
2. word of YHWH	$3b\beta$
B. Consequences/Results	4
1. YHWH's action: judgment and arbitration	4a
a. judgment	$4a\alpha$
b. arbitration	$4a\beta$
2. peoples' reaction: conversion of weapons to farm tools	$4b\alpha$
3. result: no war	$4b\beta$
a. nations not lift sword	$4b\beta^1$
b. nations not learn war	$4b\beta^2$

4. Isaiah 2, 5

This verse is an invitation to Jacob to join with YHWH. As stated above, the verse is syntactically separated from v. 2 – 4, yet it is clearly

---

[98] Kaiser, Isaiah 1 – 12, 49, labels the unit as "description of salvation" (*Heilschilderung*). Wildberger, Jesaja 1 – 12, 78, and Fohrer, Das Buch Jesaja, I 47, label it *Verheissungswort*.

composed with those verses as a model. Furthermore, it is linked syntactically to v. 6 by an adversative *kî*[99] which relates the antithesis to the
implied joining of Jacob with YHWH in v. 5 (i. e., YHWH's rejection
of Jacob in v. 6–22). This indicates that structurally, v. 5 belongs with
v. 6–22. Its relation to v. 2–4, however, indicates that it is a connecting
verse designed to link v. 2–4 and 6–22. Before final conclusions can
be made, however, the unit beginning with v. 6 must first be studied to
determine its function.

5. *Isaiah 2, 6–22*

As stated above, v. 6 is connected to v. 5 by *kî*, yet the two verses
have little in common with respect to content. Both deal with the House
of Jacob but v. 5, with its imperative and first person plural imperfect
verbs, is a vocative address to the House of Jacob. V. 6, on the other
hand, with its second person singular perfect verb, is addressed to
YHWH since *bêt ya'ᵃqob* is an accusative which specifies *'ammᵉkā*.
Furthermore, v. 5 invites Jacob into YHWH's good graces but v. 6 begins
a section dealing with YHWH's rejection of Jacob. The theme of
rejection, and consequently judgment, continues at least through v. 22
which pleads for an end to the judgment. The theme of judgment is also
found beginning in 3, 1 which is joined to 2, 6–22 by *kî*. In chapter 3,
however, Judah and Jerusalem are concerned whereas in chapter 2, the
House of Jacob or *'ādām/'ᵃnāšîm* are involved. Thus, on the grounds
of theme and subject, 2, 6–22 should for the present be regarded as a
unit separate from the preceding v. 5 and the following unit beginning
in 3, 1. Certainly, these units are connected syntactically to 2, 6–22 by
kî in v. 6 and 3, 1, but a discussion of their interrelationships must be
postponed.

In order to discuss the structure of this section, it is first necessary
to take up two textual problems in v. 6a and 9b. Their resolution is
crucial to the understanding of the structure of this text.

In v. 6a, MT reads *kî nāṭaštā 'ammᵉkā bêt ya'aqob*, "For You have
rejected your people, the House of Jacob." The LXX, however, reads
aneken gar ton laon autou ton oikon tou Israel, "for He rejected His
people, the House of Israel." Many commentators have emended this
text, accepting the LXX as the preferred reading since the third person
singular verb fits easily into the third person context of the rest of the
passage.[100] Others emend the verb to third person, but view *bêt ya'ᵃqob*

---

[99] Cf. Gesenius, sec. 163b.
[100] Gray, Isaiah I–XXVII, 57, wavers (cf. p. 52); Duhm, Das Buch Jesaia, 39; Budde,
ZAW 49 (1931), 191.

as the subject of the verb.[101] TJ, however, reads *'arê š*ᵉ*baqtûn dah*ᵃ*lā' taqîpā' dah*ᵃ*wa p*ᵉ*rîq l*ᵉ*kôn d*ᵉ*bêt ya'ᵃqōb*, "For you (pl.) have forsaken the fear of the Protector which is apportioned to you, O people of the House of Jacob." This involves only a very slight textual change, reading the second person singular verb of the MT as a second person plural. Also, *bêt ya'ᵃqob* is read as a vocative instead of an accusative. This reveals the central problem at hand. In MT, *bêt ya'ᵃqob* in v. 6a can function either as an accusative, which appositionally defines *'amm*ᵉ*kā*, or as a vocative. The consonantal text gives no clue as to which is the proper reading. The LXX opted for an accusative understanding and changed the verb to third person singular to accommodate that understanding and to remove the possibility of any other. TJ opted for a vocative reading and changed the verb to second person plural for similar reasons. Both LXX and TJ are merely trying to make sense out of an ambiguous Hebrew text. Thus, the text presupposed by MT should not be emended.[102] Furthermore, *bêt ya'ᵃqob* is best viewed as an accusative there, appositionally defining *'amm*ᵉ*kā*. A vocative understanding would require that the "you" of v. 6a refers to *bêt ya'ᵃqob* in the third person. The resulting shift from the second person perspective in v. 6a to the third person perspective of *bêt ya'ᵃqob* in v. 6b – 9a would be awkward. An accusative understanding of *bêt ya'ᵃqob* in v. 6a, however, would present no such problem since "you" in v. 6a would refer to YHWH and the third person references to *bêt ya'ᵃqob* in v. 6b – 9a would easily be understood as part of a statement describing Jacob's situation to YHWH who is addressed in v. 6a.

In v. 9b, MT reads *w*ᵉ*'al tiśśā' lahæm*, "and You shall not raise (i. e., pardon) them." LXX reads *kai ou me aneso autous*, "and I will not let them be," but this is just a reflex of the exegetical decision made in v. 6a. That LXX understands v. 9b in relation to v. 6a is evident from its use of the verb *aniemi* in both instances.[103] Changing from the second person perspective of v. 6a required changing the second person perspective of v. 9b, again to avoid the confusion of determining who the "you" is. By changing "you" to "I," LXX clearly identifies the subject of *nś'* in v. 9b as YHWH. At the same time, it transforms v. 6b – 9b into a speech by YHWH, introduced by v. 6a, which relates His reasons for punishing Jacob. Thus, LXX presupposes the consonantal text found in MT, but reinterprets it.[104]

---

[101] Scott, IB V, 183; Kissane, The Book of Isaiah, I 27 f.

[102] Note that the Peshitta and Vulgate follow the MT (cf. Wildberger, Jesaja 1 – 12, 92).

[103] The LXX apparently binds these two verses together through a word play on the meaning of this verb. Thus, "he has left (forsaken) them" in v. 6a and "I will not leave (pardon) them" in v. 9b.

[104] Another reason for this change would be that the second person form is a command directed to YHWH, which the LXX translator would have found theologically offensive (cf. E. Tov, IDB[S], 810, sec. b. i.).

1QIsa[a] omits v. 9b entirely along with v. 10. This supports scholars who claim that v. 9b is a marginal gloss.[105] A closer look at the text of 1QIsa[a], however, reveals that it had a purpose for this elimination. The scroll reads 2, 3 as follows: *lkw wn'lh 'l byt 'lhy y'qb wyrwnw mdrkyw,* "Come, and let us go up to the House of the God of Jacob and they shall teach us His ways." It eliminates *'æl har yhwh* and changes the third person masculine singular verb *weyorenû* to the plural *weyorûnû.* "They" here refers to the people or priests of Jacob who will teach YHWH's ways to the nations.[106] V. 9b – 10 imply that Jacob has sinned and should hide but these words are eliminated in 1QIsa[a]. This leaves the whole oracle, v. 6 – 22, directed against *'anāšîm/'ādām* which the Qumran sect would have identified with the nations. One might object, however, that v. 6a prevents such an interpretation since it states that Jacob has been rejected.[107] This is true if *bêt ya'aqob* is read as an accusative, but it can also be vocative as noted above. If this is the case, then v. 6a is addressed to Jacob and states that Jacob has rejected his people (i. e., the nations) which it was supposed to teach (v. 3). Jacob rejected them because of their corruption (v. 6b – 9a) and their corruption requires a future judgment by YHWH (v. 11 – 21). Such a conception of the mission of Jacob (Israel) and its subsequent failure corresponds well with the beliefs of the Qumran sect. 1QIsa[a], therefore, does not represent a true alternative to the Hebrew text presupposed by MT. It is merely the result of an interpretation of that text with respect to the ideology of the Qumran community.[108]

The versions offer no real alternative to the MT reading.[109] Yet critics have seen a problem here in that the MT of v. 9b, with its second person address and imperfect verb form, does not seem to fit into the context of v. 6b – 9a. This has caused many of them to emend the text,[110] but this problem is contrived. V. 6a and 9b form the boundaries of a sub-unit, v. 6 – 9. With their second person address form, they indicate that the whole sub-unit is a statement directed to YHWH. V. 6b – 9a are in third person form, but they provide the reason why YHWH rejected His people and why He should not pardon them. Thus, the sub-unit v. 6 – 9 is an address directed by the prophet to YHWH.

---

[105] E. g., Wildberger, Jesaja 1 – 12, 94.

[106] Brownlee, The Meaning of the Qumran Scrolls, 157.

[107] 1QIsa[a] has the same consonantal text for v. 6a as MT.

[108] Cf. G. Vermes, The Dead Sea Scrolls: Qumran in Perspective, 1978, 163 ff., esp. sections 1, 2, and 4.

[109] TJ reads *welā' tišbûq lehôn,* which is a direct translation of the Hebrew as in MT.

[110] Duhm, Das Buch Jesaia, 41; Kissane, The Book of Isaiah, I 25, 29; Gray, Isaiah I – XXVII, 59; Scott, IB, V 184.

Because v. 6aα and 9b are second person addresses whereas v. 6aβ – 9a have a third person perspective, one might conclude that the unit should be divided into three parts. There are other considerations, however. Certainly, the *kî* in v. 6aβ + b is causative since it introduces an explanation of the reasons for YHWH's rejection of Jacob mentioned in v. 6aα. Thus, there is a connection between v. 6aα and 6aβ + b. Furthermore, the statement in v. 6aβ + b is linked to verses 7 – 8a by *waw*. There is a syntactic break at v. 8b since there is no copulative but this statement[111] merely relates the significance of the preceding. It is, therefore, part of the explanation of YHWH's reasons for rejecting Jacob. V. 9a is linked to v. 8b by *waw* and spells out the moral consequences for man of the action related in v. 8b. Although v. 9b is linked to v. 9a by *waw*, it can not be considered as part of the explanation of YHWH's reasons for rejecting Jacob. Instead, it is a petition to YHWH not to pardon the people. Thus, there are two main sections in v. 6 – 9. V. 6 – 9a are an address to YHWH stating His rejection of the House of Jacob (v. 6aα) and His reasons for rejecting them (v. 6aβ – 9a). V. 9b is a petition to YHWH that He not forgive them.

The syntactic break at v. 8b indicates that the explanation for YHWH's rejection of the House of Jacob in v. 6aβ – 9a consists of two parts, v. 6aβ – 8a, which discuss the corruption of the land with false gods, and v. 8b – 9a, which discuss the corruption of the people with false gods. This division is also supported by the parallel content of the two sections. Within v. 6aβ – 8a, v. 6aβ + b is formulated with third person plural verbs which describe the people's practices, i. e., they are full of diviners (v. 6aβ) and they associate themselves with foreigners (v. 6b). V. 7 – 8a, which are formulated with third person singular verbs, describe the resulting situation of the land, i. e., it is full of war equipment (v. 7b), and it is full of false gods (v. 8a). Within v. 8b – 9a, v. 8b discusses the people's practices, i. e., their idol worship and v. 9a describes the situation of the people resulting from such action, i. e., they are abased.

Generically, v. 6 – 9 initially appear to be the indictment or accusation speech from a prophetic judgment speech. This speech is directed to YHWH, however, explaining to Him the wrongdoings of Jacob which led to His rejection of the people. But YHWH hardly needs to be informed of this. The prophet's petition not to forgive the people in v. 9b suggests that v. 6 – 9 are an acknowledgement of the people's guilt and YHWH's right to reject them. The structure of this sub-unit is as follows:

---

[111] Grammatically, v. 8bα and v. 8bβ constitute one sentence. Although v. 8bβ contains the verb *ʾāśû*, it is a nominal clause parallel to *lᵉmaʿᵃśæh yādâw* in v. 8bα. The verb *yištaḥᵃwû* governs the two parallel clauses, both of which serve as objects to *yištaḥᵃwû*.

Beginning in v. 10 is an address directed not to YHWH, but to the people. This is indicated by the imperative verbs which introduce the sub-unit in v. 10 and the third person references to YHWH throughout. The sub-unit continues until v. 22 which contains another address directed to YHWH.

The sub-unit begins with an announcement of the coming punishment of the people and the corresponding exaltation of YHWH in v. 10 – 11. These are followed by an elaboration in v. 12 – 21 which are connected to v. 10 – 11 by an explanatory *kî*. The announcement in v. 10 – 11 consists of two parts. The first is v. 10 which contains a two-fold command to hide in v. 10a expressed with imperative verbs and a two-fold explanation of what to hide from, i. e., YHWH's "fear" and "splendid might" in v. 10b. The second part of the announcement provides the explanation for the command to hide, i. e., YHWH's exaltation. This is stated from two perspectives, the humiliation of man in a two-fold statement (v. 11a) and the exaltation of YHWH in v. 11b. Thus, it is clear that the exaltation of YHWH represents a threat to man.

V. 12 – 21 elaborate on the announcement in v. 10 – 11 by explaining man's humiliation and YHWH's exaltation in terms of the Day of YHWH.[112] The unit breaks down into two parts. V. 12 – 19, which are linked together by conjunctive *waw*'s, discuss the characterization of the Day of YHWH as against all the symbols of pride, highness, arrogance, etc. V. 20 – 21, introduced by the formula, *bayyôm hahû'*, describe the

---

[112] On the Day of YHWH, see Everson, IDB[S], 209, and the literature cited there, esp. G. von Rad, Old Testament Theology, II 119 ff., and L. Černý, The Day of YHWH and Some Relevant Problems, 1948.

results of this day for mankind, i. e., YHWH's assault on man's physical symbols of pride leads to the abandonment of those symbols before the terror of YHWH who is portrayed as the true source of power.

V. 12 – 19 consist of two parts. V. 12 is a basic statement concerning the characterization of the Day of YHWH and its consequences. V. 12a + bα is a two-fold statement of what the day is against, i. e., pride and arrogance (v. 12a) and all that is uplifted (v. 12bα). V. 12bβ is a basic statement of consequences, i. e., it shall fall. A specification of the meaning of these two basic aspects follows in v. 13 – 19. V. 13 – 16 correspond to v. 12a + bα and describe in detail that which is proud, high, and lifted up. The contents of v. 13 – 16 are categorized as follows: v. 13 includes trees consisting of the Cedars of Lebanon (v. 13a) and the oaks of Bashan (v. 13b); v. 14 includes mountains which consist of alps (v. 14a) and hills (v. 14b); v. 15 includes fortifications which consist of towers (v. 15a) and walls (v. 15b); v. 16 includes boats consisting of the ships of Tarshish (v. 16a) and the beautiful craft (v. 16b). Thus, v. 13 – 16 are a catalogue of what the Day of YHWH is against. V. 17 – 19 specify the meaning of the consequence, $w^e \check{s} \bar{a} pel$, in v. 12bβ. V. 17 first states the consequences generally in terms of the humiliation of man (v. 17a, a two-fold statement) and the exaltation of YHWH (v. 17b). V. 18 – 19 explicate v. 17 in relation to false gods. V. 18 states YHWH's actions against the false gods and v. 19 states the reaction of the false gods to YHWH, i. e., they will hide.

Because this section consists of an announcement to the people of coming punishment in the form of the Day of YHWH and an elaboration which explains that announcement, the unit may be labeled as a Prophetic Announcement of the Day of YHWH. Its structure is as follows:

Prophetic Announcement of the Day of YHWH	10 – 21
I. Announcement Proper	10 – 11
A. Command to hide	10
1. command proper	10a
a. enter rocks	10aα
b. hide in dust	10aβ
2. what to hide from	10b
a. fear of YHWH	10bα
b. His splendid might	10bβ
B. Reason for command: YHWH's exaltation	11
1. humiliation of man	11a
a. proud eyes fallen	11aα
b. haughtiness brought low	11aβ
2. exaltation of YHWH	11b
II. Elaboration concerning the Day of YHWH	12 – 21
A. Concerning the Day of YHWH: Characterization and consequences	12 – 19

The third major section of v. 6 – 22 is v. 22. This verse appears to be a wisdom saying which instructs the reader to avoid reliance on man.[113] Such a saying is quite appropriate following the Day of YHWH oracle which stresses the power of God over that of man. This verse appears to be a very late addition as it is missing from LXX. It consists of two parts. V. 22a, which contains a plural imperative verb, is the instruction of the wisdom saying. V. 22b, connected to v. 22a by an explanatory *kî*, is a rhetorical question, a typical wisdom device, which

---

[113] Cf. Ps 118, 8 – 9; Isa 31, 1 – 3; 1QS 5, 17.

provides the reason for desisting from man. Man is mortal, unlike God, and is therefore not to be relied on. The structure of v. 22 is as follows:

I. Instruction   22a

II. Reason for Instruction   22b

The above discussion indicates a three-part structure for Isa 2, 6—22, with the parts differentiated by their addressees. V. 6—9, addressed to YHWH, are a prophetic acknowledgement of the people's guilt. V. 10—21, addressed to the people, are an announcement of the Day of YHWH, a day of coming punishment. V. 22, addressed to the reader, is a wisdom saying which instructs the reader not to rely on men. Generically, the passage seems to be based on a prophecy of judgment,[114] in that v. 6—9 are very similar to an accusation speech and v. 10—21 are an announcement of judgment. However, the form has been modified by the statements directing portions of the unit to YHWH. Here, the prophet speaks to both YHWH and the people as mediator. But this is still ultimately addressed to the people, since the prophet need not inform YHWH of His rejection of Jacob and His reasons for doing so. The passage explains to the people the need for their punishment and the need for YHWH's intervention in the form of the Day of YHWH. V. 20—21 make it clear, however, that this is intended as a "cleansing" operation, designed to get rid of the corrupting false gods. It is not intended to destroy Jacob, but serve as a lesson to him (cf. v. 22). Therefore, the passage may be labeled as a Prophetic Acknowledgement of the Need for Cleansing Punishment. The superstructure is as follows:

Prophetic Announcement of the Need for Cleansing Punishment
for Jacob   2, 6—22

   I. Acknowledgement of the People's Guilt   6—9

   II. Announcement of the Day of YHWH: Day of Coming
      Punishment   10—21

   III. Wisdom Saying to Desist from Reliance on Man   22

6. Isaiah 3, 1—4, 6

Isa 3, 1 begins with *kî* which ties the following verses to the preceding material (cf. 2, 6). But Isa 3, 1 also states that the passage is concerned with Jerusalem and Judah, whereas the preceding material

[114] Cf. Wildberger, Jesaja 1—12, 96, who labels this section *Predigtähnliche Drohrede* and Fohrer, Das Buch Jesaja, I 54, who labels it *scheltende und drohende Worte*.

dealt with *bêt ya'ᵃqob* and *'ᵃnāšim/'ādām*. While concern with Judah falls into the background, an interest in Jerusalem extends from 3, 1 to 4, 6. There is a distinction within this section, however, in that 3, 1 – 4, 1 deals with judgment against Jerusalem and Judah whereas 4, 2 – 6 describes coming blessing for Jerusalem. Unfortunately, there is a great deal of disagreement among scholars concerning the identification of the various sub-units of 3, 1 – 4, 1 and their interrelations with each other and with 4, 2 – 6. The following outline of scholarly opinions on this matter should illustrate the difficulty:

1) Wildberger[115]
   a) 3, 1 – 11
      i. 3, 1 – 9a
      ii. 3, 9b – 11
   b) 3, 12
   c) 3, 13 – 15
   d) 3, 16 – 24
   e) 3, 25 – 4, 1
   f) 4, 2 – 6

2) Kaiser[116]
   a) 3, 1 – 11
      i. 3, 1 – 9a
      ii. 3, 9b – 11
   b) 3, 12 – 15
      i. 3, 12
      ii. 3, 13 – 15
   c) 3, 16 – 24
   d) 3, 25 – 4, 1
   e) 4, 2 – 6

3) Vermeylen[117]
   a) 3, 1 – 11
   b) 3, 12 – 15
   c) 3, 16 – 24
   d) 3, 25 – 4, 1
   e) 4, 2 – 6

4) Clements[118]
   a) 3, 1 – 12
   b) 3, 13 – 15
   c) 3, 16 – 24
   d) 3, 25 – 4, 1
   e) 4, 2 – 6

5) Fohrer[119]
   a) 3, 1 – 9
   b) 3, 10 – 11
   c) 3, 12 – 15
   d) 3, 16 – 24
   e) 3, 25 – 4, 1
   f) 4, 2 – 6

6) Duhm[120]
   a) 3, 1 – 12
   b) 3, 13 – 15
   c) 3, 16 – 4, 1
   d) 4, 2 – 6

7) Gray[121]
   a) 3, 1 – 12
   b) 3, 13 – 15

8) Scott[122]
   a) 3, 1 – 15
   b) 3, 16 – 4, 1

---

[115] Jesaja 1 – 12, 116 ff.
[117] Du prophète Isaïe, I 144 ff.
[119] Das Buch Jesaja, I 58 ff.
[121] Isaiah I – XXVII, 60 ff.

[116] Isaiah 1 – 12, 66 ff.
[118] Isaiah 1 – 39, 46 ff.
[120] Das Buch Jesaia, 44 ff.
[122] IB V, 187 ff.

c) 3, 16 – 4, 1   c) 4, 2 – 6
d) 4, 2 – 6

9) Budde and Kissane[123]
a) 3, 1 – 15
b) 3, 16 – 4, 6

Naturally, these commentators further sub-divide their units, but it is clear that there is no consensus on which to depend. The discussion below will indicate that, based on formal and thematic grounds, the unit should be divided into three sub-units. These include 3, 1 – 15, which deals with judgment against the male leaders; 3, 16 – 4, 1, which deals with judgment against the leading females; and 4, 2 – 6, which describe the future blessings for the remnant of Israel in Jerusalem. In order to best deal with so large a unit as 3, 1 – 4, 6, each sub-unit will be individually analyzed to determine its structure and function. Afterwards, the three sub-units will be studied in relation to each other to determine the structure and function of the whole.

a. Isa 3, 1 – 15

As noted above, Isa 3, 1 begins with an introductory *kî* which links the following material to the preceding verses. The following *hinneh*, however, indicates that this is a new unit. Throughout the passage is a concern with judgment against the male leaders of Jerusalem and Judah which binds together the various generic entities which are found in these verses. The sub-unit continues until the closing oracular formula in v. 15b. The following unit is introduced by a YHWH speaking formula which indicates a new unit. There is an *inclusio* in v. 15, which includes the name, *'ªdonāy yhwh ṣᵉbā'ôt*, and v. 1, which includes the name, *hā'ādôn yhwh ṣᵉbā'ôt*.

Within 3, 1 – 15, v. 1 – 7 describe a situation in which Jerusalem and Judah are being judged. V. 1 – 3, which are one continuous sentence built around the participle *mesîr*, describe the present or impending removal of the leading citizens on which Jerusalem and Judah depend for support. V. 1a is a basic statement that YHWH is removing stay and staff. This basic statement is appositionally defined in v. 1b so that "stay and staff" of v. 1a are understood in terms of food and water. A second appositional statement in v. 2 – 3 specifies that "stay and staff" actually refer to the leading citizens of the community who are then listed in catalogue fashion according to their categories.[124] Thus, the first group

---

[123] ZAW 49 (1931), 202 ff.; ZAW 50 (1932), 38 ff.; The Book of Isaiah, I 32 ff.

[124] Note that the various elements of each category are linked by *waw*. However, there is no conjunction between the categories themselves.

in v. 2a includes the major military officials, the mighty man and the man of war. The second group in v. 2b includes the major administrative functionaries, the judges, prophets, magicians, and elders. The third group, listed in v. 3, includes lesser officials, the military unit commanders, the honored men, the counselors, the craftsmen and the charmers. By defining "stay and staff" in terms of both food and civil officials, the prophet has made it clear that these terms refer to the support of both the physical and the social life of the community. This association also indicates the interrelationship of the physical and the social support of the community. Without a stable, organized society, proper distribution of food, and thus, physical survival, will not be possible.

The relationship between civil administration and physical survival is made quite clear in v. 4—7 which describe the problems that the community will have to face when its leaders are replaced by incompetents.[125] V. 4—5a are a series of three statements which describe the appointment of youths to positions of authority and the purpose of such appointments. The statement of appointment is made in v. 4, including the appointment statement proper in verse 4a and the implication of such an appointment, i. e., that incompetents shall rule the people in v. 4b.[126] V. 5a, connected to v. 4 by *waw*-consecutive, describes the social aggravation which will result from such an appointment. V. 5b—7 discuss the consequences of this situation, i. e., the breakdown of authority in the community. The statement of consequences proper appears in v. 5b, which is syntactically unconnected to v. 5a, and an illustration of the breakdown of authority appears in v. 6—7, connected by *kî*. V. 6—7 describe a hypothetical situation in which a first man offers the leadership of the community to another man. This verse includes both a statement of the first man's action (v. 6aα) and a quotation of what he says to the second man (v. 6aβ + b). V. 7 contains the second man's refusal of the offer, including both a statement formula (v. 7aα¹) and a quotation of what he says (v. 7aα² + β + γ + b).

Thus, v. 1—3 and 4—7 together describe the removal of the leaders of the Jerusalem/Judah community and the implications of that removal. Although v. 4—7 project the implications into the future, the participial construction of v. 1—3 make it clear that this removal is currently taking

---

[125] While it is clear that v. 4a is a speech by YHWH due to its first person perspective, it is not clear how far this speech extends. Only in v. 8 is there a third person reference to YHWH which indicates that the prophet speaks there. Here, it will be assumed that the speech by YHWH extends through v. 7, but this can be neither proved nor disproved.

[126] Note the *waw*-explicativum which connects v. 4b to v. 4a. Cf. Gesenius, sec. 154a, n. (b).

place. V. 1 − 7, therefore, deal with the present situation of the Jerusalem/ Judah community.

V. 8 − 15, which are connected to v. 1 − 7 by *kî*, provide an explanation for that calamity.

In v. 8 − 11, the prophet explains the calamity by accusing the people of having caused Jerusalem and Judah to stumble. V. 8 explains the reason for Jerusalem and Judah's fall by first making a two-fold statement of that fall (v. 8a) and claiming that the reason for the fall is that the people have rebelled against YHWH (v. 8b).[127] V. 9a, which is not syntactically connected to v. 8, provides the evidence of the people's rebelliousness by referring to their looks (v. 9aα) and their speech (v. 9aβ), stated both positively and negatively.[128] V. 9b, which is also syntactically unconnected to what precedes, is a woe statement against the people for their wickedness including both the woe statement proper in v. 9bα, and the basis for the woe in v. 9bβ. Interestingly, v. 9b is qualified by two statements in v. 10 − 11. The first is a command to assure the righteous, including the command proper (v. 10a) and the basis for the command of assurance, i. e., that the righteous shall be rewarded for his righteous deeds (v. 10b). The second statement in v. 11 is another woe statement which is directed to the wicked. It includes the basic woe statement (v. 11a) and the basis for the woe (v. 11b), i. e., that the wicked shall be repaid for his wicked deeds. Thus, v. 10 − 11 make it clear that the woe statement in v. 9b, which seemed to include all the people, applies only to those people who are wicked. Those who are righteous will not be punished.

V. 12 − 15 build on the distinction made between the righteous and the wicked in v. 10 − 11 by singling out a specific group among the people of Jerusalem and Judah to blame for the present calamity described in v. 1 − 7. This group is the leaders of the people and it is with them that v. 12 − 15 are concerned. These verses begin with v. 12 which is a lament by YHWH[129] concerning the leaders' corruption of the people. It consists of two parallel statements. The first, v. 12a, deals with the nature of the leaders and contains two parts joined by *waw*-conjunctive. V. 12aα labels the leaders as capricious and v. 12aβ calls them women.[130] The second

---

[127] Note the infinitive construct, *lamrôt*, with understood *hyh* in v. 8b. This indicates purpose or motive. Cf. Gesenius, sec. 114o.

[128] V. 9a is made up of two parts constituted by the verbs *higgîdû* and *lo' kiḥēdû*. Both state the same thing, one positively and the other negatively, and should therefore be taken together.

[129] As indicated by the first person perspective. Cf. v. 4a.

[130] The original reading of *wᵉnāšîm* "and women" appears to have been *wᵉnošîm* "and creditors" as indicated by the readings of LXX and TJ. "Creditors" fits best in the context of Isa 3, 1 − 15 but "women" seems to relate only to 3, 16 − 4, 1. It is likely that MT read "and women" due to the influence of the later passage.

statement, v. 12b, also contains two parts linked by *waw* and charges the leaders with having led the people astray. V. 12bα states that the leaders have erred and v. 12bβ states that they have therefore confused the people. Thus, v. 12 holds the leaders responsible for the corruption of the people outlined in v. 8−11. In v. 13−15, the prophet relates a trial scene in which YHWH confronts the leaders of the people in court.[131] V. 13−14a relate YHWH's actions in the suit, first with a two-fold statement of His taking the stand in court (v. 13) and then with a statement of the purpose for His taking the stand, to judge the leaders (v. 14a). V. 14b−15 contain YHWH's courtroom speech and concluding oracular formula (v. 15b). The speech itself is in v. 14b−15a and consists of three parts, the accusation (v. 14bα) that the leaders have devoured the vineyard, the evidence (v. 14bβ) that the plundered goods are found in their possession, and the questioning of the defendants (v. 15a), which consists of two parts and asks what justification they can offer for what they have done.

Thus, v. 8−15, in attempting to assign the blame for the calamity described in v. 1−7, first blames the people on account of their wicked behavior, but then inquires further and assigns the blame for the wicked behavior of the people on the leaders. Ultimately, the leaders are responsible for what has happened, which is appropriate, since they are the ones whom YHWH is removing. The prophet was an important connection here between the leaders and the people. Just as the people are affected by suffering when their leaders are removed, so they are also effected by corruption when their leaders misguide them. Even though the leaders are ultimately responsible, the people still suffer.

Generically, some might call v. 1−15 a prophecy of punishment but this would be inaccurate. The unit is based on the prophecy of punishment since it includes elements of an announcement of punishment and an accusation. However, instead of projecting punishment from the present situation of corruption, as is typical in the prophecy of punishment, v. 1−15 begin with a present situation of punishment to explain that situation as the result of past corruption. By reversing the sequence of accusation and punishment from the prophecy of punishment, v. 1−15 have turned the genre's perspective into that of retrojection rather than projection. It is an inquiry into cause, not a prediction of result. Since the intent of the unit is to explain the present situation by assigning blame, it may be labeled as an accusation. The structure of the unit is as follows:

---

[131] Boecker, Redeformen des Rechtslebens, 84 ff., 89 f., labels the speech contained within these verses as an accusation speech (*Anklagerede*).

Accusation Speech Against the Leaders of Jerusalem/Judah for
Bringing about Downfall   3, 1 − 15

  I. Prophetic Announcement concerning the Present Calamity:
    Removal of Leaders and Its Implications   1 − 7
     A. Description of present calamity: Removal of leaders   1 − 3
       1. basically stated: stay and staff   1a
       2. first appositional specification: food and water   1b
       3. second appositional specification: catalogue of
         leaders   2 − 3
         a. 1st group: major warriors   2a
           1) mighty man   2aα
           2) man of war   2aβ
         b. 2nd group: major administrative functionaries   2b
           1) judge   2bα¹
           2) prophet   2bα²
           3) magician   2bβ¹
           4) elder   2bβ²
         c. 3rd group: lesser officials   3
           1) military unit commanders   3aα
           2) honored men   3aβ
           3) counselors   3bα
           4) craftsmen   3bβ
           5) charmers   3bγ
     B. Prediction of future social chaos: Installation of incom-
       petent leaders   4 − 7
       1. statement concerning the appointment of youths as
         leaders and its results   4 − 5a
         a. concerning appointment of youths   4
           1) appointment statement proper   4a
           2) purpose: incompetent leaders   4b
         b. result: social aggravation   5a
       2. consequences: breakdown of authority   5b − 7
         a. consequences statement proper   5b
         b. illustration: refusal of people to assume leadership   6 − 7
           1) 1st man's offer of leadership to another   6
             a) actions of first man   6aα
             b) speech of first man   6aβ + b
           2) 2nd man's refusal of offer   7
             a) statement formula   7aα¹
             b) speech of 2nd man   7aα² + β + γ + b
 II. Explanation for Present Calamity: The Leaders have Cor-
    rupted the People   8 − 15
     A. Accusation against people for causing fall of Jerusalem/
       Judah   8 − 11
       1. reason for fall: rebellious people   8
         a. two-fold statement of fall   8a
           1) Jerusalem has stumbled   8aα
           2) Judah has fallen   8aβ
         b. reason: rebellious people   8b

2. evidence for people's rebelliousness	9a
a. their looks	9aα
b. their speech	9aβ
1) stated positively	9aβ¹
2) stated negatively	9aβ²
3. qualified woe statement against the people	9b–11
a. woe statement against people	9b
1) woe statement proper	9bα
2) basis for woe	9bβ
b. qualification	10–11
1) command to assure righteous	10
a) command proper	10a
b) basis for command	10b
2) woe statement concerning wicked	11
a) woe statement proper	11a
b) basis for woe	11b
B. Accusation against leaders for corrupting the people	12–15
1. lament concerning leaders' corruption of the people	12
a. concerning nature of leaders	12a
1) capricious	12aα
2) women (usurers)	12aβ
b. concerning leaders' corruption of people	12b
1) their corrupting influence	12bα
2) result: confusion of people	12bβ
2. trial scene: YHWH's confrontation with the leaders	13–15
a. YHWH's action: lawsuit	13–14a
1) takes stand	13
a) to contend	13a
b) to judge	13b
2) purpose: judge leaders	14a
b. oracular report of YHWH's court speech	14b–15
1) speech proper	14b–15a
a) accusation	14bα
b) evidence	14bβ
c) questioning of defendant	15a
i. why oppress people?	15aα
ii. why grind face of poor?	15aβ
2) oracular formula	15b

b. Isa 3, 16–4, 1

Following the closing oracular formula of v. 15, this unit begins with a YHWH speaking formula in v. 16 which indicates a new unit. The unit is concerned with the punishment of women throughout. Isa 4, 2 marks the beginning of a unit concerned with the restoration of Jerusalem so that the present unit ends thematically with Isa 4, 1.

Many scholars would object to considering 3, 16 – 4, 1 as a unit, however, due to the view that 3, 25 – 4, 1 is an independent announcement of punishment which is directed against Jerusalem, whereas 3, 16 – 24 is directed against the women.[132] Such a judgment may be unjustified, however, in view of the textual problem in v. 24b. The MT reads, *kî taḥat yopî*, "for instead of beauty," and appears to be an incomplete statement. The verse does not occur in LXX, although it adds *kallistos*, "beautiful," to v. 25. 1QIsaᵃ reads, *ky tḥt ypy bšt*, "for instead of beauty, shame," which makes sense since it completes the statement. But this reading is attested nowhere else so that it is very likely an addition made by the Qumran scribe to complete the statement. Both LXX and 1QIsaᵃ seem to presuppose the text as found in MT.

Targum Jonathan reveals an interesting phenomenon. It reads *dāʾ pûrᶜᵃnûtāʾ titᶜᵃbîd minhôn ʾᵃrê tᵉᶜāʾâ bᵉšuprᵉhôn šᵉpar gibbārayik bᵉḥarbāʾ yitqaṭṭᵉlûn.* "This retribution shall be made on them because of (their) going astray due to their beauty. The beauty of your young men shall be killed by the sword..." The word *šæpær*, which is Aramaic for *yopî*, is used twice, once in a statement derived from *kî taḥat yopî* of v. 24b and once in a construct form with *gibbārayik* in TJ, v. 25. It appears that TJ had two understandings of *yopî*, one in relation to the Hebrew *kî taḥat* of v. 24b and one with *mᵉtayik* of v. 25.[133] The first corresponds with the understanding of 1QIsaᵃ. The second corresponds with LXX which eliminates v. 24b but reads *kai ho huios sou ho kallistos* in v. 25. This indicates a traditional association between v. 24b and v. 25, preserved in LXX and TJ, which supplies a clue for understanding these verses. The problem is that one expects an antonym to follow *yopî*, such as those found in v. 24a and in v. 24b of the Qumran scroll.[134] But in v. 25, it appears that an oracle has taken the place of the expected antonym. Rather than using a noun to provide a contrast with the preceding noun, *yopî*, the prophet used an oracle. The tragic scene portrayed in 3, 25 – 4, 1 is certainly a contrast to *yopî*. Thus, v. 24b – 25a would translate, "for instead of beauty, your men shall fall by the sword..." The MT can stand without emendation and 3, 25 – 4, 1 is connected structurally to v. 24.[135]

---

[132] E. g., Clements, Isaiah 1 – 39, 52.

[133] This would require repointing *yopî* as *yᵉpî*.

[134] The understanding of *kî* as "branding," i. e., "branding instead of beauty," can not be accepted. This form would be a *hapax legomenon* in the Bible. Furthermore, this understanding reverses the sequence of the pairs of images found in the preceding v. 24a from positive-negative to negative-positive. Finally, the understanding of *kî* as "branding" does not appear in the versions.

[135] Cf. Wiklander, Prophecy as Literature, 80 f.

Within 3, 16-4, 1 are two basic units, v. 16-17 and v. 18-4, 1, as indicated by the formula *bayyôm hahû'* in v. 18 and the syntactic connections within these units. V. 16-17 contain the prophet's announcement of YHWH's judgment against the women of Jerusalem and verses 18-4, 1 discuss the consequences of that judgment.

Scholars have generally viewed the statement beginning with *ya'an kî* in v. 16 as a causal statement or protasis for an announcement of judgment or apodosis in v. 17,[136] the whole being a judgment oracle. There is a problem with this interpretation, however. The speaking formula in v. 16aα[1] mentions YHWH as the speaker, but v. 17 refers to Him in the third person as *'adonāy*.[137] This leads Wildberger, who views the statement as a speech of Isaiah, to regard the speaking formula as a redactional addition.[138] One might suggest that YHWH refers to Himself in the third person, but this forces the meaning of the text. Instead, since v. 17 refers to YHWH in the third person, it must be a statement by the prophet, not by YHWH. This leaves v. 16aα[2] + β + γ + b as the quotation by YHWH. If one accepts the usual interpretation of this verse, one would object that YHWH's quote would be an incomplete sentence. A closer look at v. 16 indicates that the usual understanding is mistaken. The quote begins in v. 16aα[2], using the perfect verb, *gāb[e]hû*. This is followed by the imperfect *waw*-consecutive *wattelaknâ* of v. 16aβ. This syntactic unit, v. 16aα[2] + β + γ, ends with the syntactic break at v. 16b. V. 16b has two imperfect verbs, *telaknâ* and *t[e]'akkasnâ*, which govern clauses joined by *waw*. The first syntactic unit, v. 16aα[2] + β + γ, is based on a perfect verb indicating completed or past action, and the second syntactic unit, v. 16b, is based on imperfect verbs indicating incomplete or future action. V. 16aα[2] + β + γ must therefore be the causal statement (protasis) for the announcement of judgment (apodosis) in v. 16b.

One will immediately object that walking with minced steps and tinkling feet does not seem to be much of a punishment. This is generally considered to be the characteristic manner of walking for a stylish Israelite woman. A closer look at the words, *w[e]ṭāpop* and *t[e]'akkasnâ*, however, indicates that they also may have been misunderstood. The verb root *ṭpp* occurs only here in the Bible and is taken to mean, "to trip, take quick little steps."[139] But in late Hebrew, *ṭpp* I means "to

---

[136] Wildberger, Jesaja 1-12, 136, 137 ff.; Kaiser, Isaiah 1-12, 79. Cf. RSV, NJV, NEB, and JB.

[137] There is also a stylistic difference in that v. 17 uses the feminine plural pronoun suffix (*pâthen*) whereas v. 16 uses the masculine suffix (*ûb[e]raglêhæm*) to refer to Daughters of Zion.

[138] Jesaja 1-12, 136.

[139] BDB, 381. The noun, *ṭap*, "children," is derived from this meaning as they walk "with quick, tripping steps" (p. 381 f.).

touch closely" or "to join, add."[140] The verb root 'ks also occurs only
here in the Bible and is taken to mean, "to shake bangles, rattle,
tinkle."[141] Its Arabic cognate means, "to reverse, tie backwards" and
"to hopple, of camel." These imply restricted movement. Likewise,
Hebrew 'ækæs means "chain."[142] Therefore, the verb 'ks can imply
restriction. Both ṭpp and 'ks convey a sense of confinement, as in
chaining together. Admittedly, these would be secondary meanings but
they allow for a play on words. The women of Jerusalem, who walk
with mincing (ṭpp) steps and rattling ('ks) feet, according to the dictates
of fashion, will continue to walk with short (ṭpp) steps and rattling ('ks)
feet when they are chained together as captives. The statement attached
to YHWH's quote by the prophet in v. 17 makes this clear since exposed
genitals are characteristic of captives (cf. Isa 7, 20).

Therefore, v. 16 – 17 contain the prophet's announcement of
YHWH's judgment against the women of Jerusalem. V. 16 contains the
prophet's report of YHWH's announcement and includes the speaking
formula in v. 16aα¹ and YHWH's speech in v. 16aα² + β + γ + b. The
speech includes a protasis accusing the women of pride, basically stated
(v. 16aα²) and exemplified by their manner of walking (v. 16aβ + γ), and
an apodosis which announces judgment in reference to their tripping
walk and their rattling walk (v. 16b). V. 17, spoken by the prophet,
reports YHWH's actions against the women, including smiting their
foreheads with a scab (v. 17a) and uncovering their genitals (v. 17b).

The second basic section of 3, 16 – 4, 1, v. 18 – 4, 1, begins with a
catalogue of items of women's clothing and furnishings which the Lord
is taking away. The catalogue is organized according to the same
syntactic arrangement employed in v. 2 – 3 above. Each sub-section of
the catalogue is set off by the absence of waw while its individual
members are joined by waw. There are five groups of items in the
catalogue. Group 1 (v. 18) contains three items. Group 2 (v. 19) contains
three items. Group 3 (v. 20) contains five items. Group 4 (v. 21) contains
two items. Group 5 (v. 22 – 23) contains eight items.

The second section of 3, 18 – 4, 1, v. 24 – 4, 1, discusses the consequences of YHWH's removal of the women's finery. This section contains a series of parallel statements governed by the verb sequence of
wᵉhāyâ and yihyæh. These are v. 24aα¹, 24aα², 24aα³, and 24aα⁴. Each
statement contrasts a positive image of what is lost with a negative
image of what is replaced to demonstrate the results of YHWH's taking

---

[140] M. Jastrow, Dictionary of the Targumim, 548. Cf. ṭæpæp, "addition to city limits,
    suburb" and ṭap, "children," derived from the meaning "joined to, dependent" (Jas-
    trow, Dictionary, 545).

[141] BDB, 747. This meaning is derived from 'ækæs, "anklet, bangle."

[142] Jastrow, Dictionary, 1079.

away specific items of women's finery. V. 24b – 4, 1 differ slightly from the other statements in the series in that they begin with *kî*. The positive substantive, *yopî*, is a general term whereas the four positive substantives of v. 24a are specific. The explanatory *kî* and the general *yopî* indicate that 3, 24b – 4, 1 are a general summation of the specific examples in v. 24a. As in v. 24a, the section begins with a statement of what is lost in v. 24b. The replacement for what is lost is described by an oracle which announces punishment in 3, 25 – 4, 1. The announcement of punishment begins with a two-fold announcement proper in v. 25 directed to an unnamed city that its men would fall in battle. V. 26 – 4, 1 describe the results of the men's deaths. For the city, it will mean mourning (v. 26a) and dejection (v. 26b). For the women of the city, it will mean humiliation (4, 1). Their humiliation is indicated by their action, i. e., when seven women seize one man (4, 1aα), and their statement to the one man proposing a marriage contract (4, 1aβ + γ + b). This marriage proposal states that the women will provide their own food and clothing (4, 1aβ + γ) in return for the man's name which gives them honorable status (4, 1b).

Thus, Isa 3, 16 – 4, 1 is a prophetic announcement of YHWH's judgment against the women of Jerusalem, including the prophet's announcement proper and his announcement of the consequences of that judgment. The structure is as follows:

Prophetic Announcement of YHWH's Judgment Against the Women of Jerusalem	3, 16 – 4, 1
I. Prophetic Announcement of YHWH's Judgment Proper	16 – 17
A. Report of YHWH's announcement of judgment	16
1. YHWH speaking formula	16aα¹
2. YHWH speech (announcement of judgment)	16aα² + β + γ + b
a. protasis: accusation	16aα² + β + γ
1) basically stated: pride	16aα²
2) exemplified: manner of walk	16aβ + γ
b. apodosis: announcement of punishment	16b
1) tripping walk	16bα
2) rattling walk	16bβ
B. Announcement of YHWH's actions against the women	17
1. smiting foreheads	17a
2. uncovering genitals	17b
II. Prophetic Announcement of Consequences of YHWH's Judgment against the Women	18 – 4, 1
A. Concerning YHWH's removal of finery	18 – 23
1. group 1	18
a. anklets	18a + bα
b. necklaces	18bβ
c. crescents	18bγ

2. group 2	19
a. pendants	19a
b. bracelets	19b
c. amulets	19c
3. group 3	20
a. headdresses	20aα
b. armlets	20aβ
c. sashes	20aγ
d. boxes of perfume	20bα
e. charms	20bβ
4. group 4	21
a. signet rings	21a
b. nose rings	21b
5. group 5	22 – 23
a. robes	22aα
b. tunics	22aβ
c. cloaks	22bα
d. handbags	22bβ
e. mirrors	23aα
f. linens	23aβ
g. turbans	23bα
h. veils	23bβ
B. Concerning the results of YHWH's removing the women's finery: degradation	24 – 4, 1
1. specific examples	24a
a. stink instead of perfume	24aα¹
b. rope instead of girdle	24aα²
c. baldness instead of coiffed hair	24aα³
d. sackcloth instead of fine robe	24aα⁴
2. general summation	24b
a. what is lost: beauty	24b
b. replacement: degradation (announcement of punishment)	25 – 4, 1
1) announcement proper	25
a) concerning men	25a
b) concerning power	25b
2) results for city and women	26 – 4, 1
a) for city	26
i. mourning	26a
ii. dejection	26b
b) for women: humiliation	4, 1
i. action	4, 1aα
ii. statement (marriage contract)	4, 1aβ+γ+b
aa. what they provide	4, 1aβ+γ
i) food	4, 1aβ
ii) clothing	4, 1aγ
bb. what they receive	4, 1b
i) name	4, 1bα
ii) honorable status	4, 1bβ

c. Isa 4, 2 – 6

Following the oracles which describe the punishment of the men and women of Jerusalem, this unit, with its introductory formula *bayyôm hahû'*, describes the protection which YHWH will offer to the remnant of Israel in Jerusalem. It is followed by the parable of the vineyard in chapter 5 which discusses the judgment against the people of Israel and Judah.

Within v. 2 – 6 are two parts. V. 2 is a prophetic announcement concerning the restoration of the remnant of Israel, expressed in terms of the new growth in the land. V. 3 – 6, which begin with an introductory *wᵉhāyâ*, focus more specifically on the remnant that is left in Jerusalem. In doing so, these verses discuss what YHWH will do for the city of Jerusalem, not what He will do for the land.

Within v. 3 – 6, v. 3 discusses YHWH's protection of the remnant in Jerusalem. It also includes a statement that the remnant in Jerusalem shall be called holy (v. 3a) as well as an appositional definition of this remnant as all who are inscribed for life in Jerusalem (v. 3b). V. 4 – 6 discuss YHWH protection of the city of Jerusalem itself. V. 4 – 5a are a conditional statement concerning YHWH's creation of a cloud and flame. The conditions, introduced by *'im*,[143] are stated in v. 4 (the protasis) in two parts. One states that the filth of the Daughters of Zion must be rinsed away (v. 4aα) and the other states that the blood stains of Jerusalem must be washed out (v. 4aβ + b).[144] The apodosis is in v. 5a, which states that YHWH will create a cloud and flame over Jerusalem. The purpose of this cloud and flame is stated in the explanatory clause, introduced by *kî*, in v. 5b – 6. This purpose is the protection of Jerusalem, stated in terms of both a protective *huppâ*, "canopy," in v. 5b and a *sukkâ*, "booth," in v. 6 so that the glory in Jerusalem will not be exposed to the elements.

Generically, 4, 2 – 6 is a prophecy of salvation for the remnant of Israel.[145] It includes a prophetic announcement concerning

---

[143] Some scholars see v. 4 as a temporal clause dependent on v. 3 (e. g., Skinner, Isaiah I – XXXIX, 30 f.; cf. RSV, JPS, KJV. Duhm, Das Buch Jesaia, 52, is unsure whether to connect v. 4 with v. 3 or with v. 5). V. 4 is a temporal clause but it belongs with v. 5 since temporal or conditional clauses introduced by *'im* are always used as protases. This is the case for every example cited for the temporal use of *'im* in Gesenius, sec. 164d. When a temporal clause follows a statement, it generally uses *'ašær* or *bᵉ* plus infinitive construct.

[144] Note the use of the menstrual imagery to symbolize the cleansing of Jerusalem, i. e., just as a menstrual woman must be cleansed of her impurity (Lev 15, 19 – 30), so Jerusalem must be cleansed of hers, the sins of her people.

[145] Cf. Kaiser, Isaiah 1 – 12, 84, who labels it "prophecy of salvation" (*Heilsweissagung*).

the restoration of the remnant in Jerusalem which apparently constitutes the remnant of Israel.[146] The structure is as follows:

Prophetic Announcement of Salvation for the Remnant of Israel in Jerusalem	4, 2 – 6
I. Prophetic Announcement Concerning the Restoration of the Remnant of Israel	2
II. Specification Concerning the Remnant in Jerusalem	3 – 6
A. Concerning YHWH's protection of the remnant in Jerusalem	3
1. designation of the remnant as holy	3a
2. appositional definition of the remnant as all inscribed for life in Jerusalem	3b
B. Concerning YHWH's protection of Jerusalem	4 – 6
1. conditional statement concerning the creation of cloud and flame	4 – 5a
a. protasis: cleansing of Jerusalem	4
1) filth of Daughters of Zion rinsed away	4aα
2) bloodstains of Jerusalem washed out	4aβ + b
b. apodosis: creation of cloud and flame over Jerusalem	5a
2. statement of purpose: protection of Jerusalem	5b – 6
a. expressed in terms of *huppâ*	5b
b. expressed in terms of *sukkâ*	6

d. Formal overview: Isa 3, 1 – 4, 6

As indicated in the commentaries, there is good reason to believe that 3, 1 – 4, 1 is a composite of disparate pieces. Yet, there are indications that 3, 1 – 4, 1 were placed together to form a unit, sub-divided into 3, 1 – 15 and 3, 16 – 4, 1. Both of these sections are concerned with judgment and both have the overarching theme of Jerusalem. V. 1 – 15 refer to the male leaders of Jerusalem, the military, religious, and professional men. V. 16 – 4, 1, as indicated by the sumptuous clothing, refer to the leading women of society. V. 25 – 4, 1, which are a part of 3, 16 – 4, 1, refer to the effects of the city's devastation on both men and women.[147] Although the primary intent of 3, 25 – 4, 1 is to illustrate the situation of the women, it depicts catastrophe for the men as well. Thus, Isa 3, 1 – 4, 1 forms a single unit concerned with judgment against the people of Jerusalem and Judah. The first part accuses the men of having brought about the downfall of Jerusalem and Judah while the second

---

[146] This identification is made by the juxtaposition of v. 2, which deals with the remnant of Israel, and v. 3 – 6, which specify the remnant of Israel as the persons remaining in Jerusalem.

[147] Cf. E. E. Platt, AUSS 17 (1979), 189 ff.

part announces judgment against the women, presupposing judgment against the men. Isa 3, 1−4, 1 is therefore a judgment speech against the people of Jerusalem and Judah.

Although the perspective of 3, 1−4, 1 is essentially the present, that of 4, 2−6 is the future. Its concern with the remnant of the people presupposes punishments such as those described in 3, 1−4, 1, in that it refers to a purge which is necessary to remove the guilt of Jerusalem. There is a purpose for this punishment. By punishing the country and its people, YHWH intends to purify it. The result will be a purified city and a holy population. Thus, Isa 4, 2−6 serves as a conclusion to 3, 1−4, 1[148] by defining the purposes and goals of the punishment announced in this section.

Generically, Isa 3, 1−4, 6 is a Prophetic Announcement concerning the Purification of Zion. It superstructure is as follows:

Prophetic Announcement concerning the Purification of Zion   3, 1−4, 6
   I. Prophetic Judgment Speech against the People of Jerusalem
      and Judah   3, 1−4, 1
      A. Accusation speech against the male leaders for causing
         downfall   3, 1−15
      B. Prophetic announcement of judgment against the wom-
         en   3, 16−4, 1
   II. Prophetic Announcement of Salvation for the Cleansed
      Remnant of Israel in Jerusalem   4, 2−6

7. Structural Overview: Isaiah 2, 1−4, 6

This study has identified five units in Isa 2, 1−4, 6, including 2, 1, the superscription for the entire section; 2, 2−4, a prophetic announcement concerning the future establishment of Zion as the locus of YHWH's rule over the world; 2, 5, an invitation to Jacob to join with YHWH; 2, 6−22, a prophetic acknowledgment of the need for a cleansing punishment of Jacob; and 3, 1−4, 6, a prophetic announcement concerning the purification of Zion. It now remains to determine the functions of these units in relation to one another in order to determine the structure and meaning of Isa 2, 1−4, 6 as a whole.

In the course of study, several features appeared which indicate that these units should be joined together. First, Isa 2, 5 betrays a great deal of influence from 2, 2−4 with respect to syntax and vocabulary. Second, there is a *kî* at the beginning of 2, 6−22 which indicates a link to v. 5. The mention of *bêt ya'ªqob* in v. 6 also indicates such a link, since *bêt*

---

[148] Cf. Skinner, Isaiah I−XXXIX, 29.

ya'aqob is mentioned in v. 5. Finally, there is another *kî* at the beginning of 3, 1 − 4, 6 which also suggests a connection with the preceding material. The emphasis on *bayyôm hahû'* in this section (3, 18; 4, 2; cf. 3, 7; 4, 1), which refers directly to 2, 12, supports such a connection.

Clearly, 2, 5 and 2, 6 − 22 belong together as a unit. The syntactic link with *kî* and the concern with the House of Jacob demonstrate this. V. 5 issues an invitation to the House of Jacob to walk in the light of YHWH. But v. 6 − 22 describe the crimes of the House of Jacob and the coming punishment. Obviously, the House of Jacob can not accept the invitation since its crimes have rendered it unfit to walk in the light of YHWH. Therefore, v. 6 − 22 imply a negative response to the invitation in v. 5. The *kî* at the beginning of v. 6 has an adversative function since it introduces the reasons for this implicit negative response.[149] Furthermore, the connections between v. 5 and 2, 2 − 4 mentioned above indicate that 2, 2 − 4 and 2, 5 − 22 must stand together as two parts of a larger whole. Isa 2, 2 − 4 describes an ideal time when Jerusalem will attract the nations to follow YHWH's Torah. Isa 2, 5 − 22, however, demonstrates that Jacob is not qualified to join.

With regard to 3, 1 − 4, 6, the introductory *kî* in 3, 1 links this unit syntactically to the preceding material while the special concern with "that day" links it thematically.[150] There are distinctions between the units which indicate that they were not originally intended to be part of the same composition, but in their present context, they function as one unit. Isa 2, 5 − 22 discusses the need for a cleansing punishment of the people and 3, 1 − 4, 6 discusses the process of that cleansing for both the people and Zion. The two units together constitute a prophetic announcement concerning the cleansing of Zion. This is to prepare Zion for its role as the locus of YHWH's rule as mentioned in 2, 2 − 4. The whole of 2, 1 − 4, 6 is a prophetic announcement concerning the cleansing of Zion for its role as the locus of YHWH's rule over the world. Isa 2, 1 is the superscription for this unit and 2, 2 − 4, 6 is the announcement proper. The superstructure of this unit is as follows:

Prophetic Announcement Concerning the Cleansing of Zion for
its Role as the Locus for YHWH's Rule over the World   2, 1 − 4, 6

   I. Superscription   2, 1

   II. Announcement Proper   2, 2 − 4, 6
      A. Concerning the future establishment of Zion as the
         locus of YHWH's rule over the world   2, 2 − 4

---

[149] Cf. Gesenius, sec. 163a and especially 163b.

[150] Isa 2, 2; cf. 1, 17; 2, 11; 2, 20.

8. Redaction Analysis: Isaiah 2, 1 – 4, 6

The above discussion demonstrates that Isa 2, 1 – 4, 6 has a coherent structure and that the various sub-units of this text function together with a specific intent. The entire unit discusses the cleansing of Zion in order to prepare it for its role as the locus of YHWH's world rule. As seen above in the discussion of the structure of the book as a whole, this unit announces YHWH's world rule as the goal to which the rest of the book is directed. In its final form, the book of Isaiah dates to the late fifth century. Isa 2 – 4, with its concern for the restoration of Jerusalem and the nations' acknowledgement of YHWH at Zion, would certainly address the concerns of this period.

Certainly, Isa 2 – 4 is governed by this intent, yet there are a number of discrepancies in the text which indicate that it was not entirely written as a single composition. For example, Isa 2, 2 – 4 is concerned with Jerusalem/Zion as the site where the nations will come to learn YHWH's ways. This section does not presuppose that Jerusalem must first be cleansed nor does it in any way concern the inhabitants of the country. Yet, Isa 2, 5 – 4, 1 deals precisely with the punishment of the people. The need for such punishment is clearly presupposed by 4, 2 – 6 but the purpose is so that YHWH will provide protection for the purified city. His plans for imparting Torah to the nations are not mentioned here. One would assume that YHWH would protect His teaching center and that the place would be pure, but such a requirement is not explicitly stated, it is only implied by the juxtaposition of 2, 2 – 4 and 2, 5 – 4, 6. The only thematic connection between 2, 5 and 2, 6 – 22 is the mention of *bêt ya'ᵃqob* in v. 6. Throughout the rest of 2, 6 – 22, the party concerned is labeled *'ādām* (v. 20, 22) or a combination of *'ādām* and

ʾîš or ʾᵃnāšîm (v. 9, 11, 17). Apart from v. 6aα, where the mention of *bêt yaʿᵃqob* provides a sloppy syntactical construction, no mention of *bêt yaʿᵃqob* is made nor is there any clue that the oracle is concerned with *bêt yaʿᵃqob*. The repeated mention of ʾādām and ʾîš/ʾᵃnāšîm indicated that the oracle is directed against humans in general, not just a specific group. Isa 2, 5 (+6aα) appears to be a literary seam designed to join 2, 6−22 with 2, 2−4, which otherwise have little in common. In Isa 4, 2−6, v. 4 places the blame for Jerusalem's impurity solely on the Daughters of Zion. But 3, 1−4, 1 accuses the men and women of Jerusalem/Judah, especially the male leaders, of wrongdoing. V. 12 explicitly assigns blame for the sin of the people on their leaders who misled them. When considered in this context, Isa 4, 4 would have to assume that the women caused the leaders to err. This could be the implication of v. 12aβ in the MT, but apart from this questionable reference, there is no allusion to the responsibility of the women in v. 1−15. Furthermore, Isa 3, 16−4, 1 does not suggest that the women corrupted the men. Only the juxtaposition of 3, 16−4, 1 with 3, 1−15 and the inference drawn from that juxtaposition could justify blaming the Daughters of Zion exclusively for the impurity of the city. If 3, 16−4, 1 and 3, 1−15 were composed independently and later combined, however, this would have justified the blaming of the women in 4, 2−6. It also would have resulted in the reinterpretation of *wnšym* in 3, 12 from "usurers" to "women." In fact, such a redactional interpretation could explain most of the discrepancies in this text. Because the sub-units of Isa 2−4 betray so little awareness of one another, yet function together with a single intent, they were composed independently and later were brought together by a redactor for a purpose different from that for which they were originally composed. Therefore, each of the sub-units of Isa 2−4: 2, 1; 2, 2−4; 2, 5−22; 3, 1−15; 3, 16−4, 1; and 4, 2−6, will be studied in order to determine their dates and the circumstances for which they were composed as well as their literary integrity. This will indicate whether the material was composed by an author or redactor and the purposes of the authors or redactors who created this material.

a. Isa 2, 2−4

Isa 2, 2−4 also appears, with minor textual differences, in Mic 4, 1−3:

> And it shall come to pass in the later days that the mountain of the House of YHWH shall be established at the head of the mountains and it (shall be) elevated higher than the hills. And peoples shall flow upon it and many nations shall come and say, "Come, and let us go up to the Mountain of YHWH and the House of the God of Jacob and He will teach us His ways that we may walk in His paths."

For from Zion, Torah goes forth, and the word of YHWH from Jerusalem. And
He shall judge between many peoples and arbitrate for mighty nations far away
and they shall beat their swords into plowshares and their spears into pruning hooks
and they shall not lift up a sword, nation against nation, nor shall they learn war
any more.

Unlike Isa 2, 2 – 4, Mic 4, 1 – 3 continues with another verse:

And they shall sit, each under his vine and under his fig tree and there shall be no
one to frighten (them) for the mouth of YHWH Sebaot has spoken.

The debate concerning the authorship and dating of Isa 2, 2 – 4/
Mic 4, 1 – 4 has been long and vigorous, but it remains unresolved.
There are four basic positions:[151]

1) Micah was the author and Isaiah borrowed it from him. This
thesis, advanced by Naegelsbach in 1877, was based primarily on the
superior poetic style of the Micah passage.[152]

2) The passage is a liturgical oracle from a time earlier than that
of Isaiah or Micah which both prophets used for their own purposes.
This position is based on a supposed liturgical character of the passage
and the dating of the Zion theme from the early period of the monarchy.[153]

3) Isaiah, who has strong connections with the Jerusalem traditions,
composed this passage in order to give his interpretation of the Zion
traditions. Micah then borrowed it from him. This thesis is based on
the correspondence of the Zion theme and vocabulary of the passage
with other oracles by Isaiah.[154]

4) The passage is a later interpolation in the prophecies of Isaiah
and Micah. This position is based primarily on the universalistic element
in the oracle which is viewed as a late development in Biblical thought.[155]

The first position, that Micah was the author of this passage, has
long been abandoned. Its main support, that Mic 4, 1 – 5 is poetically
and textually superior to Isa 2, 2 – 5, is no real basis for the claim since
a person copying another work is likely to make improvements to suit
his own taste. The extra v. 4, which does not appear in Isaiah, also plays

---

[151] For convenient summaries of the debate, see Wildberger, Jesaja 1 – 12, 78 ff.; B. Renaud,
La Formation du Livre de Michée, 1977, 160 ff.

[152] Wildberger, Jesaja 1 – 12, 78; Renaud, La Formation, 160.

[153] H. Wildberger, VT 7 (1957), 62 ff.; G. von Rad, The City on the Hill, The Problem
of the Hextaeuch and Other Essays, 232 ff.; Duhm, Das Buch Jesaia, 36 f.; Junker,
Sancta Civitas, Jerusalem Nova, 17. Cf. Wildberger, Jesaja 1 – 12, 79 f.; Renaud, La
Formation, 161.

[154] J. Gray, VT 11 (1961), 14 f.; A. Kapelrud, VT 11 (1961), 395 f. Cf. Wildberger, Jesaja
1 – 12, 79; Renaud, La Formation, 161.

[155] Scott, IB V, 180; Gray, Isaiah I – XXVII, 42 ff.; Kaiser, Isaiah 1 – 12, 49 ff.; Clements,
Isaiah 1 – 39, 39 f. Cf. Wildberger, Jesaja 1 – 12, 79; Renaud, La Formation, 162 f.

a role. Mic 4, 4, with its converted perfect verb, $w^e y\bar{a}\check{s}^e b\hat{u}$, fits perfectly into the syntax of Mic 4, 1–3. The theme also fits the context well, especially following v. 3b. It would be difficult to prove that v. 4 does not belong here. It is an integral part of the text which illustrates the peaceful situation of v. 3 quite well, thus enhancing the image presented in the text. If Isaiah had copied this section from Micah, he would have had no reason to eliminate Mic 4, 4 from his text.[156] On the other hand, Mic 4, 4a does seem to have been a sort of folk saying which was used to describe a peaceful situation[157] and could easily have been added by Micah to an originally Isaianic text without disturbing the syntax. In sum, it is unlikely that Micah composed this text.

Proponents of the second position, that the passage is an older liturgical piece used by both Micah and Isaiah, tend to be a bit speculative when suggesting festival settings for the passage.[158] Also, the characterization of this text as liturgical is a somewhat subjective judgment. Certainly, it gives one the impression of a liturgical poem, but this does not mean that it actually had a place in Israelite worship. Yet, the passage does tie into the Zion traditions which extend back into the time of the establishment of the Davidic monarchy and have their roots in Canaanite ideology.[159] The designation of YHWH as $^{\,\prime\!\!\alpha}loh\hat{e}\ ya^{\,\alpha}qob$ (Isa 2, 3; Mic 4, 2) occurs elsewhere only in psalms associated with Zion (2 Sam 23, 1; Ps 20, 2; 46, 8, 12; 75, 10; 76, 7; 81, 2, 5; 84, 9; 94, 7).[160] Referring to Ps 46, 48, and 76, Wildberger points out the prominent position of Zion as the home of YHWH, the pilgrimage of the nations and peoples to Zion, and the resulting peace as common motifs in the Zion tradition.[161] Thus, there seems to be a case for associating the passage with the Zion tradition.

A closer look at the evidence indicates that there is a difference between Isa 2, 2–4/Mic 4, 1–4 and the Zion psalms. In Isa 2, 2–4/Mic 4, 1–4, the nations come voluntarily to Zion after seeing its elevation. They recognize that YHWH's Torah comes from Zion and they wish to learn and submit to YHWH's rule. YHWH will settle their disputes and they will in turn convert their weapons into agricultural tools and live together in peace. The psalms cited by Wildberger present

---

[156] Contra. Wildberger, Jesaja 1–12, 77 f.
[157] Cf. 1 Reg 8, 5; 2 Reg 18, 31 = Isa 36, 16; Zach 3, 10.
[158] Gray, VT 11, 14 f., suggests the feast of Sukkot (cf. Junker, Sancta Civitas, 27; von Rad, The City on the Hill, 234 f.) and Kapelrud, VT 11, 395 f., suggests the enthronement festival.
[159] J. J. M. Roberts, JBL 92 (1973), 329 ff.
[160] Wildberger, VT 7, 66 f. Cf. Ps 114, 7 ($^{\,\prime\!\!\alpha}l\hat{o}ah\ ya^{\,\alpha}qob$ with Leningradensis).
[161] Wildberger, VT 7, 68 f.

a different picture. In Ps 46, weapons will be destroyed, but it is YHWH who destroys them:

> Come, behold the deeds of YHWH who has wreaked havoc on earth, stopping wars unto the ends of the earth. He breaks the bow and cuts down the spear. Chariots, He burns with fire. (v. 9 – 10)

The reason for this is especially instructive. The nations have come to Zion, but they have come to attack and YHWH acts to defend His city:

> God is in her midst, she shall not fall. God will help her before morning. The nations are confounded, the kingdoms fall. He shouts, the earth trembles. YHWH Sebaot is with us, the God of Jacob is our protection. (v. 6 – 8)

Ps 48 also portrays YHWH's defeat of the nations. As Wildberger notes, v. 1 – 3 begin with statements praising YHWH and His high, holy mountain, similar to those in Isa 2, 2 – 4/Mic 4, 1 – 4. But this section is followed by v. 5 – 9 with a description of the defeated kings:

> For behold, the kings were assembled, they advanced together. They saw (and) so they were terrified, they were frightened, they bolted. Trembling seized them there, shaking like a woman giving birth. With the East wind, You destroyed the ships of Tarshish. Just as we heard, so have we seen in the city of YHWH Sebaot, in the city of our God, which God established forever.

Likewise, YHWH breaks weapons in Ps 76. The nations do not give them up voluntarily:

> God is known in Judah, great is His Name in Israel. And His tent is in Salem and His dwelling place is in Zion. There, He broke the flashings of the bow, shield and sword and war. (v. 2 – 4)

Finally, the nations will come to Zion to submit to YHWH, but their motivation is fear of Him, not a desire to receive His Torah and learn His ways:

> And now, O Kings, be prudent and be warned, O Rulers of the earth. Serve YHWH in fear and frightful trembling. Kiss His feet [162] lest He become angry and you perish by the way for He is easily provoked. (Ps 2, 10 – 12a)

Thus, Isa 2, 2 – 4 and Mic 4, 1 – 4 have motifs similar to those of the Zion tradition, exaltation of Zion, gathering of peoples at Zion, destruction of weapons, and submission of peoples to YHWH, but they use them in a different manner. Whereas the Zion psalms portray the defeat of the nations by YHWH at Zion, the destruction of their weapons by YHWH, and their consequent submission to Him in fear, Isa 2, 2 – 4/ Mic 4, 1 – 4 picture a situation where the nations come to the exalted

---

[162] Cf. the note in BHS.

Mt. Zion to seek YHWH out, to learn His ways. He will make peace among them by settling their disputes so that they can convert their weapons to peaceful uses. Clearly, Isa 2, 2 – 4/Mic 4, 1 – 4 is heavily influenced by the Zion tradition, but the themes differ.

Wildberger recognizes the difficulty of identifying Isa 2, 2 – 4 with the Zion songs. He knows that the interest of the Zion tradition is to magnify Jerusalem (and thus Israel), not the nations.[163] This leads him to the third position cited above, that Isaiah is the author of this passage.[164] He claims that Isaiah has borrowed the themes of Zion's exaltation, YHWH's rulership, etc., from the Zion psalms and combined them with other elements concerned with the welfare, not the submission, of the nations.[165] He then does an exhaustive study of the vocabulary of the section to show that it is characteristic of Isaiah and the Zion tradition.[166]

E. Cannawurf has already noted that Wildberger's vocabulary statistics do not prove that Isaiah wrote this section.[167] There is no doubt that Isaiah had close connections with the Zion traditions for he relies on them frequently.[168] Isa 31, 4 – 5 illustrates this point:

> For thus said YHWH unto me, "Just as the lion or young lion roars over its prey when a group of shepherds is called against it, by their voice, he is not alarmed, and from their noise, he does not cower. So shall YHWH Sebaot come down to battle upon Mt. Zion and upon its hill. Like birds flying, so shall YHWH Sebaot guard over Jerusalem, to guard and to save, to spare and to deliver."

The same problem applies here as with the examples of the Zion tradition cited above. According to Isa 8, 9 – 10, YHWH aligns Himself with the people of Israel and the nations are His foes:

> Be shattered and frightened, O Peoples, and give ear, all of you from the far reaches of the land. Arm yourselves and be dismayed. Arm yourselves and be dismayed. Consult in counsel, but it will be frustrated. Speak a word, but it will not stand, for God is with us.

Isaiah even goes so far as to say that YHWH will defend Zion from the nations even after punishing Zion Himself. Isa 29, 1 – 4 describes YHWH's punishment of Zion (Ariel) but v. 5 – 8 follow:

---

163 VT 7 (1957), 71.

164 Cf. the works by von Rad and Junker cited above.

165 E. g., Ps 102, 14 – 28 [VT 7 (1957), 71]. Cf. von Rad, The City on the Hill, and Junker, Sancta Civitas, Jerusalem Nova, who see this as Isaiah's response to the feast of Sukkot and the reform of Hezekiah, respectively (cf. Wildberger, Jesaja 1 – 12, 80 f.).

166 VT 7, 73 ff.

167 VT 11 (1961), 30. He notes that Wildberger had condemned Naegelsbach for using word statistics to prove Micah's authorship.

168 Cf. von Rad, Old Testament Theology, II 155 ff.

And the mob of your foes shall be like fine dust and the mob of tyrants shall be like passing chaff and at a sudden moment, you will be visited by YHWH Sebaot and with thundering and quaking and great noise, whirlwind and tempest and a flame of consuming fire. And like a dream, a vision of the night, shall the mob of all the nations that gather against Ariel be and all going forth against her and her fortress and besieging her. And it shall be as when a starving man dreams, and behold! Food! And he awakens and he is hungry. And as when a thirsty man dreams and behold! Drink! And he awakens, and behold, he is faint and he thirsts. So shall the mob of all the nations which gather against Mt. Zion be.

As in the Zion psalms, the nations will attack Zion and YHWH will defeat them. Nowhere does Isaiah use the Zion tradition to illustrate any benefit to the nations or show their voluntary acceptance of YHWH's rule. At best, they are tools for YHWH to use (cf. Isa 5, 26 – 30) and if they do not perform their proper function, they will be punished (cf. Isa 10. 5 – 11). According to Isaiah, they will receive no benefits from YHWH nor will they seek Him out. Therefore, Isaiah would not have written Isa 2, 2 – 4.

These considerations leave only one of the four options for the authorship and date of Isa 2, 2 – 4; that Isa 2, 2 – 4 is from a hand later than Isaiah. There are a number of reasons for dating this passage to the late sixth century.

The reference to Isa 2, 2 – 4 in Joel 4, 9 – 12 aids in specifying the date of this passage:

Proclaim this among the nations, prepare for war, arouse the warriors. Let them draw near, let them go up, all the men of war. Beat your plowshares to swords and your pruning hooks to spears. The weak shall say, "I am a warrior." Hurry and come, all you nations round about, and be gathered there. Bring down Your warriors, O YHWH. Let the nations be aroused and let them go up unto the Valley of Jehoshaphat because there I will sit to judge all the nations round about.

Except for the substitution of $r^e m\bar{a}h\hat{i}m$ for $h^a n\hat{i}t\hat{o}t\hat{e}h\alpha m$, the statement in v. 10a is an explicit reversal of Isa 2, 4bα. Furthermore, v. 12b brings in the idea of judging the nations which is also found in Isa 2, 4a, although in Joel, the transitive use of $li\check{s}pot$ indicates that the nations themselves will be judged whereas in Isaiah, the construction, $w^e\check{s}\bar{a}pat$ $b\hat{e}n$, which is parallel to $w^eh\hat{o}k\hat{i}ah$ $l^e...$, indicates that YHWH will settle their disputes by ruling in favor of one over the other. There can be no doubt that Joel borrowed this material from Isaiah or Micah since studies have shown that Joel borrows heavily from other prophetic traditions.[169] He uses Isa 2, 2 – 4/Mic 4, 1 – 4 because of their specific imagery of universal peace in order to deliberately reverse that imagery to universal war. Joel's intent is to announce the coming of eschatological combat. By borrowing Isa 2, 2 – 4/Mic 4, 1 – 4, he drives his point home

---

[169] Wolff, Joel and Amos, 10 f.; Renaud, La Formation, 179 f.

in an especially forceful manner since those texts would be well known statements of universal peace. Since Joel is dated to the first half of the fourth century, following the era of Ezra and Nehemiah,[170] Isa 2, 2 − 4/ Mic 4, 1 − 4 must have been written no later than the early fourth century.

Another indication of the *terminus ad quem* is found in 2 Reg 19, 29 − 31/Isa 37, 30 − 32. The oracle is part of the narrative relating the siege of Jerusalem by Sennacherib in 701 B. C. E. It follows an oracle delivered by Isaiah which condemns Sennacherib for the threatening YHWH's domain and announces a sign to Hezekiah that Judah will be preserved:

> And this shall be the sign to you: eat what grows of itself this year and in the second year, the aftergrowth. And in the third year, sow and harvest and plant vineyards and eat their fruit. And the survivors of the house of Judah who remain will again take root downward and produce fruit above, for from Judah shall a remnant go forth and a group of survivors from Mt. Zion. The zeal of YHWH (Sebaot) shall accomplish this.

A comparison of v. 31a and Isa 2, 3b shows that the two are very similar:

2 Reg 19, 31a: kî mîrûšālayim teṣeʾ šᵉʾerît ûpᵉlêṭâ mehar ṣiyôn qin'at yhwh taʿᵃśæh zoʾt

Isa 2, 3b: kî miṣṣiyôn teṣeʾ tôrâ ûdᵉbar yhwh mîrûšālāyim

Both verses have the same syntactical structure: *kî* + object #1 + *teṣeʾ* + subject #1 + subject #2 + object #2. However, they have exchanged the positions of the objects so that 2 Reg 19, 31a has Jerusalem first and Mt. Zion second whereas Isa 2, 3b has Zion first and Jerusalem second. The subjects have also changed. 2 Reg 19, 31a has "remnant" and "group of survivors" for subjects whereas Isa 2, 3b uses "Torah" and "word of YHWH." It is obvious that either 2 Reg 19, 31a or Isa 2, 3b was modeled on the other. But which is original and which is secondary? One clue is 2 Reg 19, 31b, "the zeal of YHWH (Sebaot)[171] will do this," which also occurs in Isa 9, 6.[172] A second clue is the subjects of 2 Reg 19, 31a, *šᵉʾerît* and *pᵉlêṭâ*. The second term occurs in Isa 4, 2 which, as this study has shown, is closely associated with Isa 2, 2 − 4. Likewise, 2 Reg 37, 29 − 31 associates the remnant with growth and fruit as in Isa 4, 2. Furthermore, *pᵉlêṭâ* is paired with *šᵉʾerît* in Isa 15, 9. It seems that the author of 2 Reg 19, 31 has brought together some pieces from the text of Isaiah to form a new statement. Isa 2, 2 − 4; 4, 2 − 6; and 9, 1 − 6 all refer to a coming age of restoration. By bringing

---

[170] Wolff, Joel and Amos, 5 f.
[171] Add with Isa 37, 32. Cf. *masora ketana* to 2 Reg 19, 31.
[172] Cf. Kaiser, Isaiah 13 − 39, 397.

these pieces together, the author has created a new statement which concisely describes this age.

Most scholars recognize that 2 Reg 19, 29–31/Isa 37, 30–32 belongs to a legendary source or stratum of the Sennacherib invasion narrative which dates to post-exilic times.[173] They also recognize that the oracles in 2 Reg 19, 21–28 and 29–31 (= Isa 37, 22–29, 30–32) are later interpolations into the text.[174] Some regard them as authentic Isaianic oracles since they correspond so well with Isaiah's thought.[175] It is certainly possible that authentic oracles could be inserted into a later text, yet there is evidence of late influence in these oracles. The statements which begin 2 Reg 19, 25/Isa 37, 26, "Have you not heard that from long ago, I did it? That from days of old, I conceived it? Now, I have brought it about," are typical of Deutero-Isaiah, not Isaiah.[176] If these verses contain authentic Isaianic material, they have been reworked. Therefore, the post-exilic dating of these texts must be maintained and it must be concluded that the text of Isa 2, 2–4, together with that of 4, 2–6, was known in post-exilic times.

This "post-exilic" *terminus ad quem* is vague but it is significant. This is because many texts which discuss the nations' participation in the cult of the Jerusalem Temple date to the time of the return of the exiles to Jerusalem and their rebuilding of the Temple.[177] One text from the period which relates to Isa 2, 2–4 is Zach 8, 20–23:[178]

> Thus, says YHWH Sebaot, "Again shall peoples come and the inhabitants of many cities. And the inhabitants of one shall go to the inhabitants of another saying, 'Let us indeed go to implore the face of YHWH and seek YHWH Sebaot. I will go, indeed I will.'" And many peoples shall come and numerous nations to seek YHWH Sebaot in Jerusalem and to implore the face of YHWH. Thus says YHWH Sebaot, "In those days, when ten men from all the peoples shall seize, then shall they seize the skirt of a man of Judah saying, 'Let us go with you, for we have heard that the God is with you.'"

As in Isa 2, 2–4, the peoples come voluntarily to Jerusalem to implore the face of YHWH. As Renaud noted, this is similar to their seeking

---

[173] On the source division of this narrative, cf. Childs, Isaiah and the Assyrian Crisis, 96 f.; Kaiser, Isaiah 13–39, 369 ff., 384 f.

[174] Childs, Isaiah and the Assyrian Crisis, 96 f.; Kaiser, Isaiah 13–39, 376.

[175] J. Gray, I & II Kings, OTL, 1970², 688, 692; J. A. Montgomery and H. S. Gehman, Kings, ICC, 1951, 494 ff.; G. Hasel, The Remnant, AUM 5, 1980³, 332, n. 437.

[176] Isa 40, 21, 28; 44, 8; 45, 21; 46, 8–11. Cf. Kaiser, Isaiah 13–39, 396.

[177] Cf. Renaud, La Formation, 166 ff.

[178] W. Rudolph, Sacharja 1–8, KAT XIII/4, 1976, 151 f.; P. R. Ackroyd, Exile and Restoration, 1968, 216 f.; Eissfeldt, The Old Testament: An Introduction, 432 f.; Kaiser, Introduction to the Old Testament, 277; and Fohrer, Introduction to the Old Testament, 463, think they are later but with little basis.

YHWH's Torah.[179] He also noted that the expressions, *'ammîm rabbîm* and *gôyim 'ᵃṣûmîm*, occur only here (v. 22) and in Mic 4, 3, the sister text to Isa 2, 2−4.[180] The expression *nelᵉkâ*, also occurs in these texts (Zach 8, 21; Isa 2, 3; Mic 4, 2).[181] These considerations indicate that the author of Zach 8, 20−23 was familiar with Isa 2, 2−4/Mic 4, 1−4.

A thematically similar text from the same period,[182] but with fewer linguistic parallels, is Zach 2, 14−16:

> "Shout and rejoice, O Daughter of Zion, for behold! I have come and I will dwell in your midst," utterance of YHWH. And many nations shall attach themselves unto YHWH in that day and they shall be a people to Me and I shall dwell in your midst. And you shall know that YHWH Sebaot has sent me unto you and YHWH shall inherit Judah as His portion upon the holy ground and He shall again choose Jerusalem.

The text is somewhat confused but the meaning is clear. The nations accept YHWH's lordship, yet Jerusalem maintains its special significance to YHWH.[183] There are a number of other important texts in which the nations undertake a pilgrimage to Jerusalem.[184] These also stem from the period of the return to Jerusalem and include Isa 56, 6−8; 60, 1−22;[185] 66, 18−19, 21;[186] and Hag 2, 7−9.[187] Thus, the theme of the pilgrimage of the peoples to Zion is characteristic of the early post-exilic period when the exiles began to return to Jerusalem to rebuild the Temple. Isa 2, 2−4/Mic 4, 1−4 corresponds well with the concerns of this period.

There is an earlier text from Deutero-Isaiah which has important connections with Isa 2, 2−4.[188] Isa 51, 4−6 describes YHWH's sending Torah, justice, and salvation to the peoples and affirms His rule over them. V. 4 is especially interesting in that it includes the following statement, *kî tôrâ me'ittî teṣe' ûmišpāṭî lᵉ'ôr 'ammîm*, "For Torah goes

---

[179] Renaud, La Formation, 167.

[180] Renaud, La Formation, 167 f. Cf. *'ammîm rabbîm* in Isa 2, 3, 4.

[181] Cf. D. L. Petersen, Haggai and Zechariah 1−8, OTL, 1984, 316 ff., 319 f. Note the correspondence between *'ᵃlohîm 'immākæm*, "God is with you," in Zach 8, 23 and *'immānû 'el*, "God is with us," in Isa 7, 14; 8, 8; 8, 10.

[182] Rudolph, Sacharja 1−8, 89, 90 f.; Ackroyd, Exile and Restoration, 181; Fohrer, Introduction to the Old Testament, 463; Eissfeldt, The Old Testament, 432 f. Kaiser, Introduction to the Old Testament, 277, says it is later.

[183] Rudolph Sacharja 1−8, 91.

[184] Cf. Renaud, La Formation, 167 f.

[185] Cf. von Rad, The City on the Hill. Westermann, Isaiah 40−66, 296 f., considers this text to be authentic to Trito-Isaiah.

[186] Westermann, Isaiah 40−66, 423, considers this text to be secondary.

[187] Cf. von Rad, The City on the Hill.

[188] Cf. Renaud, La Formation, 168 f.

forth from Me and My justice shall be a light of the peoples." The syntactic structure is very similar to that of Isa 2, 3b, especially with regard to the particle *kî*, the use of the preposition *min* plus object, the verb *teṣeʾ*, and the subject *tôrâ*. This verse and Isa 2, 2−4 make very similar statements, that Torah shall go forth to the nations. But there are differences. Isa 51, 4 pairs *tôrâ* with *mišpāṭ* whereas Isa 2, 3 uses *dᵉbar yhwh*. Also, Isa 2, 3 states that Torah will go forth from Jerusalem and Zion, but Isa 51, 4 states that "it will go forth from Me," i. e., YHWH. Isa 51, 4 does not mention Jerusalem at all. According to Deutero-isaiah, Jerusalem is where YHWH is returning (cf. Isa 40, 9−11; 52, 7−10) but Isa 2, 2−4 presupposes that He is already there. Deutero-Isaiah likewise says little about a pilgrimage of the nations to Zion. His concern is that the exiles return.[189] The only context in which the nations come to Jerusalem in Deutero-Isaiah portrays them as bringing the exiles back and submitting to them (Isa 49, 22−23). As demonstrated above, the pilgrimage motif whereby the nations come to Jerusalem to revere YHWH and receive benefits from Him is characteristic of Trito-Isaiah and Zechariah in the period of the return. Furthermore, Westermann has shown the direct dependence of Isa 51, 4−6 on the servant song in Isa 42, 1−4 where the servant takes YHWH's justice to the nations. They wait for the servant, they do not come to him.[190] There appears to be a development from Deutero-Isaiah to Trito-Isaiah and Zechariah. Deutero-Isaiah states that YHWH will send His Torah and justice to the nations, but Trito-Isaiah and Zechariah claim that the nations will come to Him in Jerusalem. Isa 2, 2−4 contains the concept of Torah going out to the nations, but it also contains the pilgrimage motif. Therefore, Isa 2, 2−4 should be dated after the time of Deutero-Isaiah to the period of the return when Jerusalem was reestablished as YHWH's home.

Finally, the vision of universal peace portrayed in this oracle corresponds well to the expectations for the final years of Cyrus' reign after his accession to the throne in Babylon. His designation as YHWH's anointed (Isa 45, 1; cf. 44, 28), his enlightened treatment of subject populations,[191] and the general peace which followed the fall of Babylon after years of Assyrian and Babylonian military oppression would have prompted the writing of such a vision. The renewal of political unrest during the reigns of Cambyses (530−522) and Darius I (522−486) and the deterioration of conditions under their successors make it unlikely

---

[189] von Rad, Old Testament Theology, II 244 f.
[190] Isaiah 40−66, 235.
[191] ANET, 316. Cf. 2 Chr 36, 22−23; Ezr 1, 1−4; 6, 3−5.

that the oracle would have been written much later than the completion of the Second Temple.[192] Thus, Isa 2, 2 – 4 dates to the late sixth century.[193]

b. Isa 2, 5 – 22

As noted above, Isa 2, 5 – 22 has very little to do with Isa 2, 2 – 4. Isa 2, 2 – 4 is concerned with Jerusalem, Torah, and the nations, but Isa 2, 5 – 22 deals with the "House of Jacob." The mention of the "House of Jacob" is the only conceivable link between Isa 2, 5 – 22 and 2, 2 – 4 since it occurs twice in v. 5 – 6 and "House of the God of Jacob" occurs in v. 3. But after v. 6a, no mention of Jacob appears again in 2, 5 – 22. Instead, the oracle refers to the people as *ʾādām, ʾîš*, or *ʾanāšîm*. This suggests that 2, 5 – 6a may be a redactional addition to 2, 6b – 22, designed to link it to 2, 2 – 4. The mention of *bᵉʾôr yhwh* in v. 5 suggests that such is the case for this verse. Certainly, there is an association between "light" (*ʾôr*) and Torah (v. 3) in the wisdom traditions[194] and in the hymnic tradition, light (*ʾôr*) guides the faithful to YHWH's mountain.[195] Most important is the association of light with Torah and justice in Deutero-Isaiah. In Isa 51, 4, YHWH sends out His Torah as "a light to the peoples."[196] Furthermore, Isa 2, 5 was composed with 2, 2 – 4 as a model. It seems likely that it was composed by someone who was influenced by the thinking of Deutero-Isaiah in order to link 2, 6 – 22 with 2, 2 – 4. This is not the case with v. 6a, however. V. 6a is quite important to 2, 6 – 22 since it introduces the discourse to YHWH in v. 6 – 9. Yet, the syntax of v. 6a is confused due to the mention of the "House of Jacob." Because "House of Jacob" in v. 6a is clearly linked with v. 2 – 4 and 5 but not to the rest of 2, 6 – 22, and because it is so syntactically awkward, it must be an insertion made by the redactor who composed v. 5 to link v. 2 – 4 with v. 6* – 22. The purpose of inserting "House of Jacob" would have been to identify the people of v. 6* – 22 (*ʾādām/ʾanāšîm*) with the "House of Jacob" of v. 5 and "Jacob" of v. 3 and thus insure an easier transition from 2, 2 – 4 to 2, 6* – 22.

Within v. 6* – 22, there is evidence that parts of this text are later expansions.

---

[192] For an account of political conditions during these years, see J. Bright, A History of Israel, 1981³, 361 f., 364 ff., 374 f.

[193] Cf. Werner, Eschatologische Texte, 151 ff., who dates Isa 2, 2 – 4 to the late 6th/early 5th century on the basis of thematic and motific correspondences with texts from this period.

[194] Prov. 4, 18; 6, 23. Cf. S. Aalen, TDOT, I 162.

[195] Ps 43, 3.

[196] Cf. Isa 42, 6; 49, 6; and 42, 16.

V. 22 is the most obvious example of a later addition to the text. It does not fit well with the structure of the rest of the unit since it is a wisdom saying placed in the context of what is basically a judgment speech. Its second person plural form of address, directed to the reader, does not correspond to the singular address to YHWH (v. 6, 9) or to the people (v. 10) in the rest of the unit. Furthermore, it does not appear in the LXX, one of the earliest versions available, although it does appear in 1QIsaᵃ and 1QS 5, 17.[197] Because the LXX text is consistently faithful to the consonantal text of the MT,[198] whereas 1QIsaᵃ is not, v. 22 must be considered as a late addition to the text whose place was not completely secure by the time of LXX and 1QIsaᵃ.[199] Its purpose is to draw out the lesson of v. 6–22, that one should not rely on the works of man, but on God.

V. 20–21 are another case in point. These verses borrow most of their language from other parts of the oracle, e. g., *bayyôm hahû'* also appears in v. 12 and 17; *'ᵉlîlê kaspô* and *'ᵉlîlê zᵉhābô* corresponds to terminology from v. 7a and 8a: *ᵃšær 'āśû lô lᵉhištaḥᵃwot* uses terminology from v. 8b: *lābô' bᵉniqrôt haṣṣurîm ûbisʿipê hassᵉlāʿîm* borrows terminology from v. 10a and 19a; *mippᵉnê paḥad yhwh ûmehᵃdar gᵉʾônô bᵉqûmô laʿᵃroṣ hāʾāræṣ* also appears in v. 19b and in shorter form in v. 10b. Furthermore, these verses seem to be modeled on v. 18–19 as an attempt to clarify their meaning.[200] They also appear to change the meaning of v. 18–19. Whereas v. 18–19 state that the false gods will "pass away" and will enter into rocks, v. 20–21 explain that men will cast the false gods away and that it is men who will hide in the rocks. If the oracle had originally ended with v. 19, YHWH's actions would have been directed against the false gods and the commands in v. 10 would also have been addressed to them. V. 20–21, however, assume that YHWH's actions are directed against the people and that the commands in v. 10 are directed to the people as well. Thus, v. 20–21 understand that the people are to blame for the introduction of false gods into their land. V. 18–19, on the other hand, with the force of punishment directed against the false gods, would have viewed the false gods as the party responsible for the people's guilt. Thus, v. 20–21 are

---

[197] A. van der Kooij, Die Alten Textzeugen des Jesajabuches, OBO 35, 1981, 21, 112, places both LXX Isa and 1QIsaᵃ in the earliest period of textual witnesses to Isaiah, i. e., 200–75 B. C. E.

[198] S. Jellicoe, The Septuagint and Modern Study, 1968, 300. Furthermore, the text critical comments above have noted that LXX generally tries to work with a difficult text, especially in the case of 3, 24–25, rather than eliminate material. Sometimes it does eliminate repetitious material (e. g., 3, 15; 4, 6), but v. 22 is not repetitious.

[199] Cf. Wildberger, Jesaja 1–12, 96.

[200] Wildberger, Jesaja 1–12, 96.

a later addition, perhaps by a member of an Isaianic school, which reinterprets an aspect of the oracle in v. 6* – 19.[201]

V. 18 – 19 also appear to be a later addition to the original oracle. The syntactic construction of v. 18 is problematic in that $w^e h \bar{a}^{,æ} l \hat{\imath} l \hat{\imath} m$ and $y a h^a l \bar{o} p$ do not agree with respect to number. This requires that $y h w h$ from v. 17b is the subject of the verb and $w^e h \bar{a}^{,æ} l \hat{\imath} l \hat{\imath} m$ is the object, an awkward reading at best. The passage also picks up themes and some language from earlier parts of the oracle, e. g., the mention of the false gods from v. 8, the hiding in the rocks from v. 10, and the refrain, "From before the fear of YHWH and from His magnificent splendor" from v. 10. However, it combines them in such a way so as to understand YHWH's anger and actions as directed against the false gods, which is not apparent from the rest of the oracle. The language of v. 6* – 17 is ambiguous enough to allow for such an interpretation. But according to the accusations in v. 6 – 9, it is the people who have done wrong, whereas in v. 18 – 19, it is the false gods who are punished. V. 18 – 19 therefore are an addition made to clarify the oracle in v. 6* – 17 with the understanding that the false gods were responsible for the people's guilt. Consequently, they should be punished.

A number of scholars have claimed that v. 9b is a marginal gloss. Its appearance in the *Vorlage* of the LXX indicates that this is not the case.

Other scholars have attempted to claim that v. 10 and 11 are secondary additions which were intended to tie together v. 7 – 9a and v. 12 – 17 which they believe were originally separate. This position depends on the view that v. 12 – 17 are a "closed unit" and that grammatical inconsistencies in v. 6* – 9a require that v. 6* be secondary.[202] This would leave two fragmentary units, i. e., an accusation (v. 7 – 9a) without a statement of judgment, and a statement of judgment (v. 12 – 17) without an accusation. Furthermore, grammatical inconsistencies are common in this text. To separate these sections would destroy the point of the whole oracle, i. e., that man's desire to lower himself with false gods (v. 6 – 9) leads to YHWH's lowering man. This demonstrates the impotency of the false gods and His own supreme power (v. 10 – 17). V. 6* – 17, therefore, represent the original oracle.

The historical setting of this oracle seems to be in the period before Sennacherib's invasion when Hezekiah was making alliances with his neighbors to oppose Assyrian suzerainty. The principle allies would be

---

[201] J. Blenkinsopp, ZAW 93 (1981), 60 f., considers this expansion analogous to the "pesher" technique employed at Qumran.

[202] E. g., Wildberger, Jesaja 1 – 12, 95 f.

Egypt and Philistia, but Phoenicia seems to have been involved as well.[203] Elsewhere, Isaiah has given his opinion of foreign alliances, particularly with Egypt, and has foreseen the problems of false gods and sorcery which accompany such alliances.[204] Egypt would also have supplied the chariotry mentioned in verse 7[205] as well as the main financial backing since Phoenicia, Philistia, and Judah were already paying tribute to Assyria. Likewise, Clements notes that the $\check{s}^e k\hat{\imath}y\hat{o}t$ mentioned in v. 16 are an Egyptian type of watercraft.[206] The oracle alludes to the Philistines in v. 6 and possibly to the Phoenicians in v. 13. The intent of this oracle, composed by Isaiah, was to express his opposition to Hezekiah's alliances against Assyria.[207] The oracle underwent expansion in two stages within the Isaianic school (i.e., the additions of v. 18–19 and 20–21) before it was connected to 2, 2–4 by a redactor who added 2, 5–6*. V. 22 is an addition made some time after this section found its place in the book as whole.

c. Isa 3, 1–15

Within Isa 3, 1–15, v. 1–9 are a self-contained oracle which explain that the deportation of Jerusalem's and Judah's leaders is a result of the people's rebellion against YHWH. However, other material follows which must be analyzed.

As noted in the discussion of the structure of this passage, v. 10–11 modify the woe statement of v. 9b. Whereas v. 9b condemned every one of the people of Jerusalem and Judah, v. 10–11 make a distinction between the righteous and the wicked which is found nowhere else in the oracle. Furthermore, v. 10–11 appear to have borrowed some vocabulary from other parts of the oracle. Thus, $ma'all\hat{e}h\alpha m$ in v. 10 also appears in v. 8. The occurrence of $r\bar{a}'$ in v. 11 could be derived from $r\bar{a}'\hat{a}$ in v. 9. The word $g^em\hat{u}l$ in v. 11 is derived from $g\bar{a}m^el\hat{u}$ in v. 9. Finally, the '$\hat{o}y$ form of v. 11 is modeled on the '$\hat{o}y$ form of v. 9b. Such a distinction between right and wrong and the rewards or consequences for each has connections in the Deuteronomistic tradition, the wisdom tradition, and Trito-Isaiah. As noted in the discussion of the structure

---

[203] On the political background and alliances of Hezekiah's revolt against Assyria, see B. Oded's remarks in Israelite and Judaean History, ed. by J. Hayes and J. M. Miller, 1977, 441 ff.

[204] Isa 19, 1–3; 30, 1–7; cf. 18, 1–7.

[205] Cf. 2 Reg 18, 24 = Isa 36, 9.

[206] Isaiah 1–39, 46.

[207] It is unlikely that this oracles date to the Syro-Ephraimitic War as Clements, Isaiah 1–39, 43, and others maintain. Judah was militarily weak at this time and lacked allies.

of this unit, v. 12 – 15 substantially modify this oracle in that they focus the blame for Jerusalem's and Judah's downfall on the leaders. There is some inconsistency here as well. In v. 13 – 15, the leaders are accused of oppressing the people but v. 8 – 9 presuppose that the people are corrupt, not oppressed. Furthermore, the leaders mentioned here are elders and commanders, hardly the comprehensive catalogue of v. 1 – 3. Also, from the perspective of v. 13 – 15, punishment has not yet come to the leaders, whereas in v. 1 – 9 it has.

V. 12, on the other hand, appears to have connections with v. 1 – 9 and with v. 13 – 15. Thus, *nogᵉśâw* in v. 12 recalls *wᵉniggaś* of v. 5; *mᵉʿôlel* of v. 12 recalls *wᵉtaʿᵃlûlîm* of v. 4; and *māśᵉlû bô* in v. 12 recalls *yimśᵉlû-bām* of v. 4. Likewise, *ʿammî* in v. 12 corresponds to *ʿammî* in v. 15 and *wᵉnošîm* (LXX) in v. 12 identifies the crimes mentioned in v. 14. It seems that v. 12 is an editorial link which connects v. 13 – 15 with v. 1 – 9. The historical situation of v. 1 – 9 appears to be the aftermath of Sennacherib's siege against Jerusalem when a number of people were deported to Assyria.[208] V. 13 – 15 could have been spoken at any time during Isaiah's career. Isaiah's opinion of the leaders of Jerusalem and Judah is well known and it is very likely that he is the one who made the connection between v. 13 – 15 and 1 – 9 with v. 12. V. 10 – 11 are very likely much later due to their affinities with Trito-Isaiah and Deuteronomistic thought, i. e., about the fifth century.

d. Isa 3, 16 – 4, 1

Within 3, 16 – 4, 1, it is evident that 3, 25 – 4, 1 is originally from another context. This oracle is not addressed to the women of Jerusalem as is the rest of passage. Its second person feminine singular address in v. 25 and the imagery of v. 26 indicate that this passage is directed against a city. While the identification of the city is not clear from the oracle itself, in the present context it is Jerusalem. The manner in which this oracle was worked into the structure of Isa 3, 16 – 4, 1 has already been noted. There is no reason to dispute the Isaianic authorship of 3, 25 – 4, 1 or 3, 16 – 4, 1 as a whole.[209] The peace and prosperity presupposed by the unit indicate that it refers to the time of Hezekiah,

---

[208] Cf. ANET, 288.

[209] Some scholars claim that the catalogue in v. 18 – 23 is a later expansion due to its *bayyôm hahûʾ* formula and Aramaic influence in the names of some of the items mentioned (e. g., Clements, Isaiah 1 – 39, 50 f.). However, the catalogue technique appears in Isa 3, 1 – 3 and 2, 12 – 16, both of which are Isaianic. As for foreign influence in the names of the items, many of them would have been acquired by trade and their names could easily reflect foreign influence.

before his revolt against Sennacherib.[210] At this time, Hezekiah had the money to restore the Temple but his predecessor would have been too burdened by the Syro-Ephraimite encounter and tribute to Assyria to allow for prosperous times.

e. Isa 4, 2 — 6

Isa 4, 2 — 6 presents a problem. It begins by stating that the "shoot of YHWH" and the "fruit of the land" shall be objects of beauty, pride, etc., to the escaped portion of *Israel*. Yet v. 3 — 6 are concerned exclusively with the fate of the remnant in *Jerusalem*. Surely Isaiah understood that Jerusalem and Israel were distinct.[211] Furthermore, he almost never singles out a remnant from Jerusalem alone for restoration. He speaks of the remnant of Jacob (Isa 10, 21) or Israel (Isa 10, 20) or His (YHWH's) people (Isa 11, 11, 16; 28, 5). An exception to this is in Isa 37, 32, which possibly contains authentic Isaianic material but is influenced by later ideology. Thus, it can not serve as a reliable witness to Isaiah's thought.

With regard to the date of this passage, the phrase, "all who are inscribed for life in Jerusalem," (v. 3) should be noted. This is a reference to YHWH's book of life which scholars identify as a late concept in Biblical literature.[212] More important is the cloud by day and the smoke and fire by night which will protect Zion (v. 5). As noted in Chapter II, this is a direct reference to the Exodus traditions in which YHWH's Presence was symbolized by a pillar of cloud by day and a pillar of fire by night which protected the people and led them through the wilderness. The use of Exodus motifs is not characteristic of Isaiah of Jerusalem.[213] Exodus motifs do play a major role in the prophecies of Deutero-Isaiah, however.[214] Deutero-Isaiah was among the first to combine Exodus and Jerusalem traditions.[215] Furthermore, the use of creation language, such as *bārā'* in v. 5, is characteristic of Deutero-Isaiah.[216] However, the passage also has an unmistakable priestly stamp which is not characteristic of Deutero-Isaiah but does appear in the Trito-Isaiah materials. Thus,

---

[210] Cf. 2 Chr 32, 27 — 31.

[211] Cf. Isa 8, 14.

[212] Cf. Ps 69, 29; Ex 32, 32; Dan 12, 1 (also Mal 3, 16; Est 6, 1). Wildberger, Jesaja 1 — 12, 157 f.

[213] C. Stuhlmueller, Creative Redemption in Deutero-Isaiah, AnBib 43, 1970, 64 f.

[214] Anderson, Exodus Typology in Second Isaiah; Kiesow, Exodustexte im Jesajabuch.

[215] Anderson, Exodus and Covenant in Deutero-Isaiah and Prophetic Tradition. On Deutero-Isaiah's use of tradition in general, see von Rad, Old Testament Theology, II 238 ff.

[216] Stuhlmueller, Creative Redemption, 209 ff.

the purification of Jerusalem borrows the imagery of the cleansing of a menstrual woman found in the priestly purity laws (Lev 15, 19−31). The terminology is also priestly: *rāḥaṣ* and *yādîaḥ* for cleansing;[217] *qādôš* for the people;[218] and *miqrā'* for the congregation.[219] Even the concept of the Presence of YHWH at His sanctuary, represented by cloud, smoke, and fire, is characteristic of the priestly traditions of the Torah.[220] Such priestly concerns are characteristic of the period following that of Deutero-Isaiah, when the exiles returned and the building of the second Temple began. However, they are particularly stressed in the period of Ezra and Nehemiah, when the Jerusalem community was established as a theocracy.[221]

In its present form, Isa 4, 2−6 must date to the post-exilic period.[222] While knowledge of this period is somewhat lacking, the most likely time for the writing of this text is the mid- to late-fifth century, in the time of Ezra and Nehemiah. The priestly influence and the focus on Jerusalem confirm this for v. 3−6.[223] V. 2 is probably not from the same

---

[217] The term *rāḥaṣ* appears twenty-six times in Lev and in many other places in the P source of the Torah. For *yādîaḥ*, cf. Ex 40, 38; 2 Chr 4, 6.

[218] This is not to suggest that *qādôš* is exclusively a priestly term, however.

[219] Lev 23, 2, 3, 4, 7, 8, 21, 24, 27, 35, 36, 37; Num 10, 2; 28, 18, 25, 26; 29, 1, 7, 12. Cf. Neh 12, 6; Isa 1, 13.

[220] G. H. Davies, IDB III 817, notes that *'āmûd*, "pillar," is the term that distinguishes the JE use of cloud and fire from P which does not use it. No pillar is mentioned in the present context.

[221] Cf. S. Hermann, A History of Old Testament Times, 1975, 307 ff.; Bright, A History of Israel, 379 ff.

[222] There are two other passages which have much in common with Isa 4, 2−6. These are Isa 28, 5−6 and 37, 30−32. Scholars have noted the strong correspondence between the vocabulary and concepts of Isa 28, 5−6 and 4, 2−6 and suggest that they were written by the same hand (cf. D. L. Petersen, Isaiah 28, A Redaction Critical Study, SBL 1979 Seminar Papers, II ed. by P. Achtemeier, 1979, 107). The dating of this passage is disputed, however. Some claim that it is from a later hand since its apparent salvation perspective appears to intrude into a judgment oracle (cf. Petersen's summary of scholarship on pp. 102 ff.). Others claim that the juxtaposition of salvation and judgment is perfectly in line with Isaiah's thinking (e. g., Hasel, The Remnant, 301 f. Cf. his notes on the positions of other scholars.) The evidence can go either way. Therefore, Isa 28, 5−6 can provide no sure indication of the dating of Isa 4, 2−6, especially for v. 2. Isa 37, 30−32, especially v. 31 with its agricultural portrayal of the survival of the remnant is similar in thought to 4, 2. The influence of later ideology on this passage was noted above, however. Isa 37, 30−32 may contain early material, but in its present form, it is post-exilic.

[223] Werner, Eschatologische Texte, 91 ff., dates 4, 2−6 to the period after Ezra and Nehemiah in the mid-4th or 3rd centuries. His view is based primarily on a supposed dependence of v. 6 on Isa 25, 4. Wildberger, Jesaja 13−27, 910, indicates that Isa 24−27 borrowed from previous prophetic traditions. On the use of Isaianic textual

hand as v. 3 – 6, however. V. 2 focuses on Israel in general whereas
v. 3 – 6 specify the survivor(s) of Israel as the remaining Jerusalem
community.[224] There apparently were tensions in the post-exilic community between people who remained in the land and those who returned
from exile in Babylon claiming to be the true remnant of Israel.[225] Since
v. 3 – 6 specify v. 2, it may be assumed that v. 2 was written at an earlier
time, perhaps at the end of the sixth century or the beginning of the
fifth. This would have been before the exclusionary policies of Ezra and
Nehemiah were able to take hold of the post-exilic community, i. e., at
a time when the restoration of Israel was conceived in broader terms.

f. Redactional reconstruction: Isaiah 2, 1 – 4, 6

The above discussion demonstrated that Isa 2 – 4 consists of a
number of previously independent units and editorial material which
are dated as follows:

1)	Isa 2, 2 – 4:	late 6th century
2)	Isa 2, 5 – 6*:	(editorial) late 6th century or later
3)	Isa 2, 6* – 17:	(Isaiah), prior to 701 B. C. E.
4)	Isa 2, 18 – 19:	(Isaianic school), 7th century?
5)	Isa 2, 20 – 21:	(Isaianic school), 7th century?
6)	Isa 2, 22:	(marginal gloss), 4th – 3rd century?
7)	Isa 3, 1 – 15*:	(Isaiah), after 701 B. C. E.
	v. 1 – 9:	(Isaiah), after 701 B. C. E.
	v. 10 – 11:	(Dtr. oriented writer), 5th century
	v. 12:	(Isaiah?), after 701 B. C. E.
	v. 13 – 15:	(Isaiah), 735 – 701 B. C. E.
8)	Isa 3, 16 – 4, 1:	(Isaiah), prior to 701 B. C. E.
9)	Isa 4, 2 – 6:	mid- to late-5th century
	v. 2:	late 6th/early 5th century
	v. 3 – 6:	mid- to late-5th century

Thus, with the exception of minor insertions and expansions, such as
2, 18 – 19; 2, 20 – 21; 2, 22; 3, 10 – 11; and perhaps 3, 12, Isa 2, 6* – 4, 1
contains entirely Isaianic material which focuses primarily on the invasion of Judah by the Assyrians in 701 B. C. E. The three major sections
of this material, 2, 6* – 22; 3, 1 – 15; and 3, 16 – 4, 1, are mainly concerned with the guilt of the people and the punishment which they

---

material in Isa 24 – 27 (including the use of 4, 6 in 25, 4), see M. Sweeney, Textual
Citations in Isaiah 24 – 27: Toward an Understanding of the Redactional Function of
Chapters 24 – 27 in the Book of Isaiah, forthcoming in JBL.

[224] Cf. Hasel, The Remnant, 258, n. 155, for the various opinions.

[225] Bright, A History of Israel, 365 f.

receive in the form of the Assyrian invasion. Interestingly, Isa 2, 2–4 and 4, 2, which frame this block of material, both date to the late sixth or early fifth century. Rather than focusing on the guilt of the people and their punishment, these sections emphasize themes of restoration. However, they do not seem to stem from the same hand. Isa 2, 2–4 is concerned with Jerusalem in relation to the nations and has very little to say about Israel in general. Isa 4, 2 focuses specifically on Israel and is not concerned with Jerusalem or with the nations. As noted above, Isa 2, 5–6* is an editorial unit, the purpose of which is to join 2, 2–4 with 2, 6*–22. It was formed with 2, 2–4 as a model but its concerns are different in that it deals specifically with the House of Jacob instead of Jerusalem and the nations. By joining 2, 2–4 and 2, 6–22, it relates the situation of Israel in general (here called to House of Jacob) to the projected future world in which YHWH rules the nations from Zion. By implication, it claims that Israel has a role in this new world but that it first had to be punished and cleared of its false gods before it could play its part. It is with this purpose in mind that Isa 4, 2 becomes significant. This verse focuses on Israel as does 2, 5–6*. Furthermore, it states that the "shoot of YHWH" and the "fruit of the land" shall be for beauty, glory, pride, etc., for the remnant of Israel. This reverses the situation portrayed in 2, 6–22 in which the people considered their own creations, military might, wealth, sailing ships, and idols, as objects of pride, glory, and splendor. This theme was also stressed in the clothing catalogue of 3, 18–23. The differences in vocabulary and the lack of direct reference to anything in 2, 6*–4, 1 indicate that 4, 2 was not composed for its present position. On the other hand, the concern with Israel's relation to YHWH and the allusion to correcting the situation presupposed by 2, 6*–22 and 3, 1–4, 1 lead to the conclusion that the redactor who wrote 2, 5–6* also selected 4, 2 as the conclusion for 2, 2–4, 2. The dates and themes of 2, 2–4 and 4, 2 make it clear that this unit would have been in existence in the early fifth century. Its purpose would have been to proclaim YHWH's world rule as well as to explain Israel's (and Jerusalem's) punishment as necessary to prepare it for its role in this new world. The conclusion of this unit at 4, 2 indicates that Israel, like the nations, will recognize YHWH's sovereignty. Such a unit would have helped to provide moral support to the returning exiles who at that time were working to reestablish the Jewish community.

As noted above, Isa 4, 3–6 is specifically focused on the remnant of the people in Jerusalem rather than on the people of Israel in general. It therefore defines the remnant of Israel as those who are in Jerusalem. Because these verses date to the mid- or late-fifth century, they are a later supplement to 4, 2 in particular and 2, 2–4, 2 in general. Their purpose was to define the remnant of Israel as the Jerusalem community and thus legitimate its claim as the true remnant of Israel. It does this by portraying the Jerusalem community as the holy and pure remnant that was left after YHWH had cleansed the city of the crimes which were mentioned in the previous sections.[226] It also mentions YHWH's special protection for this community which further legitimizes its claim.

Isa 3, 10–11 focuses on the distinction between the righteous and the wicked and the rewards or consequences which they will receive as a result of their actions. As noted above, this concern corresponds with Deuteronomistic and Trito-Isaianic thought. It also corresponds with the concerns of the Deuteronomistically oriented redactor of chapter 1.

Finally, the title for this section, Isa 2, 1, dates to the post-exilic period due to its mention of "Judah and Jerusalem," a stereotypical expression for the post-exilic community centered in Jerusalem.[227] It was very likely in place before the supplementary material in 4, 3–6 was added to 2, 2–4, 2.[228]

---

[226] Note that these verses take special care to blame the Daughters of Zion for the defiled state of the city (v. 4) which indicates that the writer of these verses presupposed the assignment of responsibility represented in 3, 1–15, i.e., the people were corrupt because their leaders were corrupt and the leaders were corrupt because of the women (cf. 3, 12 and the reading "and women" there).

[227] Cf. Jones, ZAW 67 (1955), 239 f. According to Jones, oracles authentic to Isaiah use the sequence Jerusalem/Judah.

[228] Wiklander's dating of the final form of Isa 2–4 to ca. 734–622 must be rejected (Prophecy as Literature, 175 ff.). Although a number of the texts within these chapters were originally composed during this period, the present analysis demonstrates that the key organizing texts (Isa 2, 1; 2, 2–4; 2, 5–6*; 4, 2; and 4, 3–6) were composed at a much later time. Because of his focus on covenant as the underlying concept of this text and the sociopolitical assumptions he makes concerning the meaning of this concept, he overlooks a number of tensions and indications of later material within these chapters in an attempt to demonstrate the metaphorical expression of this concept. Consequently, he is forced to choose a pre-exilic setting for this text which accounts for a time when Judah was a vassal to a foreign power and enjoyed relative peace and prosperity. Nevertheless, Wiklander's dating may be correct for an earlier form of these chapters. The 7th century additions to Isa 2, 6*–17 (i.e., 2, 18 f.; 2, 20 f.) suggest that this material circulated in some form during the 7th century. If this is the case, the aftermath of Sennacherib's invasion of Judah, including the final years of Hezekiah's reign (701–687) and the reign of Manasseh (687–642), would provide an appropriate setting for Isa 2, 6*–21 + 3, 1–9; 3, 12–4, 1. The addition of 2, 18 f. and 2, 20 f., which accentuates the world-wide perspective of 2, 6*–17 (n. b. the references to 'ādām and 'anāšîm throughout these verses), was probably motivated by the extension of Assyrian power into Egypt during the reign of Esarhaddon (681–669). The reference to deported officials in 3, 1 ff., not including the king (cf. Wiklander, Prophecy as Literature, 177 ff.), would also correspond to the situation in Judah during these years. Finally, although 3, 1–9 and 3, 25–4, 1 demonstrate that Jerusalem has been defeated, there is no indication in 2, 6*–21 + 3, 1–9; 3, 12–4, 1 that the city

Thus, by composing 2, 5−6* and adding 2, 2−4 and 4, 2, a late sixth or early fifth century redactor was able to transform a collection of Isaiah's oracles concerning Sennacherib's invasion of Judah into the substance of a theological explanation for Israel's suffering, the destruction of its land, and the deportation of the people. By calling attention to YHWH's future world rule from Zion in the context of the early years of the Persian empire, this redaction was able to claim that the suffering which Israel had endured served a purpose. Before this purpose could be accomplished, however, Zion required cleansing as her people had defiled her with their transgressions. Once this cleansing was completed, YHWH's purpose, the manifestation of His rule over the entire world, could be realized. Thus, the punishment which the people of Israel endured did not bring about their downfall and disappearance from the world. Instead, it enabled them to reestablish themselves as the chosen people of the world's ruler, YHWH.

---

was destroyed. Consequently, a 7th century edition of this material would present the rise of Assyria and Judah's vassal status as an act of YHWH to punish the people and project His power throughout the world (n. b. 3, 13−15). The addition of the later exilic and post-exilic materials emphasize the role of Jerusalem, including its destruction and restoration, in YHWH's plan for the entire world.

Chapter V
Conclusion

This study is an attempt to understand the redactional formation of the book of Isaiah. Because a full redaction analysis of the entire book of Isaiah would far exceed the bounds of a single monograph, this study has focused on chapters 1 – 4 of Isaiah in order to provide a basis for future research on the rest of the book. The results of this study may now be summarized and conclusions drawn concerning their meaning.

Whereas past scholarship viewed Isaiah as a combination of several independent prophetic books or collections stemming from Isaiah, Deutero-Isaiah, Trito-Isaiah, and anonymous authors or editors, recent advances indicate that the book of Isaiah is a redactional unity. Studies have indicated that not only do chapters 40 ff. build upon the themes, language, and historical presentation of chapters 1 – 39, but that chapters 1 – 39 are presented in such a manner that anticipates the concerns of chapters 40 – 66. This has important implications for understanding the redactional formation of the book, especially of chapters 1 – 39, in that it indicates that the editors of the book fashioned chapters 1 – 39 as a preface for chapters 40 – 66. This means that the early Isaianic tradition found in chapters 1 – 39, was interpreted, supplemented, edited, and presented in relation to Deutero-Isaiah and Trito-Isaiah. In essence, the concerns of the latter part of the book dictated the final redaction of the first part. Consequently, an understanding of the redactional formation of the first part of the book requires that it be considered in relation to the entire book of Isaiah, i. e., as a component of the book as a whole. Therefore, the structure, genre, setting, and intent of the entire book must be determined in order to understand the overarching concerns which led to its formation and the role which its component texts play as part of the larger framework. Afterwards, the component texts can be analyzed in order to determine how they were redactionally formed to fulfill their tasks within the book as a whole.

The examination of the book of Isaiah as a whole demonstrates that it functions as an exhortation to reestablish and maintain the Jewish community in Jerusalem in the mid- to late-fifth century B. C. E. It is directed to the post-exilic Jewish population in general and attempts to convince them that YHWH is the God of all creation, that His covenant with them is still in effect, and that it is still necessary for them to adhere to Him as God and fulfill His requirements. The book is structured to serve this purpose. It begins with a prologue in chapter 1 which is a summary of the message of the book as a whole, i.e., YHWH's offer of redemption to the people. Chapters 2 – 35 announce YHWH's plan for a new world order centered at Zion. This includes both the announcement proper (chapters 2 – 4) and an elaboration on the implementation of this plan (chapters 5 – 35), explaining that the chastisement of Israel/Judah and the nations leads to His assumption of world kingship at Zion. Chapters 36 – 39 explain why the implementation of the plan was delayed from the time when Assyria dominated Judah to the time when Babylon invaded and destroyed the country in the early sixth century. Chapters 40 – 66 exhort the people to participate in YHWH's plan. The announcement of YHWH's return to Zion appears in 40, 1 – 11 and this is substantiated in 40, 12 – 54, 17 by a series of arguments designed to demonstrate that YHWH is the master of all creation and that He is restoring His relationship with Zion. Chapters 55 – 66 attempt to convince the people to join in the covenant and discuss the requirements for participation.

While the final form of the book of Isaiah displays unity of purpose and setting, the same can not be said for the process of the formation of the book. The examination of chapters 1 – 4 showed that a number of authors and redactors were operative in the formation of this material over a period of three centuries or more. Within these chapters, two blocks of redactional material were identified, chapter 1 and chapters 2 – 4*, each with its own history of composition.

Isa 1 is the prologue of the entire book in its present form. It presents YHWH's offer of redemption to the people and thus serves as an exhortation which summarizes the message of the entire book. Its final form dates to the mid- to late-fifth century, the time of the final redaction of the book as a whole. It contains much older material including three Isaianic oracles: 1, 2 – 9; 1, 10 – 18; and 1, 21 – 26, which deal with Sennacherib's invasion of Judah in 701 B. C. E., and a late preexilic or exilic oracle, 1, 29 – 31, concerning those who participate in fertility cults. The redactional materials which organize these older materials into the present arrangement of the chapter are found in 1, 1; 1, 19 – 20; and 1, 27 – 28. These passages indicate that the redactor was heavily influenced by Deuteronomistic ideology, especially in regard to the distinction of the righteous and the wicked, and the consequences which each can expect. Accordingly, those who fulfill YHWH's requirements as stated in the Isaianic oracles of this chapter, are righteous and can expect redemption. Those who refuse to meet His requirements are wicked and can expect to perish. By portraying the contrasting fates of the righteous and the wicked, the chapter attempts to convince the people to choose the path of righteousness so that they will share in the coming redemption of Zion.

Isa 2 – 4 is the announcement proper of YHWH's plan for a new world order centered at Zion. In their present form, these chapters have been supplemented by the redactor of chapter 1 in 3, 10 – 11 and 4, 3 – 6 and by a much later addition in 2, 22. Apart from these additions, the unit dates to the late sixth or early fifth century B. C. E. As in chapter 1, there is much originally Isaianic material here, including 2, 6* – 17; 3, 1 – 9, 12, 13 – 15; and 3, 16 – 4, 1. Furthermore, there are two supplements to 2, 6* – 17 dating to the seventh century, 2, 18 – 19 and 2, 20 – 21; a late exilic salvation oracle in 2, 2 – 4; and a late exilic statement focusing on the restoration of Israel in 4, 2. Material supplied by the redactor appears in 2, 1 and 2, 5 – 6*. This redactional material and the present arrangement of the previously existing oracles shows the redaction's concern with demonstrating YHWH's efficacy and role as world ruler. Accordingly, it portrays the establishment of YHWH's rule of the world at Zion and explains the past suffering of Jerusalem as a necessary part of YHWH's plan to purify the city in preparation for its role as His capital. Unlike the redaction of chapter 1, the redaction of chapters 2 – 4* does not distinguish between the righteous and wicked. The wicked have been eliminated or punished and redemption is available to all.

The materials in these chapters were composed for quite diverse situations over a long period of time. Yet, in order for all of the materials within these chapters to be put together for a common purpose in a common situation, a process of adaptation must have taken place. The texts have been identified according to the periods and situations for which they were written by working backwards chronologically from the latest stages in the composition of the text to the earliest. But in order to fully understand the hermeneutics operative at the time of the writing of these texts as well as the times of their reinterpretation and adaptation to later situations, they must be discussed according to the chronological order of their formation.[1]

---

[1] This discussion of the hermeneutics employed by Isaiah and the subsequent redactions which formed the book of Isaiah presupposes the "hermeneutical triangle" proposed by J. A. Sanders ("Hermeneutics in True and False Prophecy," Canon and Authority, ed. by G. W. Coats and B. O. Long, 1977, 21 – 41, esp. 21 f.). According to Sanders, ancient Israelite prophecy is best understood in the interaction of three major factors: ancient traditions (texts), situations (contexts), and hermeneutics. He states that texts are "the common authoritative traditions employed and brought forward (re-presented) by the prophet to bear upon the situation to which he or she spoke in antiquity" (p. 21). Contexts are "the historical, cultural, social, political, economic, national, and international situations to which the prophets applied the 'texts' " (p. 21). Hermeneutics is "the ancient theological mode, as well as literary technique, by which that application was made by the prophet, true or false, that is, how he read his 'texts' and 'contexts' and how he related them" (p. 22). There are two basic theological or hermeneutical

At the first stage of composition are the prophecies of Isaiah ben
Amoz which he delivered in the latter part of the eighth century B. C. E.
According to the above analysis, these include 1, 2 – 9; 1, 10 – 18;
1, 21 – 26; 2, 6* – 17; 3, 1 – 9; 3, 12; 3, 13 – 15; and 3, 16 – 4, 1. The situation presupposed by these oracles centers in Hezekiah's revolt against
Assyria and Assyria's subsequent invasion of Judah and siege of Jerusalem, including the events leading up to the revolt, the invasion itself,
and the consequences of the revolt. It is clear from these oracles that
Isaiah was very much concerned with Hezekiah's policies in preparing
Judah to oppose the Assyrian empire. To this end, Hezekiah made
entreaties to Egypt and his more immediate neighbors to form a military
coalition against Assyria. Furthermore, Hezekiah's cultic reforms, his
repair and cleansing of the Temple, served his political goals as a public
signal that Hezekiah would no longer tolerate Assyrian hegemony.

Isaiah opposed this policy of revolt against Assyria just as he earlier
opposed Ahaz's policy of political alliance with Assyria to thwart the
Syro-Ephraimitic threat. He knew that the alliance which Hezekiah had
formed would never be a match for the Assyrian army. Yet, he did not
voice his opposition to Hezekiah in strictly political terms. Rather, he
viewed history theologically, not as an arena in which only humans were
involved, but in which YHWH was involved as well. Thus, with respect
to this situation, Isaiah employed a prophetic hermeneutic in making
known his opposition to Hezekiah's preparations for revolt. He challenged the actions and attitudes of the people of Judah, accusing them
of rebellion against YHWH (1, 2 – 3) in that their reliance on their own
military power and that of their allies was a deliberate rejection of the
protection offered by their God. He maintained that the people had
become proud and arrogant, that they considered themselves and their
works as sources of power and might, but they had forgotten that
YHWH is the source of all power and the creator of all that is high
(2, 6* – 17). Isaiah claimed that the people's attitude of arrogance and
self importance corrupted their moral judgment as well as their political
judgment. Thus, the people had become dishonest, cheating in the
market place, ignoring the plight of widows and orphans, and harboring
murders in their midst (1, 21 – 26). They had become misguided in
their focus on material goods (3, 16 – 4, 1) and this caused them to
misunderstand their relationship with YHWH. According to Isaiah, they
pictured YHWH in their own image, as one who desires material goods
such as sacrifices. This view is quite evident in Isaiah's critique of

---

modes which ancient Biblical thinkers employed: the constitutive and the prophetic
(Sanders, IDB[S], 405). The constitutive mode is essentially a "supportive" reading of
the situation and tradition. The prophetic mode is a "challenging" reading of the
situation and tradition.

Hezekiah's cultic reforms where he claims that YHWH's priorities are not sacrifice and festival observance but righteousness in the people, so that they will recognize their social responsibilities to all elements of society (1, 10 – 18). Hezekiah's reliance on political allies to solve his problems was not only an indication of a lack of political judgment to Isaiah, it was a rejection of YHWH which was reflected in the people's behavior and attitudes as well.

In employing his prophetic hermeneutic to interpret the political and historical events of his time, Isaiah made substantial use of tradition current in the culture of his day. Much discussion has already taken place of his use of the Zion and royal traditions in his oracles.[2] Yet, while the Isaianic oracles of chapters 1 – 4 contain elements of the Zion traditions, other traditions are operative here as well. Isaiah was a master at reversing the understanding of the constitutive traditions of Israel, that is, taking the traditions of the people which they understood as supporting or justifying their existence, beliefs, and practices, and reapplying them so that they contributed to his critique. Thus, in announcing the Day of YHWH in 2, 6* – 17, Isaiah took up an ancient tradition from Israel's early days and applied it against the people.[3] According to the traditions about the period of wandering in the desert and the conquest of the land, YHWH had fought for His people as a holy warrior, defeating Israel's enemies, protecting her, and leading her to the promised land in order to establish them as His special people. The Day of Midian referred to one of His battles as the Holy Warrior, when He defeated the Midianites in the time of Gideon.[4] When Isaiah announced the Day of YHWH, he employed the Holy War tradition but modified it so that YHWH did not come to defend the people, but to punish them. Because Hezekiah rejected YHWH's protection as Holy Warrior, the Holy Warrior would turn on him. Rejection of the Holy Warrior by the people leads to the Holy Warrior's rejection of the people.

In referring to the people in terms of Sodom and Gomorrah (1, 10; 3, 9; cf. 1, 9), Isaiah reapplied another constitutive tradition in a prophetic mode. In ancient Israelite tradition, Sodom and Gomorrah were the wicked cities of the patriarchal age which YHWH destroyed precisely because of their extreme wickedness. In this respect, they were the paradigms of evil behavior in the ancient world. But while their destruction testified to their wickedness, the continued existence of other cities testified to their righteousness relative to the Sodomites and the people

---

[2] Cf. von Rad, Old Testament Theology, II 147 ff.

[3] On the Day of YHWH and the holy war tradition, see von Rad, Old Testament Theology, II 119 ff.; F. M. Cross, Jr., Canaanite Myth and Hebrew Epic, 1973, 91 ff.; P. Miller, The Divine Warrior in Early Israel, HSM 5, 1973.

[4] Isa 9, 3; cf. Jud 7, 15 – 25.

of Gomorrah. Yet, it was Isaiah's contention that the people of Judah and Jerusalem were not better than the people of Sodom and Gomorrah. His observations of their behavior and attitudes convinced him of that. When Isaiah saw the destruction of the land of Judah inflicted by the Assyrians (1, 4 – 9) and the deportation of the leading elements of Jerusalem society in the aftermath of Sennacherib's siege (3, 1 – 9), he drew his conclusions. The people of Judah and Jerusalem were just like the people of Sodom and Gomorrah, otherwise, why would YHWH have treated them in a similar fashion? Certainly Isaiah presupposed the Zion traditions in which Zion, like the House of David, has an eternal covenant with YHWH for its protection and continued existence. The special status of Jerusalem entailed responsibilities for fidelity to YHWH and His moral and social requirements (1, 21 – 26). When these requirements were not met, the city, like the king, would be punished (cf. 2 Sam 7). YHWH's covenant marked the establishment of Israel, but according to Isaiah, YHWH's covenant also entailed Israel's punishment when the people rebelled (1, 2 – 9; 3, 13 – 15).

Finally, in accusing the people of rebellion, Isaiah used a wisdom analogy to the natural order of creation, claiming that even animals know who their master is, i. e., who provides them with sustenance. But Israel, unlike the ox and the ass, does not even understand this basic premise of the order of the world. They do not recognize that YHWH is their master and provides their livelihood. Such an accusation must have been quite a shock to people whose tradition told them that they were appointed by YHWH as custodians over the earth and everything in it, including animals (Ps 8, 7; cf. Gen 3, 20 – 21). Yet in Isaiah's view, the people had demonstrated their ignorance of the basic order of creation.

These oracles also indicate that Isaiah hoped that the people would reform themselves. If they would accept YHWH's instructions and meet His requirements (1, 10 – 18), the punishment could be averted.[5] In any case, the punishment was for the purpose of correction, not to bring a full end to the country.

There is no clear evidence that the Isaianic oracles of chapters 1 – 4 circulated as an independent collection. The evidence does indicate that the oracle concerning the Day of YHWH in 2, 6* – 17 was later supplemented with 2, 18 f. and 2, 20 f. These supplements are midrashic in character in that they attempt to interpret the oracle in 2, 6* – 17. In its Isaianic form, the oracle allows for some ambiguity in that it is uncertain to whom the command to hide in v. 10 is directed. The two

---

[5] Although Isaiah may have hoped for the people's repentance, the terms of his commission make it clear that repentance was not expected (Isa 6, 9 – 13).

supplements indicate this ambiguity in that 2, 18 f. presupposes that it is directed to the idols mentioned in v. 8a whereas 2, 20 f. presupposes that it is directed to the people. Here, there is a conflict of opinion in applying this oracle to the circumstances of the idolatrous reign of King Manasseh in the 7th century. Manasseh submitted to Assyrian rule and allowed idol worship in the country as part of his policy of placating the Assyrians. While he has been condemned in the Deuteronomistic history for his policies, it is not entirely clear that he had much choice in the matter.[6] It seems likely that two opinions are preserved in the supplements to 2, 6* − 17. By focusing on the idols, the midrashist of 2, 18 f. directed the judgment of the entire oracle on the idols, suggesting that the idols are to blame for the corruption in the country and that humans, on whom the idols were imposed, are their victims. On the other hand, the midrashist of 2, 20 f. directs the oracle against the people, suggesting that they were directly responsible for allowing idols into the country and therefore, are responsible for their own corruption. In any case, these are two attempts to apply the oracle in 2, 6* − 17 to the circumstances of the reign of Manasseh. Both presuppose that the land is full of idols as mentioned in v. 8, but the one condemns the idols for their influence in the country at this time, while the other condemns the people for allowing the idols to enter the land.

As noted at the end of chapter IV, these additions suggest the possibility that 2, 6* − 21 + 3, 1 − 9; 3, 12 − 4, 1 constituted a 7th century edition of these texts. If this is the case, the redactors of this material apparently understood the Assyrian conquest of Egypt during the reign of Manasseh as the ultimate fulfillment of the "Day of YHWH" oracle in 2, 6* − 21. By stating that YHWH will terrorize the "land/earth" and that *'ādām* and *'anāšîm* will suffer the consequences, the supplements in 2, 18 f. and 2, 20 f. emphasize the world-wide implications of 2, 6* − 17. Esarhaddon's conquest of Egypt in 671 would provide an international context for Isaiah's understanding of YHWH's use of Assyria for punishment in relation to this passage. The following references to the deportation of Judah's officials and the suffering of Jerusalem's women in 3, 1 − 9 and 3, 16 − 4, 1 would emphasize Judah's and Jerusalem's fate in relation to YHWH's world-wide action. Likewise, the placement of 3, 12 − 15, with its reference to YHWH's punishing "peoples" (v. 13), demonstrates this international context. Such an understanding of Isaiah's oracles would have been the product of Isaiah's later disciples who applied the prophet's oracles to later circumstances. Such interpreta-

---

[6] For the Deuteronomistic account of Manasseh's reign, see 2 Reg 21, 1 − 18. As a vassal of the Assyrian empire, Manasseh felt that he had to submit to the Assyrian gods as well as to the government, although the evidence suggests that he went far beyond what was necessary (cf. Bright, A History of Israel, 310 ff.).

tive activity would have laid the basis for the hermeneutics of the later
post-exilic redactions which understood the Isaianic tradition in relation
to the destruction and restoration of Jerusalem, concluding that these
events demonstrated YHWH's kingship over the entire earth.

The next major stage in the formation of this material is the
redaction identified in chapters 2 – 4*. According to the above analysis
of this material, a late sixth or early fifth century redaction used the
oracles in 2, 6* – 21; 3, 1 – 9, 12, 13 – 15; and 3, 16 – 4, 1 as the basis for
a new composition dealing with the circumstances of the Jerusalem
community at the time of the rebuilding of the Temple. To this end, it
also used non-Isaianic oracles in 2, 2 – 4 and 4, 2 and supplied its own
material in 2, 1 and 2, 5 – 6* in organizing and framing the material.
Like Isaiah, this redaction was very much concerned with the political
and religious circumstances of its time. These circumstances were quite
different from those of Isaiah. At this time, some of the people were
just returning to Jerusalem after years of exile in Babylonia. The Temple
and Jerusalem had been destroyed by Nebuchadrezzar in 587 B. C. E.
and the population deported. However, when the Babylonian empire fell
to the Medes and Persians in the latter part of the sixth century, the
new emperor, Cyrus, took steps to reestablish the exiled Jews in their
own homeland and allowed them to reestablish their religion.

All of this was part of Cyrus' policy for governing the subject
territories, but like Isaiah, this redaction interpreted these historical
events theologically. In its interpretation of these events, the redaction
of chapters 2 – 4* resignified the previously existing Isaianic material in
relation to these events. Of course, this work was facilitated by the fact
that nowhere in these oracles from the time of Isaiah is there any specific
historical reference to Sennacherib, Hezekiah, or the Assyrians. Without
historical referents in the material and with the typological analogy of
the invasion of Judah by the Assyrians with the invasion by Nebuchadrezzar, the redaction of chapters 2 – 4* was able to apply these oracles in
reference to the Babylonian invasion and their destruction of Jerusalem.
According to this redaction, the Day of YHWH oracle in 2, 6* – 21
referred not to the impending invasion by the Assyrian army in 701
B. C. E., but to Nebuchadrezzar's invasion in 587. The deportation of
the leading citizens of Jerusalem mentioned in 3, 1 – 9 referred not to
Sennacherib's deportation of the leading elements of Jerusalem after
Hezekiah's capitulation, but to Nebuchadrezzar's deportations of 597
and 587. The oracle concerning the women of Jerusalem which ends
with an oracle mourning the defeat of a city by the Assyrians, now
refers to the defeat of Jerusalem by the Babylonians. YHWH's judgment
against the people mentioned in 3, 13 – 15, refers not to the Assyrian
punishment but to the Babylonian debacle. Finally, the complaint concerning incompetent leaders in 3, 12 refers to the administrations of
Jehoiakim, Jehoiachin, and Zedekiah, not to that of Hezekiah.

This redaction also selected other materials, such as 2, 2 – 4. According to the above analysis, this oracle was written at the end of the sixth century, during the time of the rebuilding of the Temple in Jerusalem. It presupposes the Zion tradition in viewing Zion as the home of YHWH but modifies it by portraying the nations as peacefully approaching Zion to ask for YHWH's Torah, whereas earlier Zion traditions indicated that the nations approached Zion to attack and were soundly defeated by YHWH. Such a change in the tradition looks forward to a time of peace among nations, which is what would have been expected in the early years of Persian rule. The redaction also selected 4, 2, which recognized the people's past tragedy by referring to them as the remnant, but it also looked forward to the renewal of their relationship with YHWH and the land which they would enjoy at the time of the return.

On the surface, this redaction's use of the Isaianic oracles with their judgmental perspective and the later materials in 2, 2 – 4 and 4, 2, with their promissory perspective, seems somewhat contradictory. Yet these two groups of materials, with their differing outlooks, corresponded to the two periods of history at whose crossroads this redaction stood. In the view of this redaction, the past was a period of punishment which was required on account of the people's wrongdoings. The Babylonians had done their divinely motivated work. The purpose of punishment had been for cleansing and this cleansing was now complete. It was now possible to look forward to the future under the Persians. This would be a time of rebuilding and reconstituting the Jewish community in the newly purified Jerusalem. Thus, the hermeneutic employed by the redaction of chapters 2 – 4* was constitutive, it provided support for the people when they needed it most. After the Babylonian debacle, the people would have believed that YHWH was defeated. Certainly Marduk had asserted his power over YHWH and YHWH's claims to authority were now null and void. He couldn't even protect His own home, Zion. But by arranging the Isaianic material together with the later oracles of promise in a new framework, the redaction of chapters 2 – 4* argued that the destruction of Jerusalem by the Babylonians was a part of YHWH's plan. According to 2, 2 – 4, YHWH meant to assert His power over the entire world, not just Judah and Zion. Such a vision, with its portrayal of world peace, would have corresponded well with the optimistic expectations during Cyrus' rule and would have been viewed as the goal for which YHWH employed Cyrus as His "anointed" (Isa 45, 1; cf. 44, 28). But in order for Him to accomplish this, He had to correct the people at home, cleansing His own abode so that it would be a fit capital for ruling the entire world. In such a manner, the redaction of chapters 2 – 4* argued for YHWH's efficacy and power to a people who, at best, would have been skeptical. But with the events of the beginning of the Persian period, with the promised restoration of the Temple and the cult, such an argument would certainly be credible. This argument provides the theological justification for the establishment of post-exilic Judaism at this time and derives its credibility from a theological understanding of contemporary historical events.

Finally, the viewpoint of the redaction of chapters 2 – 4*, especially with its focus on the universal aspects of YHWH's world rule, has much in common with certain parts of Trito-Isaiah, such as Isa 60 – 62, and certainly presupposes Deutero-Isaiah.[7]

The last major stage in the formation of Isa 1 – 4 is the redaction identified in chapter 1. According to the above analysis, the Isaianic materials in this section include 1, 2 – 9; 1, 10 – 18; and 1, 21 – 26. There is also a non-Isaianic oracle in 1, 29 – 31. The redaction has organized this material and provided framework materials in 1, 1; 1, 19 – 20; and 1, 27 – 28. Furthermore, it has added 3, 10 – 11 and 4, 3 – 6 to the re-dacted materials of chapters 2 – 4*. Like Isaiah and the redaction of chapters 2 – 4*, this redaction is also very much concerned with the events of its own day, it is no mere collection of tradition. It was completed toward the end of the fifth century B. C. E., about the time of Nehemiah and Ezra. At this time, the Jewish community in Jerusalem was still in the process of rebuilding the city and reconstituting Judaism, but the idealistic hopes of the early part of the century had not been realized. The nations had not acknowledged YHWH's rule as had been expected earlier, the rebuilt Temple was not the seat of YHWH's world rule, and the people were struggling just to survive. Furthermore, there were deep divisions within the community as rival factions attempted to assert their views as to what Judaism should be.[8] Finally, there was quite an assimilationist tendency at this time as the people intermarried with the pagan population and adopted their cultic practices. This was the time when Nehemiah and especially Ezra took steps which resulted in the formation of post-exilic Judaism. Ezra is credited with presenting the Torah to the Jerusalem community at this time. He sought to ensure the continuation of the Jewish people by requiring strict adherence to YHWH's requirements as expressed in the Torah. To this end, he

---

[7] Note Knierim's distinction between Deutero-Isaiah and Trito-Isaiah. Deutero-Isaiah sees the new Exodus as the consummation of YHWH's new creative activity, i. e., a reconstituted Israel is the goal of YHWH's new creative activity. Trito-Isaiah, however, sees YHWH's new creation as an entirely new cosmic world order. In this scheme, Israel is the vehicle for YHWH's goal, not the goal itself (HBT 3 [1981], 59 ff., esp. 104 ff.). The redaction of chapters 2 – 4*, with its use of 2, 2 – 4 and its invitation to Jacob to join in YHWH's new world order in 2, 5, seems to have much in common with Trito-Isaiah.

[8] On the rival factions and ideologies current at this time, see P. Hanson, The Dawn of Apocalyptic, 1975, and D. L. Petersen, Late Israelite Prophecy, SBLMS 23, 1977.

attempted to remove the syncretistic elements from the community. Intermarriage was banned and those who were not of the "holy seed" (Ezr 9, 2; cf. Isa 6, 13) were denied admission to the community. Observance of the Sabbath and festivals was instituted and proper worship of YHWH was maintained at the Temple. At this time, there was a great deal of interest in distinguishing a true Jew, i. e., one who was righteous, from one who was not a true Jew, i. e., one who was wicked.[9]

Against this background and that of the previous years of Babylonian exile, this redaction interpreted the Isaianic oracles of chapter 1. Thus, 1, 4 – 9 referred not to the devastation left by the Assyrian army in the latter part of the eighth century, but to the devastated land of the latter part of the fifth century. Nebuchadrezzar had destroyed it, but it had never been restored, even after the return under the Persians. According to this redaction, this indicated YHWH's displeasure with the people. The oracle concerning cultic practice in 1, 10 – 18 referred not to Hezekiah's cultic reforms, but to those parties in the late fifth century who sought to continue cultic service to YHWH, but lacked the teachings which were the basis of His Torah. Likewise, the oracle in 1, 21 – 26 did not refer to the corrupt practices of the people of Jerusalem in Hezekiah's time, but to those of the time of Nehemiah and Ezra. Finally, just as the people were rebellious during the time of Isaiah, so they were rebellious now (1, 2 – 3) in that many of them did not care to follow the practices promulgated by Ezra's reform. The people were apostasizing, so that the oracle in 1, 29 – 31, originally delivered against the apostasizers of the late pre-exilic or early exilic period, was just as appropriate at this time.

The redaction organized this material in such a way as to present a choice to the people. In its view, their situation was perilous, judgment was imminent. But if the people accepted instruction (i. e., Torah, 1, 10) and followed YHWH's requirements, they would be considered among the righteous and would therefore be redeemed (1, 19; 1, 27). If they refused YHWH's instruction, however, then they would be considered among the wicked and would perish (1, 20a; 1, 28). The redaction also presupposed the earlier redactional block in chapters 2 – 4*. This section promised a period of peace for all nations under YHWH's rule. Divine judgment was not imminent here. Again, there appears to be a contradiction in the redaction's use of earlier material. But the contradiction reflects the circumstances of the redaction's time. Universal peace and salvation had been promised, but had not been realized, and the redaction

---

[9] For an account of Ezra's reforms, see Ezr 7 – 10; Neh 8 – 10. Cf. Neh 13 for Nehemiah's reform activity. For a general analysis of Ezra's reform, see K. Koch, JSS 19 (1974), 173 ff. According to Koch, Ezra saw his reform as a fulfillment of prophetic tradition, including that of Isaiah.

was compelled to explain this situation. It did so by returning to a prophetic hermeneutic in line with its Deuteronomistic orientation. According to Deuteronomistic ideology, misfortune was caused by the wickedness of the people, fortune was the result of the people's righteousness. In its own time, the Jewish community had problems, therefore these problems must be explained as the result of some fault of the people. But it also had to deal with the authority of the promises contained in the earlier material. YHWH had promised restoration, but that restoration had not been realized. The redaction reconciled this situation with an element of constitutive hermeneutic together with the prophetic element in line with Deuteronomistic ideology. The promise had been made to the righteous, but judgment still remained for the wicked. Thus, YHWH's promises still held and so did His judgment, but their realization was projected into the future. Zion would still serve as YHWH's capital for His world rule. It simply needed more cleansing and this cleansing was what Nehemiah and Ezra were trying to accomplish. Therefore, the material in chapter 1 served as an explanation why the promise of chapters 2 – 4* had not been realized.[10] Furthermore, the additions in 3, 10 – 11 and 4, 3 – 6 which emphasized the distinction of the righteous from the wicked and the cleansing of Jerusalem also served this purpose. By making this clear, the redaction hoped to convince the people to choose righteousness, i. e., YHWH's Torah.[11]

These conclusions have implications for understanding the redaction of the book as a whole. As noted in chapter II, Isa 1 and Isa 65 – 66 form a redactional "envelope" around the entire book of Isaiah which suggests that these chapters were composed or placed in their present positions as part of the final redaction of the book.[12] If this is the case,

---

[10] Cf. R. Carroll, When Prophecy Failed: Cognitive Dissonance in the Prophetic Traditions of the Old Testament, 1979, 152 ff. Carroll explains the response to such disappointments in terms of a theory of cognitive dissonance. According to this theory, the non-realization of strong cognitive expectations often leads to dissonance, unrelieved tensions between expectations and results which requires resolution. Accordingly, such persons act to overcome their dissonance in various ways. They often compensate psychologically for their disappointment by developing explanations for the failure of their expectations to materialize, i. e., them into the future and claiming that they have been delayed for some reason. In applying this theory to the Isaianic tradition, Carroll focuses primarily on Trito-Isaiah. It seems that this same process is operative for the redaction identified in Isa 1.

[11] As noted in Chapter III, there is no indication in Isaiah that Torah refers to the Five Books of Moses or any specific body of teaching. This and the willingness to accept foreigners (Isa 56, 1 – 8; 66, 18 – 23) indicate that the party which produced the final form of the book did not fully agree with Ezra's program.

[12] E. Sehmsdorf, ZAW 84 (1972), 517 ff., points to Deuteronomistic influence in Isa 65 – 66 which corresponds to that in Isa 1. He also notes Deuteronomistic influence throughout the rest of Trito-Isaiah and W. Brueggemann, ZAW 80 (1968), 191 ff., finds

Isa 2 – 4* may have served as the introduction to a late-sixth or early-fifth century edition of the book of Isaiah. Its superscription in 2, 1 and its programmatic character certainly qualify it for such a role.[13] Proving the existence of such an edition and defining its extent would require much more discussion than is possible here. However, much of Trito-Isaiah and other texts such as 3, 10 – 11, 4, 3 – 6, and Isa 24 – 27 correspond to Isa 1 and Isa 65 – 66, with their emphasis on distinguishing the righteous from the wicked, the delayed expectation of the redemption of the righteous, and cosmic transformation. If these texts were removed as the final redactional layer of the book, a late-sixth or early-fifth century edition of Isaiah might encompass Isa 2 – 55* and perhaps Isa 60 – 62.[14] Likewise, Barth and Clements have demonstrated the possibil-

---

it in Isa 55. Cf. Vermeylen, Du prophète Isaïe, II 504 ff., who argues that the first edition of Trito-Isaiah was patterned after Isa 1.

[13] Cf. G. Sheppard, JBL 104 (1985), 193 – 216, who traces themes and language from Isa 2 – 4 through Isa 1 – 39 and Isa 40 ff. Sheppard follows Barth, Die Jesaja-Worte in der Josiazeit, in maintaining that Isa 2 – 4* is part of the 7th century "Assyrian Redaction" of Isa 2 – 32*. Barth's general hypothesis need not be discarded but his contention that Isa 2 – 4* forms the beginning of the "Assyrian Redaction" must be rejected. Instead, Clements' view that Isa 5 forms the beginning of this redaction should be followed (Isaiah 1 – 39, 5 f.). Barth's decision to consider 2, 1 as the beginning of the "Assyrian Redaction" is based on his inability to see Isa 2, 1 – 5, 7 as a previously existing separate collection of Isaiah's words. He therefore assumes that these materials must have been a part of the book of Isaiah in its prior forms since these chapters contain authentic words of the prophet from his earliest period (Die Jesaja-Worte, 220 f.). As seen above, most of the Isaianic material here is not from his early period but from the time of the Assyrian invasion. Furthermore, the Isaianic material in these chapters has been redacted so that it speaks to the concerns of the post-exilic community. While there is no evidence that this material existed as a previously independent collection of Isaianic oracles, neither is there indisputable evidence that it formed a section of the book of Isaiah prior to the post-exilic period. It is possible that the individual Isaianic oracles or an early 7th century edition of 2, 6* – 21 + 3, 1 – 9; 3, 12 – 4, 1 had places in an earlier form of the book, but if this is the case, they have been removed from that context for their present placement as Sheppard maintains (JBL 104, 198 ff.). Tracing such a process, however, is extremely difficult with the evidence at hand.

[14] Such an edition would correspond well to the early years of the Persian empire. Isa 2, 2 – 4, with its vision of future peace among the nations, would point to the early years of Persian rule with its promise of international peace. Such a vision would be especially appealing following the military oppression of Assyria and Babylonia. Likewise, the absence of Persia or Media in the oracles against the nations suggests that the nations listed in Isa 13 – 23, which include nearly all the nations of the ancient Near East, could have been subjugated by Persia/Media. Such a view would be supported by Isa 13, 17 ff. and 21, 2 which portray Media's overthrow of Babylon, and Isa 44, 28 and 45, 1 which portray Cyrus as YHWH's annointed. During these years, Persia would have been viewed as YHWH's instrument for acting in international

ity of a late-seventh century edition of the book of Isaiah in Isa 5 – 32*.[15]
Of course, future research will determine the validity of this hypothetical
reconstruction.

Finally, these results have implications for broader concerns within
the field of Biblical studies.

This study indicates that in its present form, the book of Isaiah
functions as a unified whole with a specific intent. Yet, it is clear that
all the materials in the book were not written to serve the purpose of
the book as a whole. They were written over a period of about three
centuries by various authors and redactors, for different purposes, and
in relation to different situations. By their placement, supplementation,
and reinterpretation in the present form of the book, they serve a
purpose for which they were not originally formed. The arrangement and
understanding of the individual texts included in the book of Isaiah is
dictated by a conception that was originally foreign to these texts.
They have been systematically arranged to serve the purposes of this
conception and it is this conception which determines their meaning in
the present form of the book. Scholars have seen this phenomenon of
systematization of older materials before, especially in the narrative
literature, such as the J source of the Torah which understands the early
traditions about the formation of Israel in relation to royal ideology,
the Deuteronomistic history, which interprets Israel's and Judah's history
in such a way so as to explain the Babylonian catastrophe, etc. As
Ackroyd notes, such systematized presentations of past tradition tend
to appear in relation to periods of great change or crisis.[16] In the case
of the J source, this was in relation to the formation of the Davidic-
Solomonic empire, and in the case of the Deuteronomistic history, this
was in relation to the end of the kingdom of Judah and its dynasty.
These are cases when Israel and Judah asked about the meaning of their
present situation in the light of past tradition, i. e., an attempt at self-
understanding in changed circumstances. These systematized presenta-

---

    affairs just as Assyria and Babylonia were viewed to have filled this role in earlier
    times. However, political instability in the Persian empire began during the reigns of
    Cambyses (530 – 522) and Darius I (522 – 486) and worsened during the reigns of their
    successors (cf. Bright, A History of Israel, 369, 373 ff.). These conditions, together with
    the persistent problems of the post-exilic Jewish community, would have led to the
    belief that the realization of YHWH's plan had been delayed. This would have
    prompted the writing of the final edition of the book of Isaiah which maintained that
    the realization of YHWH's plan had been delayed until all the wicked could be
    punished.

[15] Cf. note 12 above.
[16] The Old Testament in the Making, The Cambridge History of the Bible, ed. by P. R.
    Ackroyd and C. F. Evans, I 1970, 105 ff.

tions were a response to their questioning, i. e., new attempts at self-understanding in the light of both tradition and contemporary experience. The book of Isaiah seems to fill a similar role, but in relation to prophetic traditions, not narrative. Thus, for the post-exilic community trying to cope with the changed circumstances of its time, the rebuilding of Jerusalem and the Temple after the Babylonian destruction, the establishment of a theocratic province on the ashes of the old monarchy, the book of Isaiah represents an answer to the question of self-definition. All this is part of YHWH's plan to establish His rule over the entire world.

This means that major shifts must have taken place in the understanding of the older Isaianic traditions. Whereas Isaiah, the prophet, spoke a message that emphasized judgment against the people of Jerusalem and Judah, the message of Isaiah, the book, is directed primarily to their salvation. While Isaiah, the prophet, saw the Assyrian onslaught as the punishment of the people ordained by YHWH, Isaiah, the book, saw that punishment as the Babylonian catastrophe. In the final form of the book, the meaning of individual passages in relation to the situations and purposes for which they were composed is no longer relevant when considered in relation to the book. What is determinative in their interpretation is their meaning in relation to the conception which governs the whole book. This indicates that there must be a generic distinction between the "message" which the original texts contain, i. e., the original meaning of the text within itself, and the systematic conception or teaching of the book as a whole, i. e., the meaning of the text as a constitutive element of a larger system.

This raises a question concerning the relationship between the "messages" of the individual texts contained in the book and the systematic conception which governs the understanding of these texts in the book as a whole. Does the systematic conceptualization grow out of the messages of the individual texts? If so, how does the book arrive at its basic message of salvation when the prophet announced judgment? Is the systematic conceptualization the product of extra-textual factors, such as the historical fact of Jerusalem's restoration and the rebuilding of the Temple in the post-exilic period? If so, then why are Isaiah's prophecies of judgment in the book? The above discussion of the redaction of chapters 1 – 4 indicates that the systematic conceptualization grows out of both textual traditions and historical circumstances. The tradition announced judgment, the new situation indicated restoration, and the redactors organized the material to show that the judgment led to the restoration. This study has dealt only with chapters 1 – 4. Future research will provide a more complete picture of the relation between the "messages" of the individual texts which make up the book and the systematic conception which governs the book as a whole.

This study also has implications for an understanding of the traditio-historical process itself. The analysis of Isa 1 – 4 indicates that the transmission of older materials in later redactions does not depend solely on their authority as historical traditions. It also depends on how later redactors conceive their applicability to the contemporary situation. In recording older traditions, the redactors look to the past for authoritative statements, but they do this with eyes to the future. They are not primarily concerned with the meaning of these traditions in relation to the time and situation in which they were written but in relation to their own contemporary situation. The most important questions for the redactors are not, "where have we been in the past?" but "where are we now in the present?" and "where are we going in the future?" In this sense, they are more than mere archivists. They are theologians who interpret and apply traditions to the present. Thus, the traditio-historical process is not, strictly speaking, interested in the past for its own sake. It is interested in the past as a guide for the present and future. In short, the tradition process is concerned with the continued life of the community.

Finally, this study leads to a theological problem. Three major perspectives have been identified in relation to Isa 1 – 4. The prophet Isaiah was a prophet of judgment who saw corruption in his time and announced that this had to end. The redactor of chapters 2 – 4* employed a constitutive hermeneutic to announce that a time of restoration had begun. The redactor of chapters 1 and 2 – 4* qualified the announcement of restoration by stating that only the righteous would enjoy the restoration and that the period of judgment was not yet complete. Which of these perspectives is considered theologically authoritative in understanding the book? Should only the "authentic" words and perspective of the prophet Isaiah be considered as authoritative? In that case, a major portion of the book is excluded and the theological evaluation of the book is subject to the changing tides of critical scholarship. Should only the final form of the book and thus, the perspective of the final redaction be considered authoritative? In that case, the prophet himself loses his relevance and the authoritative basis for the tradition is undercut. Instead, it must be kept in mind that the book is received as the product of its transmission process. It presents all of its perspectives at once, but these must be uncovered. Each stage of the book, whether that of the prophet or one of the redactions, grapples with circumstances unique to its own time. Yet each considered the past traditions as authoritative[17]

---

[17] Note that this principle is explicitly stated in the announcement of YHWH's return to Zion in Isa 40, 8, "and the word of our God shall stand forever." This principle is evident in the reinterpretation of prophetic tradition, rather than its rejection, when confronted with changing circumstances. Cf. Isa 55, 10, "for the word which goes

and interpreted the past traditions and contemporary events in relation to the hermeneutic which was appropriate to the needs of the time. We have a past tradition in the book of Isaiah which includes several hermeneutical perspectives. Our problem is to determine the hermeneutic that is appropriate for applying that tradition to the needs of our own situation, for it is only so long as we are able to understand the past tradition of the prophets in relation to our own circumstances that the prophets will continue to speak.

---

forth from My mouth shall not return to Me empty, but it shall do that which I desire, and accomplish that for which I send it."

Bibliography

Ackroyd, P. R., Exile and Restoration: A Study of Hebrew Thought of the Sixth Century B. C., 1968.

Ackroyd, P. R., The Death of Hezekiah — A Pointer to the Future? De la Tôrah au Messie; Étudés d'exégèse et d'herméneutique bibliques offertes à Henri Cazelles pour ses 25 années d'enseignement à l'Institut Catholique de Paris (Octobre 1979), ed. M. Carrez, J. Doné, P. Grelot, 1982, 219 – 226.

Ackroyd, P. R., An Interpretation of the Babylonian Exile, SJT 27 (1974), 328 – 352.

Ackroyd, P. R., Isaiah, The Interpreter's One-Volume Commentary on the Bible, ed. C. M. Layman, 1971, 329 – 371.

Ackroyd, P. R., Isaiah I – XII: Presentation of a Prophet, SVT 29 (1978), 16 – 48.

Ackroyd, P. R., Isaiah 36 – 39: Structure and Function, Von Kanaan bis Kerala, Festschrift für Prof. Mag. Dr. Dr. J. P. M. van der Ploeg, O. P. zur Vollendung des siebzigsten Lebensjahres am 4. Juli 1979, ed. J. R. Nelis, J. R. T. M. Peters et al. AOAT 211, 1982, 3 – 21.

Ackroyd, P. R., A Note on Isaiah 2, 1, ZAW 75 (1963), 320 – 321.

Ackroyd, P. R., The Old Testament in the Making, The Cambridge History of the Bible, ed. P. R. Ackroyd & C. F. Evans. Vol. 1, 1970, 67 – 113.

Andersen, F. I., The Hebrew Verbless Clause in the Pentateuch, JBLMS 14, 1970.

Anderson, B. W., Exodus and Covenant in Second Isaiah and Prophetic Tradition, Magnalia Dei: The Mighty Acts of God, ed. F. M. Cross, Jr., 1976, 339 – 360.

Anderson, B. W., Exodus Typology in Second Isaiah, Israel's Prophetic Heritage, ed. B. W. Anderson & W. Harrelson, 1962, 177 – 195.

Banwell, B. O., A Suggested Analysis of Isaiah xl – lxvi, ExpT 76 (1964 – 65), 166.

Barth, H., Die Jesaja-Worte in der Josiazeit, WMANT 48, 1977.

Barth, H. & Steck, O. H., Exegese des Alten Testaments: Leitfaden der Methodik, 1980⁹.

Becker, J., Isaias — der Prophet und sein Buch, SBS 30, 1968.

Begrich, J., Das priesterliche Heilsorakel, ZAW 52 (1934), 81 – 92.

Begrich, J., Die priesterliche Tora, BZAW 66 (1936), 63 – 88.

Begrich, J., Studien zur Deuterojesaja, ThB 20, 1969².

Blenkinsopp, J., Fragments of Ancient Exegesis in an Isaian Poem, ZAW 93 (1981), 51 – 62.

Boecker, H. J., Redeformen des Rechtslebens im alten Testament, WMANT 14, 1970².

Bonnard, P.-E., Le Second Isaïe: son disciple et leurs éditeurs, Isaïe 40 – 66, 1972.

Bright, J., A History of Israel, 1981³.

Brown, F. with S. R. Driver & C. A. Briggs, A Hebrew and English Lexicon of the Old Testament, 1974.

Brownlee, W. H., The Meaning of the Qumran Scrolls for the Bible, 1964.

Brueggemann, W., Isaiah 55 and Deuteronomic Theology, ZAW 80 (1968), 191 – 203.

Budde, K., Jesajas Erleben. Eine gemeinverständliche Auslegung der Denkschrift des Propheten (Kap. 6, 1 – 9, 6), 1928.

Budde, K., Zu Jesaja 1 – 5, ZAW 49 (1931), 16 – 40, 182 – 211; ZAW 50 (1932), 38 – 72.

Cannawurf, E., The Authenticity of Micah IV 1–4, VT 13 (1963), 26–33.

Carroll, R. P., When Prophecy Failed: Cognitive Dissonance in the Prophetic Traditions of the Old Testament, 1979.

Cazelles, H., Qui aurait visé, à l'origine Isaïe ii 2–5? VT 30 (1980), 409–420.

Černý, L., The Day of YHWH and Some Relevant Problems, 1948.

Childs, B., Introduction to the Old Testament as Scripture, 1979.

Childs, B., Isaiah and the Assyrian Crisis, SBT 3, 1967.

Clements, R. E., Beyond Tradition History: Deutero-Isaianic Development of First Isaiah's Themes, JSOT 31 (February, 1985), 95–113.

Clements, R. E., Isaiah 1–39, NCeB, 1980.

Clements, R. E., Isaiah and the Deliverance of Jerusalem, JSOTSS 13, 1980.

Clements, R. E., The Prophecies of Isaiah and the Fall of Jerusalem in 587 B.C., VT 30 (1980), 421–436.

Clements, R. E., Prophecy and Tradition, 1975.

Clements, R. E., The Unity of the Book of Isaiah, Int 36 (1982), 117–129.

Conrad, E. W., The Community as King in Second Isaiah, Understanding the Word: Essays in Honor of Bernhard W. Anderson, ed. J. T. Butler, E. W. Conrad, B. C. Ollenburger, JSOTSS 37, 1985, 99–111.

Conrad, E. W., Fear Not Warrior: A Study of 'al tîrā' Pericopes in the Hebrew Scriptures, BJS 75, 1985.

Cornill, C. H., Die Composition des Buches Jesaja, ZAW 4 (1884), 83–105.

Cross, F. M., Jr., Canaanite Myth and Hebrew Epic, 1973.

Crüsemann, F., Studien zur Formgeschichte von Hymnus und Danklied in Israel, WMANT 32, 1969.

Davidson, A. B., Hebrew Syntax, 1902³.

Delitzsch, F., Biblical Commentary on the Prophecies of Isaiah, 2 vols., 1954.

Duhm, B., Das Buch Jesaia, 1968⁵.

Eissfeldt, O., The Old Testament: An Introduction, 1965.

Eissfeldt, O., The Promises of Grace to David in Isaiah 55, 1–5, Israel's Prophetic Heritage, ed. B. W. Anderson & W. Harrelson, 1962, 196–207.

Elliger, K., Deuterojesaja 40, 1–45, 7, BKAT XI/1, 1978.

Elliger, K., Deuterojesaja in seinem Verhältnis zu Trito-Jesaja, BWANT 63, 1933.

Erlandsson, S., The Burden of Babylon: A Study of Isaiah 13: 2–14: 23, CBOTS 4, 1970.

Exum, J. C., Isaiah 28–32: A Literary Approach. SBL 1979 Seminar Papers, ed. P. Achtemeier, vol. 2, 1979, 123–151.

Fichtner, J., Jahves Plan in der Botschaft des Jesaja, ZAW 63 (1951), 16–33.

Fohrer, G., Das Buch Jesaja, ZBK, 3 vols., 1964–1967².

Fohrer, G., Introduction to the Old Testament, 1968.

Fohrer, G., Jesaja 1 als Zusammenfassung der Verkündigung Jesajas. BZAW 99 (1967), 148–166.

Fohrer, G., The Origin, Composition and Tradition of Isaiah I–XXXIX, ALUOS 3 (1961), 3–38.

Fohrer, G. et al., Exegese des Alten Testaments: Einführung in die Methodik, 1976³.

Gemser, B., The RÎB- or Controversy Pattern in Hebrew Mentality, SVT 3 (1955), 120–137.

Ginsburg, C. D., Introduction to the Massoretico-Critical Edition of the Hebrew Bible, 1966.

Gitay, Y., The Effectiveness of Isaiah's Speech, JQR 75 (1984), 162–172.

Gitay, Y., Prophecy and Persuasion: A Study of Isaiah 40 – 48, FThL 14, 1981.

Gitay, Y., Reflections on the Study of the Prophetic Discourse. The Question of Isaiah i 2 – 20. VT 33 (1983), 207 – 221.

Gray, G. B., A Critical and Exegetical Commentary on the Book of Isaiah I – XXVII, ICC, 1912.

Gray, J., I & II Kings: A Commentary, OTL, 1970².

Gray, J., The Kingship of God in the Prophets and Psalms, VT 11 (1961), 1 – 29.

Graetz, H., Isaiah XXXIV and XXXV, JQR 4 (1892), 1 – 8.

Gunkel, H., Jesaja 33, eine prophetische Liturgie, ZAW 42 (1924), 177 – 208.

Habel, N., The Form and Significance of the Call Narratives, ZAW 77 (1965), 297 – 323.

Hanson, P., The Dawn of Apocalyptic, 1975.

Haran, M., The Literary Structure and Chronological Framework of the Prophecies in Is. XL – XLVIII, SVT 9 (1963), 127 – 155.

Harvey, J., Le plaidoyer prophétique contra Israël après la rupture de l'alliance: Étude d'une formula littéraire de l'ancien testament, 1967.

Hasel, G., The Remnant: The History and Theology of the Remnant Idea from Genesis to Isaiah, AUM 5, 1980³.

Hayes, J. H. & Miller, J. M., Israelite and Judaean History, 1977.

Hermann, S., A History of Israel in Old Testament Times, 1975.

Hillers, D. R., Hôy and Hôy-Oracles: A Neglected Syntactic Aspect, The Word of the Lord Shall Go Forth: Essays in Honor of David Noel Freedman in Celebration of his Sixtieth Birthday, ed. C. L. Meyers & M. O'Conner, 1983, 185 – 188.

Hoffmann, H. W., Die Intention der Verkündigung Jesajas, BZAW 136, 1974.

Huffman, H., The Covenant Lawsuit in the Prophets, JBL 78 (1959), 285 – 295.

The Interpreter's Dictionary of the Bible, ed. G. Buttrick et al., 4 vols., 1962.

The Interpreter's Dictionary of the Bible, Supplementary Volume, ed. K. Crim, 1976.

Jastrow, M., A Dictionary of the Targumim, the Talmud Babli and Yerushalmi, and the Midrashic Literature, 2 vols., 1967.

Jellicoe, S., The Septuagint and Modern Study, 1968.

Jensen, J., The Use of tôrâ by Isaiah: His Debate with the Wisdom Tradition, CBQMS 3, 1973.

Jones, D. R., Isaiah 56 – 66 and Joel, TB, 1964.

Jones, D. R., The Traditio of the Oracles of Isaiah of Jerusalem, ZAW 67 (1955), 226 – 246.

Junker, H., Sancta Civitas, Jerusalem Nova: Eine formkritische und überlieferungsge- schichtliche Studie zu Is 2: 1, Ekklesia: Festschrift für Bischof Dr. Matthias Wehr, TThS 15, 1962, 17 – 33.

Kaiser, O., Introduction to the Old Testament: A Presentation of its Results and Problems, 1977.

Kaiser, O., Isaiah 1 – 12: A Commentary, OTL, 1983².

Kaiser, O., Isaiah 13 – 39: A Commentary, OTL, 1974.

Kaiser, O. & Kümmel, W. G., Exegetical Method: A Student's Handbook, 1981².

Kapelrud, A. S., Eschatology in the Book of Micah, VT 11 (1961), 392 – 405.

Kaufmann, Y., The Babylonian Captivity and Deutero-Isaiah, 1970.

Kautzsch, E., Gesenius' Hebrew Grammar, 1974².

Kiesow, K., Exodustexte im Jesajabuch, OBO 24, 1979.

Kissane, E. J., The Book of Isaiah, 2 vols., 1960², 1943.

Knierim, R. P., Cosmos and History in Israel's Theology, HBT 3 (1981), 59 – 123.

Knierim, R. P., Criticism of Literary Features, Form, Tradition, and Redaction, The Hebrew Bible and Its Modern Interpreters, ed. D. A. Knight & G. M. Tucker, 1985, 123–165.

Knierim, R. P., Old Testament Form Criticism Reconsidered, Int 27 (1973), 435–468.

Knierim, R. P., The Vocation of Isaiah, VT 18 (1968), 47–68.

Koch, K., Ezra and the Origins of Judaism, JSS 19 (1974), 173–197.

Koch, K., The Growth of the Biblical Tradition, 1969.

Koch, K., et al., Amos: Untersucht mit den Methoden einer strukturalen Formgeschichte, 3 vols., AOAT 30, 1976.

Lack, R., La symbolique du livre d'Isaïe, AnBib 59, 1973.

Liebreich, L. J., The Compilation of the Book of Isaiah, JQR 46 (1955–56), 259–277; JQR 47 (1956–57), 114–138.

Marti, K., Das Buch Jesaja, KHAT X, 1900.

Mays, J. L., Amos: A Commentary, OTL, 1969.

McKenzie, J., Second Isaiah, AB 20, 1968.

Melugin, R., The Formation of Isaiah 40–55, BZAW 141, 1976.

Merendino, R. P., Der Erste und der Letzte: Eine Untersuchung von Jes 40–48, SVT 31, 1981.

Milgrom, J., Did Isaiah Prophesy During the Reign of Uzziah? VT 14 (1964), 164–182.

Millar, W. R., Isaiah 24–27 and the Origin of Apocalyptic, HSM 11, 1976.

Miller, P., The Divine Warrior in Early Israel, HSM 5, 1973.

Montgomery, J. A. & Gehman, H. S., A Critical and Exegetical Commentary on the Books of Kings, ICC, 1951.

Mowinckel, S., Jesaja-displene. Prophetien frå Jesaja til Jeremia, 1926.

Mowinckel, S., Die Komposition des Jesajabuches, AO 11 (1933), 267–292.

Muilenburg, J., Isaiah 40–66: Introduction and Exegesis, The Interpreter's Bible, ed. G. A. Buttrick et al., vol. 5, 1956, 381–773.

Niditch, S., The Composition of Isaiah 1, Bibl 61 (1980), 509–529.

North, C. R., The Second Isaiah, 1964.

North, C. R., The Suffering Servant in Deutero-Isaiah: An Historical and Critical Study, 1956.

Noth, M., Überlieferungsgeschichtliche Studien: Die sammelenden und bearbeitenden Geschichtswerke im alten Testament, 1957², 1–110.

Pauritsch, K., Die neue Gemeinde: Gott sammelt Ausgestossene und Arme (Jesaja 56–66), AnBib 47, 1971.

Petersen, D. L., Haggai and Zechariah 1–8: A Commentary, OTL, 1984.

Petersen, D. L., Isaiah 28: A Redaction Critical Study, SBL 1979 Seminar Papers, ed. P. Achtemeier, vol. 2, 1979, 101–122.

Petersen, D. L., Late Israelite Prophecy: Studies in Deutero-Prophetic Literature and in Chronicles, SBLMS 23, 1977.

Platt, E. E., Jewelry of Bible Times and the Catalog of Isa 3: 18–23, AUSS 17 (1979), 71–81, 189–201.

Pope, M. H., Isaiah 34 in Relation to Isaiah 35, 40–66, JBL 71 (1952), 235–243.

Pritchard, J., Ancient Near Eastern Texts Relating to the Old Testament with Supplement, 1969³.

Procksch, O., Jesaia I, KAT IX/1, 1930.

Rahlfs, A., Septuaginta, 2 vols., 1935.

Renaud, B., La Formation du Livre de Michée, 1977.

Rendtorff, R., Zur Komposition des Buches Jesajas, VT 34 (1984), 295 – 320.

Rendtorff, R., The Old Testament: An Introduction, 1986.

Richter, W., Exegese als Literaturwissenschaft: Entwurf einer alttestamentlichen Literatur-theorie und Methodologie, 1971.

Roberts, J. J. M., The Davidic Origins of the Zion Tradition, JBL 92 (1973), 329 – 344.

Roberts, J. J. M., Form, Syntax, and Redaction in Isaiah 1: 2 – 20, PSB 3 (1982), 293 – 306.

Rudolph, W., Haggai, Sacharja 1 – 8, Sacharja 9 – 14, Maleachi, KAT XIII/4, 1976.

Rudolph, W., Jeremia, HAT 12, 1968³.

Sanders, J. A., Hermeneutics in True and False Prophecy, Canon and Authority, ed. G. W. Coats & B. O. Long, 1977, 21 – 41.

Schoors, A., I am God your Saviour, SVT 24, 1973.

Scott, R. B. Y., The Book of Isaiah, Chapters 1 – 39: Introduction and Exegesis, The Interpreter's Bible, ed. G. A. Buttrick et al., vol. 5, 1956, 149 – 381.

Scott, R. B. Y., The Literary Structure of Isaiah's Oracles, Studies in Old Testament Prophecy, ed. H. H. Rowley, 1957, 175 – 186.

Segal, M. H., A Grammar of Mishnaic Hebrew, 1927.

Sehmsdorf, E., Studien zur Redaktionsgeschichte von Jesaja 56 – 66, ZAW 84 (1972), 517 – 575.

Sheppard, G. T., The Anti-Assyrian Redaction and the Canonical Context of Isaiah 1 – 39, JBL 104 (1985), 193 – 216.

Skinner, J., The Book of the Prophet Isaiah, Chapters I – XXXIX, CB, 1905.

Skinner, J., The Book of the Prophet Isaiah, Chapters XL – LXVI, CB, 1929².

Smart, J. D., History and Theology in Second Isaiah: A Commentary on Isaiah 35, 40 – 66, 1965.

Soggin, J. A., Introduction to the Old Testament, From its Origins to the Closing of the Alexandrian Canon, 1976.

Spykerboer, H. C., The Structure and Composition of Deutero-Isaiah, 1976.

Steck, O. H., Bemerkungen zu Jesaja 6, BZ 16 (1972), 188 – 206.

Steck, O. H., Beiträge zum Verständnis von Jesaja 7, 10 – 17 und 8, 1 – 4, TZ 29 (1973), 161 – 178.

Stuhlmueller, C., Creative Redemption in Deutero-Isaiah, AnBib 43, 1970.

Sweeney, M. A., New Gleanings from an Old Vineyard: Isaiah 27 Reconsidered, Early Jewish and Christian Exegesis: Studies in Memory of William Hugh Brownlee, ed. C. Evans & W. F. Stinespring, 1987, 51 – 66.

Sweeney, M. A., Textual Citations in Isaiah 24 – 27: Toward an Understanding of the Redactional Function of Chapters 24 – 27 in the Book of Isaiah, JBL, forthcoming.

Theological Dictionary of the Old Testament, ed. G. J. Botterweck & H. Ringgren, 1974 ff.

Torrey, C. C., The Second Isaiah: A New Interpretation, 1928.

Tucker, G. M., Form Criticism of the Old Testament, 1971.

Tucker, G. M., Prophetic Superscirptions and the Growth of a Canon, Canon and Authority, ed. G. W. Coats & B. O. Long, 1977, 56 – 70.

van der Kooij, A., Die Alten Textzeugen des Jesajabuches: Ein Beitrag zur Textgeschichte des Alten Testaments, OBO 35, 1981.

Vattioni, F., Ecclesiastico: Testo ebraico con apparato critico e versioni greca, latina, e siriaca, 1968.

Vermes, G., The Dead Sea Scrolls: Qumran in Perspective, 1978.

Vermeylen, J., Du Prophète Isaïe à l'Apocalyptique, 2 vols., 1977 – 78.

Volz, P., Jesaia II, KAT IX, 1932.

von Rad, G., The City on the Hill, The Problem of the Hexateuch and Other Essays, 1966, 232 – 242.

von Rad, G., Das formgeschichtliche Problem des Hexateuch, BWANT 4, 1938.

von Rad, G., Old Testament Theology, 2 vols., 1962, 1965.

von Waldow, E., Der traditionsgeschichtliche Hintergrund der prophetischen Gerichtsreden, BZAW 85, 1963.

Weis, R. D., A Definition of the Genre *Maśśā'* in the Hebrew Bible, Ph. D. Dissertation, Claremont Graduate School, 1986.

Werner, W., Eschatologische Texte in Jesaja 1 – 39: Messias, Heiliger Rest, Völker, FZB 46, 1982.

Westermann, C., Basic Forms of Prophetic Speech, 1967.

Westermann, C., Isaiah 40 – 66: A Commentary, OTL, 1969.

Westermann, C., The Praise of God in the Psalms, 1965.

Westermann, C., Sprache und Struktur der Prophetie Deutero-jesajas, CTM 11, 1981.

Whedbee, J. W., Isaiah and Wisdom, 1971.

Wiklander, B., Prophecy as Literature: A Text-Linguistic and Rhetorical Approach to Isaiah 2 – 4, CBOTS 22, 1984.

Wildberger, H., Jesaja, BKAT X, 1972, 1978, 1982.

Wildberger, H., Die Völkerwallfahrt zum Zion: Jes. II 1 – 5, VT 7 (1957), 62 – 81.

Willis, J. T., The First Pericope in the Book of Isaiah, VT 34 (1984), 63 – 77.

Willis, J. T., On the Interpretation of Isaiah 1: 18, JSOT 25 (February, 1983), 35 – 54.

Willis, J. T., Redaction Criticism and Historical Reconstruction, Encounter with the Text: Form and History in the Hebrew Bible, ed. M. Buss, 1979, 83 – 89.

Wolff, H. W., Hosea, Herm, 1974.

Wolff, H. W., Joel and Amos, Herm, 1977.

Wolff, H. W., The Kerygma of the Deuteronomic Historical Work, The Vitality of Old Testament Traditions, W. Brueggemann & H. W. Wolff, 1976, 83 – 100.

Author Index

BEIHEFTE ZUR ZEITSCHRIFT FÜR DIE
ALTTESTAMENTLICHE WISSENSCHAFT

GERALD T. SHEPPARD

Wisdom as a Hermeneutical Construct

A Study in the Sapientializing of the Old Testament

1980. Large-octavo. XII, 178 pages. Cloth DM 78,—
ISBN 3 11 007504 0 (Volume 151)

J. A. LOADER

Polar Structures in the Book of Qohelet

Edited by Georg Fohrer

1979. Large-octavo. XII, 138 pages. Cloth DM 65,—
ISBN 3 11 007636 5 (Volume 152)

PHILIP J. NEL

The Structure and Ethos of the Wisdom Admonitions in Proverbs

1982. Large-octavo. XII, 142 pages. Cloth DM 74,—
ISBN 3 11 008750 2 (Volume 158)

WILLEM S. PRINSLOO

The Theology of the Book of Joel

1985. Large-octavo. VIII, 136 pages. Cloth DM 74,—
ISBN 3 11 010301 X (Volume 163)

ANNELI AEJMELAEUS

The Traditional Prayer in the Psalms

LUDWIG SCHMIDT

Literarische Studien zur Josephsgeschichte

1987. Large-octavo. VI, 310 pages. Cloth DM 140,—
ISBN 3 11 010480 6 (Volume 167)

Prices are subject to change

Walter de Gruyter Berlin · New York

BEIHEFTE ZUR ZEITSCHRIFT FÜR DIE ALTTESTAMENTLICHE WISSENSCHAFT

CHRISTOPHER R. SEITZ

Theology in Conflict

Reactions of the Exile in the Book of Jeremiah

1988. Large-octavo. Approx. 400 pages. Cloth approx. DM 148,−
ISBN 3 11 011223 X (in preparation)

IAIN W. PROVAN

Hezekiah and the Books of Kings

A Contribution to the Debate about the Composition
of the Deuteronomistic History

1988. Large-octavo. Approx. 300 pages. Cloth approx. DM 98,−
ISBN 3 11 011557 3 (in preparation)

ETAN LEVINE

The Aramaic Version of the Bible

Contents and Context

1988. Large-octavo. Approx. 290 pages. Cloth approx. DM 118,−
ISBN 3 11 011474 7 (in preparation)

SA-MOON KANG

Divine War in the Old Testament and the Ancient Near East

1988. Large-octavo. Approx. 290 pages. Cloth approx. DM 120,−
ISBN 3 11 011156 X (in preparation)

JOHN HA

Genesis 15

A Theological Compendium of Pentateuchal History

1988. Large-octavo. Approx. 290 pages. Cloth approx. DM 82,−
ISBN 3 11 011206 X (in preparation)

BARUCH MARGALIT

The Ugaritic Poem of AQHT

Text − Translation − Commentary

1988. Large-octavo. Approx. 590 pages. Cloth approx. DM 198,−
ISBN 3 11 011632 4 (in preparation)

Prices are subject to change

Walter de Gruyter

Berlin · New York